The Mask of Nostradamus

The Mask of
Nostradamus

JAMES RANDI

CHARLES SCRIBNER'S SONS

New York

Charles Scribner's Sons
Macmillan Publishing Company
866 Third Avenue, New York, NY 10022
Collier Macmillan Canada, Inc.

Library of Congress Cataloging-in-Publication Data
Randi, James.
The mask of Nostradamus / James Randi.
p. cm.
Includes bibliographical references (p.
ISBN 0-684-19056-7
1. Nostradamus, 1503–1566. 2. Prophets—France—Biography.
I. Title.
BF1815.N8R35 1990   89-70189   CIP
133.3′092–dc20
[B]

Macmillan books are available at special discounts for bulk purchases for sales promotions, premiums, fund-raising, or educational use. For details, contact:

Special Sales Director
Macmillan Publishing Company
866 Third Avenue
New York, NY 10022

10 9 8 7 6 5 4 3 2 1

Designed by Nancy Sugihara

Printed in the United States of America

This book is dedicated to Raymond Han, a painter of incredible skill who was among the first of my friends who instilled in me an appreciation of art and artists. He enlarged my world and widened my perception in ways that I have never expressed to him, and I trust that though we see little of one another these days, he will accept my declaration that his efforts to bring me to culture were not entirely without result.

Contents

Appendixes

Bibliography

Index

Acknowledgments

THE IDEA FOR THIS BOOK was born somewhere around 46th Street and Broadway in New York City, when a lovely lady named Fifi Oscard suggested that I might apply my investigative talents to the subject of Nostradamus. I am grateful for that suggestion.

I wish to thank Everett Bleiler, who wrote on this subject under the name Liberté E. LeVert, a pseudonym which has an obvious derivation. His book, *The Prophecies and Enigmas of Nostradamus* (1979), is one of the very few that has ever critically examined the prophecies, and in his writings and in telephone conversations and letters over a period of two years he offered me many insights that assisted me greatly.

My friend Antoine Kevorkian, a resident of Grenoble, France, traveled through Provence with me and also worked as a translator. He deserves a monument of some sort for his long hours puzzling over the intricacies of Nostradamus' Renaissance language. Some of the seemingly small items of usage and word variants that he came up with by searching through his library enabled me to cut to the bone of quite a few mysteries. We covered many hundreds of kilometers of rural France and consumed many a glass of fine French cognac in our journey.

I was denied the pleasure of meeting Dr. Edgar Leroy, of St. Rémy de Provence, who passed away shortly before I first visited that picturesque town. He was a noted scholar, and I benefited greatly from his dedicated research on Nostradamus, which no major publisher has chosen to make available. Copies of his work are hard to find even in France, and most of it consists of articles in obscure journals not likely to come to the attention of the public.

The 1961 book of Edgar Leoni, by far the most thorough—though somewhat naive—investigator of the Nostradamus work, was an indispensable source of information, and I will refer to it often.

I happily chanced upon the talents of Lys Ann Shore, an American who earned a degree at the University of Toronto in medieval studies. Her suggestions and discoveries while examining the Nostradamus verses are shared with you here, and I am grateful to Dr. Shore for welcome corrections and ideas freely offered.

Paul Kellogg and David Field were available for late-night panic calls to clear up small details about French usage and my computer's word-processing eccentricities, and their help is gratefully noted.

My colleague José Alvarez, who has been an important part of many of my investigations, learned the fine art of tiptoeing to maintain quiet and inserting cups of coffee into the debris that was stacked on my desk as this work progressed. His patience is acknowledged.

My apprentice, Massimo Polidoro, acquired great agility leaping to file drawers on command and discovering various notes, books and documents that had obviously relocated themselves by still unsolved means.

My hardworking agent, Kevin McShane of Fifi Oscard Associates, who represents me in New York City, heroically refereed the various discussions involved in getting this book into production, while I suspect that Hamilton Cain and Ned Chase of Scribners played good cop/bad cop to extract the final product from me. Ned is a fierce editor, and for that I am grateful to him.

Graduate students Wade Riddick and Jim Tarver of Louisiana State University at Baton Rouge extended their courtesy by helping me to discover a very important source of information concerning my subject. My thanks for their efforts.

Penn & Teller didn't do a single thing to assist with this book, but they have kept me sane just by being their outrageous selves. My world is far richer for their trashing of it.

Finally, Denis Parsons, a valued colleague and former press officer at the British Library, opened doors at that venerable institution for me and facilitated searches, thus making my research there much easier.

Thank you all.

The Mask of Nostradamus

CHAPTER ONE

My Search Begins

I WRITE THIS from a window seat aboard a jet carrying me from Paris to Marseille on the second of what may be several more trips to the area of St. Rémy de Provence and Salon in search of the truth about Michel de Notredame and his prophecies. As I look from the aircraft to the terrain 11,000 meters below me, I observe that somehow, inserted into an area of apparent wilderness, there is a very square area of deciduous forest perhaps half a kilometer on a side, which is a bright yellow-green among the surrounding growth. I see no roads or even pathways entering that area, yet for some reason I cannot imagine, those trees appear to have resisted the urging of seasonal frost and diminished sunlight that have turned the rest of their neighbors into red, gold and brown masses.

Why? Did some long-gone culture alter that square of Provençal France so that it now nurtures its vegetation differently? Has a variety of tree that resists or delays the autumn changes been planted and cultured there purposely? Perhaps the government of La Belle France is conducting an agricultural experiment, or has perversely undertaken to confound a foreign visitor passing overhead *par avion?* I have no idea, nor am I ever likely to know what has wrought this wonder.

The aircraft passes by this apparent anomaly, and the mystery is left with me, unsolved.

It is the nature of our species to wonder over such matters. We look for solutions to every question we can invent, and seek patterns and order in the information that presents itself to us.

Unsolved puzzles and unanswered questions, order among chaos, and ripples in the fabric of our universe are all matters to ponder.

As a singularly curious individual, I am perhaps more attracted to anomalies that might fail to interest others. A patch of unexpectedly green foliage is surely one of the more minor puzzles I have encountered in the past sixty years, and it hardly compares with the purpose of my present trip to France. But I have found that most great mysteries reduce, during solution, to a number of smaller, less powerful, riddles, and so it appears to be with the overall mystery which I now undertake to examine. That mystery bears the name Nostradamus.

The man, his education, his milieu, the culture in which he was born and immersed, the fears and hopes of his day—these and other aspects must be resolved so that we may at least partly, perhaps, lift away the mask of Nostradamus.

I suspect that when we peek beneath that mask, the Seer of Provence will be smiling at us. . . .

An English translation of the Latin inscription on a marble slab set in the wall of a church in Salon de Provence tells us:

> Here rest the bones of the illustrious Michael Nostradamus, alone of all mortals judged worthy to record with his almost divine pen, under the influence of the stars, the future events of the whole world. He lived 62 years, 6 months and 17 days. He died at Salon in the year 1566. Let not posterity disturb his rest. Anne Pons Gemelle wishes her husband true happiness.

We will perhaps disturb those dusty bones a little in our search.

> *Sitting by night in my secret study,*
> *Alone, resting upon the stool of brass,*
> *A slight flame, going out of the solitude,*
> *Makes me pronounce what is not to be believed vain.*
>
> *The wand in hand, set in the middle of the branches,*
> *From the wave I wet both the hem and the foot,*
> *In fear I write, trembling in the sleeves,*
> *Divine splendor: the Divine seated nearby.*

With these lines, this remarkable 16th-century Frenchman began his masterpiece, the *Centuries,* nine hundred and forty-odd quatrains that purport to prophesy important events in the history of the world up until the very end of the planet—which date students of his writings have variously determined to be somewhere between A.D. 1999 and 7000. Interpretation of Nostradamus is not an exact science.

To write a book about Nostradamus that supports the idea that he was a prophet requires little skill or effort. So many naive scholars, over the centuries, have pored over his writings to extract every possible obscurity, that thousands of pages of drivel are readily available to be copied, shuffled about and hyperbolized. Writing a book that presents a more likely and rational point of view is a different matter, but I have undertaken to perform this task.

It is too easy to explain certain aspects of a man's fame by simply stating that he "lived in a remarkable age." All ages are remarkable, most often because of the men and women who inhabit them. Being born in an advantageous time is not a distinction reserved by Fate for the nurturing of great artists, statesmen, philosophers or academics. In the case of Nostradamus, though I would not imply an exception to that observation, it is true that certain circumstances of his period simplified his existence, encouraged his success and enabled him to survive until today as a legend, an enigma and an apparent hero of unusual proportions.

He said that his major opus, the *Centuries,* was written as a collection of prophetic quatrains with no chronological order. Together with numerous lengthy almanacs, letters, "presages," sixaines* and notes, the verses have fascinated all who have seen or only heard of them, and along with Homer, Shakespeare, the authors of Holy Scripture, and very few others, the Seer of Provence could claim that after more than four centuries, his works have been in continuous print ever since their first publication. More than four hundred books and essays about his prophecies by almost as many authors have been published since his death in 1566, along with a great number of articles and other commentaries, in numerous languages. That is a remarkable record, and there must be good reasons for it. I have set out to understand this persistent popularity of Nostradamus.

---

*The sixaines are usually treated as spurious by even the most ardent Nostradamians.

The 16th century began with intellectual revolution in the air. Academically, the excitement of newly available knowledge that threatened to supersede all previous notions in such fields as medicine, astronomy, mathematics and philosophy was intoxicating the generation of Nostradamus. The entire view of the universe was beginning to change, and with it the role of Man in its development and its very existence. Such changes in basic thinking wrenched at the emotional stability of intellectuals who until then had been accustomed to dependence upon authorities who suddenly began to seem much lesser gods than before.

Politically, Nostradamus existed in a dangerous, violent time in which anyone could come afoul of the established mores in attempting to escape mediocrity. The penalties for such transgressions were barbarous and seldom surpassed in history; heroes then were deserving of the name. France and Italy were perpetually fighting small conflicts with one another in a state of continuous low-level warfare, and a great economic depression was in effect in France. Our subject lived in a very difficult period of history.

Aside from these obvious influences on the life of Nostradamus that must constitute a good part of my investigation, another part of it is to examine the social milieu—the personal, everyday atmosphere—in which the man flourished.

I want to know more about such an illustrious person, a man who might well have survived in the history of his region even without his pursuit of arcane knowledge. Though most information about his life is at best sketchy and at worst highly fictionalized, I must attempt to sort it all out and arrive at a reasonably correct profile.

Dates of events in Nostradamus' early life are largely unknown. Many miraculous accounts of fabulous feats attributed to him, given by his fans down through the centuries, have little or no documentation, and might therefore be discounted. Though many printed copies of his works exist, beginning with a treatise on cosmetics in 1552, there are no known written manuscript copies of any of his works. The very first editions of his prophetic writings are lost and we must depend upon the accuracy and integrity of those who transcribed them. Numerous known forgeries have been published, some to prove points not originally intended by the seer and others merely to take financial advantage of a public hungry for anything in any form bearing the Nostradamus name.

Typographical errors, transpositions, changed italicization, punctuation and capitalization, altered spellings and "improvements" on his writings have bastardized his works to the point where proper scholarship is difficult. We must go as far back as possible to original sources, at the same time understanding that there is no ideal version of Nostradamus' works, and the oldest is not necessarily the best source. Since every edition is either more complete, contains changes, has less typographical errors, or shows spelling or other text changes, we must decide what to accept as a standard. Frequently I will give more than one variation so that my comments may be more fairly judged. In all cases, I will attempt to provide my reader with exactly what has presented itself to me, without alteration or embellishment.

In this book, I have simplified matters by avoiding the use of Roman numerals in designating the verses. Thus the number 2-37 means Quatrain number thirty-seven in Century (book) number two.

My critics have often declared, with great conviction, that I cannot become persuaded of any unusual claim because of my "attitude," which is admittedly skeptical. I have answered that attitudes and beliefs can have nothing to do with properly conducted research and conclusions drawn therefrom. I may choose to believe that three plus two equals six, but mixing three marbles with two pencils still results in a total of five; my personal belief, no matter how strong, can have nothing to do with that result. When it comes to unusual claims of any kind, I am more than willing to be shown.

Lest it be thought that I have no appreciation for the marvelous, I will assert here that I regard Lewis Carroll, puppy dogs and selected sunsets as a few of the "miracles" of my own life. I am not immune to such beauty. You are told, by astrologers, psychics and other such "experts," that you are not the capable, responsible and rather remarkable person that you really are. We belong to a species that has reached out a quarter of a million miles to set foot on the moon, and if that is not miracle enough for us all, I despair for our sense of wonder. The modern soothsayers suggest that you stop thinking for yourselves. They ask you to retreat to the caves from which our ancestors are said to have come, while you have the choice of going to the stars. I have opted for the stars, and I invite you to join me.

In my analysis, I will depend upon the application of the principle of parsimony, which says that complicated explanations are less likely to be correct than relatively simple ones. Some interpretations of the Nostradamus material are so very obvious and applicable that they cannot be denied; some are so far-fetched and convoluted that no reasonable person can accept them.

I must declare frankly that I have no belief in the popularly held notion that Nostradamus or anyone else ever had or now has any supernatural prophetic powers. My rather considerable professional experience and my common sense dictate against such a belief, but I will always yield to facts and probabilities that oppose my admitted yet understandable prejudice when those facts are properly derived and set forth. That, to a limited extent, is a tenet of the scientific method.

Nostradamus himself apparently had no problem about leaving life without squaring his philosophical and moral debt with those who survived and followed him. I think that it is time to re-examine his work and perhaps come to a different conclusion than the one he intended.

Investigating the validity of the *Centuries* as prophecy is only a small part of this book, and that inquiry is entered into only to develop answers to the major questions I am asking about the man Nostradamus—who was he and what drove him?

Hoping not to confound the typesetter and the proofreader, I have retained the original spelling and usage of certain passages in old English. There seems to be little uniformity involved in those items, which often prove somewhat confusing. I believe the flavor supplied by these archaic items will be effective.

In assembling the material for this research, I came upon many end-of-the-world prophecies that I hope my reader will find interesting, for they are an indication of the credulity of the public through the ages. The appendix contains a summary of more than thirty of these dire presages.

With several aging dictionaries, rolls of microfilm, old maps, atlases, history books and some thirty other source books on hand and with access to some really expert assistance, I now take on this formidable task.

CHAPTER TWO

Genesis of a Prophet

*He who boasts of his ancestors boasts of
what does not properly belong to him.*
—SENECA, A.D. 1–56

The Political Scene

THE ROMAN EMPIRE EXPANDED into southern Gaul in 125 B.C.
by establishing the first Roman province beyond the Alps in the
area now known as Provence, which took its name from that
fact. Once a country separate from France, Provence retained
its Roman laws, customs and ties well into the 17th century. In
some areas even today, the Provençal language, based upon
Latin, is still spoken.

The 13th century saw the beginning of the end of the period
when Jews and Christians could comfortably live together in
Provence, which up until then had been a tolerant ethnic and
religious haven. In earlier times Jews had been allowed their
freedom of religion in that strongly Catholic community, and
were accepted in most professions, though usually referred to
as "juif" in written records as if that served to better identify
them. Indeed, we may not assume otherwise. Thus, legal papers
would record a transaction between "Jacques Giraud and Pierre
Morel, jew," without troubling to designate Jacques as a Christian.

Then in 1481 Provence became officially a part of France, the
territory having been willed to Louis XI by the successor of
Count René, who was also King of Naples. René was an enlight-

ened man who in his stewardship of the area had treated the Moors and the Jews with great understanding. But under Louis, the status of Jews in Provence deteriorated rapidly, until in 1501, the monarch enforced a strong edict, at the urging of the Vatican, which gave Provençal Jews three months to be baptized into the Catholic Church or suffer forfeiture of their property and subsequent expulsion from their country.

Since family names were usually changed upon conversion and baptism, it has not been determined just what percentage of the Jews of Provence abandoned their faith in favor of Christianity during this period of grace. Many did, among them a man of St. Rémy named Guy Gassonet. He and his family were baptized under the new name of Notredame,* and thereby became, in theory at least, more acceptable as part of the community. Guy Gassonet became Pierre de Notredame on his conversion.

The Family History

According to the words of Nostradamus himself, grandfather Pierre was a prominent physician, having chosen one of the limited number of professions then open to Jews. He had been a physician to Count René, along with one Jean de St. Rémy, another converted Jew. The two doctors became close friends. Later, Pierre practiced in Arles, then moved to St. Rémy de Provence (also known as St. Rémy de Crau). His son, Jacques, married Renée, the daughter of Jean, and these two became the parents of Michel de Notredame, the subject of our study.

But grandfather Pierre had invented much of this history, freely bringing into existence a panoply of high-ranked ancestors for the newly created Notredame family. All of his forebears, he claimed, were poets, adventurers and scholars who were also associates of, and officeholders to, royalty. Even Pierre's own personal history underwent rather heavy revision.

*The Provençal spelling was Nostredame, the "s" substituting for an accent on the vowel previous. This was the practice in Provençal usage. The modern French for the words would be "nôtre dame." Nostradamus is the Latin version of the name. Libraries list Nostradamus and his works under one, two or three spellings, depending upon the competency of their librarians.

As he should have been very aware, such a deception was not likely to go undetected for long if his family history were looked into. In 16th-century France, almost every transaction, evaluation or event, no matter how trivial, went on official record in some way. By law, any debts, gifts, changes of status, promotions, measurements, surveys and such matters as marriages, deaths and changes of domicile were written down in detail by notaries. These records were kept in great quantities, and many of them are still extant in the local archives of France. It was a vain hope for the Notredame family to create illustrious forebears, in light of the supporting documentation that would have had to exist among those records, had those persons themselves existed.

One earnest Nostradamus scholar, Dr. Edgar Leroy, assiduously explored the extensive archives of Avignon and St. Rémy and came up with some facts about Michel de Notredame's more mundane sources. Spending prodigious amounts of time searching mountains of old documents, Leroy uncovered the truth. The family background he retrieved proves the Notredames to be quite solid and respectable, though not as romantic and scholarly as the scenario invented by grandfather Pierre might indicate.

It seems that Pierre (as Guy Gassonet) had first arrived in Avignon, the large city north of St. Rémy, some time in the 1400s. He came from a long line of grain dealers, not physicians, and he himself was in the grain business. He married a gentile woman, Blanche, after converting to Christianity. His son Jacques, Michel's father, was also a grain dealer when he moved to St. Rémy and married Reynière (Renée), daughter of the previously mentioned Jean de St. Rémy, who was actually a failed doctor who had turned to tax collecting for the king.

Enter the Prophet

Our hero was born in St. Rémy de Provence shortly past noon on December 24 (new calendar),* in the year 1503. His father,

---

*To make up for the extra eleven minutes and fourteen seconds a year that had been ignored in the old Julian system, and to bring it more in line with newly determined observations and calculations, Pope Gregory XIII revised the calendar in March of 1582. The adjustment

Jean, was by this time a successful notary, and well able to support a family. Young Michel was a favorite of Pierre's. He lived at St. Rémy until age sixteen, attended school at the city of Avignon to study the humanities, which in that day were grammar, rhetoric, logic, arithmetic, geometry, music and astronomy. The last consisted of a mixture of what we now know as the science of astronomy and the art of astrology. All of these subjects were taught in Latin. He then pursued his higher education at the University of Montpellier in Provence, famous since 1153 as a medical school. Modern historians, examining the extensive records available from university archives, rank Montpellier as a center of medical training at that time second only to the University of Salerno, which was perhaps more famous for the substantial financial support it received from those indefatigable patrons of anything Italian, the Medicis. Praises were heard for Montpellier in every court of Europe, and aristocrats urged their male offspring to aspire to attendance there.

It appears, especially in view of his eventual impact on history, that Michel was a genuinely astute individual, and probably a good student, since he graduated at an early age, twenty-two. When he had completed his studies at Montpellier, he took the name Nostradamus, a Latin form of the French name. This name change was the custom of most physicians and other scholars of the day. The practice set them above the uneducated and declared their status clearly. From then on, he was also privileged to wear the four-sided hat that identified him as a properly licensed physician of that time. All representations of the seer show him in this distinctive headgear.

Nostradamus distinguished himself as a plague doctor, during a prolonged tour to perform what would today be called an internship. He traveled among the sick and bravely treated patients in rural areas of France.

There is an interesting observation to be made here. When Michel returned to Montpellier to obtain his full medical degree, he inscribed his name and intentions in the student register. Today, those handwritten registers of former times are still

---

was made by adding ten days to the old Julian dates. Thus, though Nostradamus would have recorded his birth date as December 14, we would use the 24th to determine important matters such as a horoscope.

available for consultation at the University of Montpellier. Translated from Latin, his entry reads:

I, Michel de Notredame, of the country of Provence, of the city of Saint-Rémy, of the diocese of Avignon, have come to study at the University of Montpellier, of which I agree to observe the rules, the rights and the privileges, both present and future. I have paid the registration fees and have chosen Antoine Romier as my patron, the 23rd day of October, 1529.

What takes the attention of the careful observer, however, is that just after he wrote "I" at the beginning of this registration, he wrote what appears to be the partial word "Pet" and then crossed it out before he wrote in his name, Michel. In Latin, the name Pierre would be written "Petrus." Did Michel slip up and begin writing a name by which he was more commonly known at home and by his friends?

Michel attracted a lot of attention at the university. He had started his advanced studies at age nineteen, studying anatomy as outlined by the classical anatomist Galen, the application of astrological knowledge to diagnosis and the prescribing of medicines, pharmacology, surgical procedures and the notion of "humors" and other supposed aspects and influences of nature that played such an important part in the medical procedures of his day.

The University of Montpellier, though markedly modernist in outlook, was basically dedicated to the principles of Avicenna, a Persian physician (980–1037 A.D.) who wrote *The Canon of Medicine,* the most famous single book on the subject in the East and West, and which was *the* medical authority from the 12th to 16th centuries. The book combined theology, medicine and an early psychology. Montpellier had a faculty that consisted largely of members of a local Jewish* community. The university was at the leading edge of the dawn of what can be called modern medicine. The specialty was surgery (amputation was the most common surgical operation of the day, and developed into a specialty) rather than internal medicine, which had to await the retreat of the old idea of "humors." The foundations

*Regardless of the vows and declarations involved in conversion to Christianity, Jews still regarded themselves, and were regarded by the community, as a separate group.

of the study of metabolism were laid there, and a theory was developed that anticipated the germ theory of infection. That idea had to await the invention of the microscope, not far away in time. Nostradamus, while at Montpellier, would have studied anatomy extensively, would have become acquainted with new substances such as quinine and tobacco (used as a narcotic) and would have been surprised, during his time at Montpellier, by the discovery that a prominent pestilence of the day known as "lepra" was venereal in origin. It was soon to become known as syphilis.

Nostradamus obtained his full license to practice medicine at age twenty-six. Then he fell in with a most unusual person.

A Strange Alliance

Jules-César Scaliger (formerly "de l'Escalle," but he took the Latin version) was a prominent academic who was born in Padua, Italy. He excelled in medicine, poetry, philosophy, botany and mathematics. By his own account, he had studied under the famous artist Albrecht Dürer, and was distinguished as a military man. He had practiced medicine at Padua, then became one of the scholars who took the Renaissance with him when he and others moved to France to enjoy its relatively freer intellectual climate. He became a permanent and celebrated resident of the small town of Agen at age forty-one in the year 1526, as physician to the bishop of Agen. The presence of this learned man brought considerable prestige to the area, which was essentially bereft of any other distinction.

Scaliger, aged fifty, had just taken a young bride of sixteen when young doctor Nostradamus came to his attention, and he invited the neophyte to study with him. Flattered by this honor, Nostradamus enthusiastically moved to take up residence with the Scaligers in Agen. We can only imagine the delight of the citizens at having two such luminaries to boast of.

There Michel married his first wife, whose name is lost to us. They produced two children, also unknown. But the convenient and potentially productive intellectual alliance between the two scholars was not to last long. Along the way, Nostradamus' close association with Scaliger broke down for reasons still not understood but perhaps not difficult to guess at.

The older scholar was well known to be a generally very disagreeable individual who constantly boasted of his accomplishments and his victories over other scholars. For example, he claimed that by means of his scholarly criticism he had caused Erasmus to die of melancholy and that he had destroyed the academic standing of a famous contemporary, Girolamo Cardan, by ridiculing his astrological claims. Cardan hardly needed any destroying by another. He was a vain, pompous egocentric who contributed substantially to mathematics but made a fool of himself in almost all other ways. He confidently predicted that Edward VI of England would fall ill and die at age fifty-five years, three months and seventeen days; Edward died at age fifteen. Rationalizing his error madly, Cardan said that he now realized that Edward had not been "adequately marked by the stars," in which case it would be necessary to cast horoscopes for his close associates as well, to make up for this discrepancy. Cardan then astrologically predicted his own death at age seventy-five, and there was much talk—unsubstantiated but titillating to contemplate—that his death at that exact age was self-induced. Considering the history of the man and his abundant ego, that possibility is not totally unlikely.

Apparently Scaliger's young wife amply reflected all of her husband's unpleasant qualities. They were a battling pair who, in spite of this marital impediment, still managed to produce a brood of fifteen children, one of whom joined his father in the history books as one of the most brilliant teachers of the age.

According to one usually dependable historian, the citizens of Agen, knowing a good publicity setup when they saw it, and fearing an imminent breakup of their celebrated team, offered the Scaliger/Nostradamus duo a large stipend if they would agree to repair their differences and settle down in that city permanently. The reaction of Nostradamus to this offer is not recorded, but Scaliger spurned the city officials' appeal, replying that their money would be put to better use if distributed to the sick, the elderly and the poor. The citizens of Agen were so incensed at what they perceived as ingratitude that they rioted and tried to pull the two scholars off their horses as they rode in the street. In spite of this pressure on them to remain in association, they parted.

It might have been Michel's interest in astrology that precipitated the rift between the pupil and teacher, for Scaliger, in spite of his tumultuous life-style, was a genuine no-nonsense intellectual. Well after the schism between the two, one of the Scaligers, either *père* or *fils,* it cannot be said with certainty which, wrote a denunciation of Nostradamus when his *Centuries* appeared in 1555 to great popular acclaim. The tirade appeared in a letter circulated among scholars:

> Credulous France, what are you doing, hanging on the words of Nostradamus? What sort of jewish sorcery restrains your anger? . . . Don't you care that this guilt stains your honor? Don't you understand that this dirty rascal offers you only nonsense? . . . One must ask, in the end, who is sillier, this evil charlatan or you, who accept his impostures?

Regardless of these totally unveiled and brutal insults, Nostradamus always had a kind comment about his mentor, even long after their disagreement. Not one word of resentment against Scaliger from Nostradamus exists in print or manuscript form, nor are there reports from his biographers of such a feeling. In 1552 Nostradamus wrote,

> [Scaliger] seems to have inherited Cicero's ability in eloquence, Virgil's in poetry, and Galen's twice over in medicine. I owe him more than anyone else in the world.

The Rest of the Family

The plague visited Agen soon after this. Nostradamus was away on a tour of Provence at the time. First his two children, then his wife, succumbed to it. Sorrowing over his loss, Michel took off on a long pilgrimage as a physician, treating the plague by his own methods over a wide area of France and Italy. This eventually brought him back to Salon de Provence not far from St. Rémy, where he settled down and met his second wife, Anna Ponce Gemelle, a rich widow by whom he was to have three sons and three daughters.

The eldest of his children was César (1555–1631) who became Consul of Salon in 1598 and again in 1614. He wrote a comprehensive history of Provence, ambitiously starting at the biblical Deluge. Understandably, the book featured the history of his illustrious father prominently. It was unfinished when César died, and his nephew, another César who became governor of Provence, eventually completed and published his uncle's book.

André, the second son, went to Paris, where he lived a bohemian life and in 1587 was arrested for killing a dueling opponent. As a sentence, he was given the option of taking holy orders, which he accepted. Becoming a Capuchin monk and entering a monastery, he promptly vanished from the records. The third son, Charles, became a poet. We know little of his merits.

Just whom the three Notredame daughters married is uncertain. There were no descendants from César, the only son who married, but apparently some from the daughters.

A couple of claimant sons, Michel Junior (Le Jeune) and Anthoine Crespin Nostradamus, are credited with a number of highly successful after-the-fact prophetic quatrains. Though the task of sorting out the works that are said to have originated with Nostradamus *père* is monumental enough, scholars have identified the spurious Nostradamus *fils'* works with ease. Incompetently invented by unknown villains, they are just too specific and accurate to be genuine. Michel Junior reached too far in establishing his inheritance. A soldier, he was asked by his commanding officer to predict the outcome of an impending battle. He predicted that the enemy town would be in flames after they had been through it, and indeed it was, but only with the considerable help of Michel himself, who was observed applying a torch at strategic spots around the town, apparently in order to ensure that his prediction would succeed. He was executed on the spot, an event he evidently had *not* foreseen.

Two of Nostradamus' brothers survived him, Bertrand and Jean. The latter was also a poet, with some fair recognition in his day. He published one known work in 1575, a biographical listing of the troubadours of Provence.

Nostradamus' disciple, de Chavigny, left us a physical description of his master:

He was just under medium height, robust, agile and vigorous. He had a large, open forehead, a straight nose and gray eyes, which were usually pleasant but which blazed when he was angered. His face was both severe and jolly, but along with this severity there was a great kindness. His cheeks were ruddy, even in his old age, and his beard was long and thick. Except in his old age, his health was good and his senses were acute. His mind was lively and curious, and he had an excellent memory. He spoke little, but thought much. He slept only four or five hours a night. He praised freedom of speech, was faithful to the Catholic Church, outside of which he felt there was no salvation. He hated vice. I recall his charity towards the poor, to whom he was very generous.

The Author Is Published

Nostradamus was first published as an authority on various compotes, as well as cosmetics. His first work, and his major nonprophetic book, published in 1555, was *Excellent et Moult utile Opuscule à touts necessaire qui desirent auoir cognoissance de plusiers exquises Receptes* (Excellent and Most useful Tract of everything needed, for those who wish to become familiar with many choice Recipes). Long and comprehensive titles were all the rage at that period.

Largely a combination of two of his earlier books, the *Opuscule* contained excellent recipes, and copied versions are still extant. An enterprising French manufacturer, taking advantage of Nostradamus' name and the currently strong interest in the occult in that land, has recently produced a product known as "Nostradamus Jam" to feed the emotional and culinary needs of the faithful. I am told that no dedicated believer in psychic matters in France is without a supply of this enchanting *confiture*.

Noting the immediate success of his initial publishing venture, Nostradamus must have decided that he could add to his relatively moderate income as a physician by bringing out other books. Since he was already trained in astrology—it was a required subject at Montpellier—and he claimed descent from the Jewish tribe of Issacher, a family that was said to have "understanding of the times," the idea of an almanac was obvious. An almanac is a periodical calendar of predicted events, combining such astronomical facts as moon phases with astrological speculations. In 1550, his expectations of success were more than met when the first of his yearly almanacs was published. In 1555, he printed the first, short edition of his book of prophecy, the *Centuries*, and with that publication, his lasting fame was more than assured.

Bibliography of His Writings

The term "Centuries" refers not to a time period, but to a group of one hundred verses. It is wrongly claimed in some books, including John Hogue's *Nostradamus and the Millennium* (Doubleday, 1987), that the *Centuries* consists of ten groups of one hundred quatrains each, totaling one thousand verses. Actually, the first edition of the *Centuries* contained only Centuries One to Three and fifty-three quatrains of Century Four.

A supplemented edition of 1557 had all Centuries through Six, plus the first forty of Century Seven. The first English edition, titled *THE TRUE PROPHECIES OR PROGNOSTICATIONS OF Michael Nostradamus, PHYSICIAN TO Henry II. Francis II. and Charles IX, KINGS OF FRANCE, And one of the best ASTRONO-MERS that ever were* (1672), of which I have a fine copy, contains forty-*four* verses of Century Seven* along with verses 73, 80, 82 and 83 of the same Century. The text mentions that the last group of four was originally twelve, but eight were rejected because "they were found in the foregoing Centuries." Finally, Centuries Eight through Ten were published in 1558 as a separate book. There have been additional works printed by several other publishers, but well after the death of the purported author. I cannot give very much credence to these additions.

Another book of quatrains, Centuries Eight to Ten, appeared in 1568, still containing a 1558 dedicatory epistle to King Henry II of France expressing the author's wishes for a long and happy life. Henry failed to benefit from these blessings; he died in 1559. Nostradamus author Everett Bleiler suggests that a complete edition said to have been produced at Lyons in 1558—a few months before Henry's demise—probably did exist, but owing to the many bad guesses made by Nostradamus (in Centuries Eight through Ten) about his sovereign, all copies might have been destroyed. Negative evidence has a way of spoiling a

*What is probably verse 44 is numbered LXIV, rather than XLIV. Quatrains 7–42 and 7–43 are false, as we will see in Chapter 10.

good theory. I agree with Bleiler's view of the 6–74 quatrain (see Chapter 11), that it seems to be a direct propaganda gimmick directed against Elizabeth I of England, powerful enemy of Henry II of France, and it would appear to have been written to please Henry.

Though other editions offer slight variations and blatant inventions that provide titillating opportunities for "interpreters" to exploit, in preparing this book I have chosen to refer mainly to the edition which is considered as close to an *editio princeps* as can be obtained. It is the 1568 printing by Benoist Rigaud, at Lyon. The one I used was the variant "a," a copy of which is also found at the Musée Arbaud, in Aix-en-Provence. Surprisingly, it is a very small book, about 3" × 4", and just more than 200 pages long. A very clear film copy of this rare book was kindly provided to me by the Bibliothèque de Marseille, France.

So, in all, there are 940 to 948 quatrains that were published during the lifetime of Nostradamus. Along with those were the almanacs, sixaines, presages and the several letters and dedications, all very vague and flattering to the recipients, most very compatible in style with the *Centuries,* but some probably fakes.

Whether directed against the fake or the genuine Nostradamus product, a Latin verse began to be circulated among the intelligentsia of Europe soon after the quatrains became known. A clever pun on the prophet's name, which can mean "we give our own" in Latin, it read:

> Nostra damus cum falsa damus, nam fallere nostrum est; Et cum falsa damus, nil nisi nostra damus.

Losing all its value as a pun in English, it translates:

> We give our own when we give false things, for it is our nature to deceive; And when we give false things, we only give our own things.

It was very obvious to scholars who circulated this verse that it referred to Nostradamus, and with his aspirations for acceptance among his peers, it must have been painful to him.

Apparently struck by the success of his publishing ventures, Nostradamus essayed to produce a book that properly belonged to his primary profession as a physician. This may have been an attempt to soften the jeers of his colleagues. A paraphrase of the writings of the classical anatomist Galen issued from Nostradamus' pen in 1557. It caused little excitement and received much criticism for inaccuracy, even though the original Galen itself was quite wrong in some respects, confusing functions of the body and misconnecting major organs. Though Galen had correctly determined that the arteries contain blood rather than air, as previous authorities had taught, he erred in stating that there were imperceptible pores within the heart that conducted blood between the chambers, and he promoted belief in certain spirits that inhabited the liver, heart and brain, and controlled vital processes.

Four months after the publication of the *Centuries* in 1555, the Queen of France, Catherine de Médicis, wrote to Claude de Savoie, the Governor of Provence and a personal friend of Nostradamus. A royal invitation for Nostradamus to visit Paris followed within days. This was quite a distinct honor, since at that time Paris supported an estimated 30,000* sorcerers, alchemists, astrologers and a variety of other sayers of sooth. These were all available to the superstitious queen, and her request for Nostradamus indicated her exceptional regard for his work. Unlike most of the others, he was a rather substantial citizen. He was married into a wealthy family, was a physician with a reputation of having successfully treated the plague, and had published several times, including a book which was now being widely discussed at court.

After an arduous journey, not improved by the ill health suffered by Nostradamus but simplified by royal permission to use certain favorable routes limited to favored persons, as well as provisions for frequent changes of mount during his trip, the seer was received by the rulers in Paris. Apparently making a favorable impression, he was granted several royal appointments and a sum of money. With those honors still fresh, he returned to Salon and began production of a second, more extensive edition of the *Centuries,* and in 1558 met yet greater notoriety and sales with this expanded version.

*New York City's bunco squad estimates that there are some 8,000 fortune tellers, astrologers and other such artists working in that city presently. The Postal Service in Newark, New Jersey, adds another 1,500 mail-order psychics to that number. In the relatively unenlightened 16th century, the larger estimate is not surprising.

Nostradamus as Detective

His fame as a seer spread far and wide. He was admired, sought after, vilified, insulted and avoided all at once. No one was neutral about his reputation, and everyone had a story to tell about him. A dependable record exists in French archives relating that in 1562 the Bishop of Orange asked Nostradamus for his assistance in solving a shocking felony. A valued silver chalice and other holy objects had been stolen from the cathedral, and there was no clue concerning the perpetrators of this sacrilege. Nostradamus replied with an enigmatic and uninterpreted horoscope accompanied by a lengthy commentary in typically evasive, symbolic style, but gave no direct clue to a solution of the crime. It reads, in fact, *very* much like the material given law-enforcement officers today by the so-called "police psychics" who are consulted for similar purposes and who, like Nostradamus, freely accuse unnamed conspirators whose identities may be guessed by the authorities, often incorrectly and always unfairly. Part of it reads:

> . . . the theft of the sacred objects has been perpetrated with the collusion of two of your brothers in the church—indeed, ones who have previously extended to you private counsel on several occasions as to what had befallen your silver. . . . the silver was put in the house of one of your people and locked up; . . . But note, my venerable Lords, that unless by those of your company who are not without knowledge of the day and night when the theft of the sacred objects was perpetrated there be restored and replaced in full what was stolen, not only in its place and into the hands of those entrusted with its custody, but also returned into the temple, remembering the silver chalice, there will fall upon them the greatest misfortune that ever befell anyone, on them and on their family; and furthermore, pestilence will approach your city and within its ramparts as great as ever covered your city or was contained within its walls, and let them not object to the above. . . . if that which was stolen is not brought back one way or another, that they will die the most miserable death, more lingering and more violent and of more inconceivable intensity than ever before occurred—unless everything is restored. . . .

He closes this dire forecast and fearsome but valueless tirade with an assurance:

Have no fear whatsoever, sirs, but that shortly all will be found, and that if it be not thus, rest assured that [the thieves'] unhappy destiny approaches. . . .

Also inserted into his text is a notice that he "can err," apparently to cover the possibility that if he is wrong, it will not be unexpected by his clients. Note that he says the silver will be found, or perhaps will not be found, and the thieves will suffer whether they are apprehended or not. In other words, this is a perfect example of waffling on every statement and giving nothing really useful while stimulating the authorities to suspect everyone around them. It is classical psychic claptrap, which has changed very little in the four centuries since Nostradamus used it, and it was venerable even then.

There is no record available to tell us whether or not the stolen silver was ever recovered, or whether a couple of local Orange miscreants began oozing their innards in answer to divine wrath. I feel sure that if Nostradamus had been successful, that fact would have been trumpeted far and wide; we've heard not a note. No recorded pestilence assailed the city of Orange, either.

A Possible Scenario

Writer Charles Ward, a prominent Nostradamian, suggested in 1891 what he felt was a "straw man" notion that he could easily knock down. He said it had been unkindly suggested by critics that

[Nostradamus] set up for a gift that he did not possess, and soon found the imposture was far more lucrative than the dull routine of medical practice, as in those times the superstition of the public was unlimited. The ignorance of the Middle Ages is pointedly contrasted for us now with the wisdom and knowledge of our own day.

I believe that passage to be an excellent and probably quite correct analysis of at least part of what drove Nostradamus to become a writer of prophecies. Ward's straw man is more likely made of bricks. The "wisdom and knowledge" of the 1890s did not serve to prevent author Ward from endorsing Nostradamus' powers.

The Miraculous Anecdotes

In among all the fanciful accounts that constitute the framework of the Nostradamus legend, the real man occasionally peeks through. I am trying to get a closer look at the authentic person so fleetingly seen. There is always a clutter of tedious legend that develops in the wake of every famous person, some of it obviously invented from scratch, some of it borrowed from other legends, and much of it based upon some relatively minor event that becomes embellished to the status of a miracle. No biographical study would be complete without giving the mythology as well as the facts, and anecdotal material that has developed during the last four centuries about Nostradamus is most revealing. Here are a few of the stories, most of them related by de Chavigny, the disciple who attached himself to the prophet not long before his death, and became his biographer.

The Lost Dog

The story is told of Nostradamus during his 1556 visit to Paris at the command of Queen Catherine. He had been overworked by a heavy schedule of casting horoscopes, not only for his royal hosts, but for other lesser nobility who could afford his services. The prophet was lodged at the home of the Cardinal Bourbon-Vendôme, Archbishop of Sens, as befitted such a distinguished visitor. Abed late at night and suffering from a painful attack of the gout, which was one of his persistent physical problems in his last years, he was finally comfortably drifting off to sleep when he was awakened by a loud knocking on his door.

A young page in the employ of the noble Beauveau family had lost one of his master's favorite hunting dogs, and had come, at his wit's end, to seek the seer's help. But Nostradamus was not about to further extend himself, and certainly not for a minor servant. Angrily he shouted at the door from his bed,

> Why do you trouble me at this hour, king's page? You are making much ado about a lost dog! Go along the road that leads to Orléans. You will find the dog there being led on a leash.

The desperate lad hastened to the Orléans road and had hardly been on it for an hour when he encountered a man leading the sought dog on a leash. Stunned but grateful, the page was left wondering how the doctor from Salon had known he was a king's page and had lost a dog, let alone where the dog could be found.*

The Unlikely Pope

Another famous account tells of Nostradamus during his sojourn in Italy. Walking on the road near the town of Ancona, he encountered a group of Franciscan monks. Standing aside to let them pass on the narrow, muddy road, he suddenly exclaimed and threw himself on his knees in the mud, bowing his head and clutching at the garment of one of the monks.

All the group were astonished at this strange act of obeisance. The monk he had honored was a former swineherder of very lowly birth, one Brother Felice Peretti, a person of no distinction. Asked why he had done such a silly act, Nostradamus replied, "I must yield myself and bow before his Holiness." A moment later he was on his way again, to the amusement of the monks.

Nineteen years after the death of Nostradamus, Peretti was installed as Pope Sixtus V.

The Peasant Girl

It is said that one evening in spring, shortly after Nostradamus had attained fame as a seer, he was seated in front of his home when a young lady from a few doors away passed by on her way to the nearby woods to gather firewood. She greeted her famous neighbor. "Bonjour, Monsieur de Notredame." Replied the prophet, "Bonjour, fillette."

About an hour later, the girl returned laden with firewood. Again she greeted Nostradamus. "Bonjour, Monsieur de Notredame." The old man smiled and knowingly replied, "Bonjour, petite femme."

*This is the story, just as told and retold by many writers on the subject. No one seems to question the designation of the lad as a *king's* page. He worked for a minor member of the French court, not the king!

Should my readers be unfamiliar with basic French, I will say merely that "fillette" refers to a "little girl" and "petite femme" means "little woman."

Black Pig/White Pig

One of Nostradamus' clients was a wealthy gentleman named de Florinville. A tale is told that while the seer was visiting his estate, Monsieur de Florinville decided to put his powers to a test and have his little joke on his visitor as well. Nostradamus was shown two suckling pigs, one black, the other white. Asked to predict which of the two unfortunates would be served at the supper table that night, Nostradamus unhesitatingly pointed to the black pig.

That evening, Nostradamus was again asked which pig would be consumed at supper, and his answer was the same. Later, as the company sat down to dine and the main course was brought to the table, de Florinville announced to all present that the great prophet had failed on this simplest of all predictions, for the white pig, on the specific instructions of the master, had been prepared for their consumption. De Florinville had, so he thought, frustrated Nostradamus and was enjoying his prank to the fullest. Calmly, his celebrated guest asked that the cook be brought before the assemblage.

Questioned, the servant tearfully confessed that a minor mishap had occurred to him earlier that day. A tame wolf cub, normally kept outside, had wandered into the kitchen and seized the roasting white pig, destroying its appearance. The cook, terrified at this unexpected catastrophe, had thereupon slaughtered the remaining black piglet and substituted it for the original, not knowing that his pragmatic solution would become known to his master. The prediction was fulfilled.

(Being naturally skeptical and to some degree suspicious, I would have watched for a wink to pass between Nostradamus and the cook at this point.)

The Command Séance

Queen Catherine, ever willing to consult occult sources, asked Nostradamus to conduct a séance for her at the beautiful castle of Chaumont. Since her husband was now dead, she wanted to know the fate of her royal line, the Valois family, as applied to her sons, who Nostradamus had already told her would all be kings. Seated in a magic circle, Catherine followed the ceremony dictated by the prophet, staring into a magic mirror which acted like a window which revealed another room. The angel Anael was invoked, and soon she began to see the images of her offspring.

First to appear was Francis II, the newly crowned monarch of France. He walked around the imaginary room just once, then was gone. Next Charles appeared, who was to succeed Francis as king. He walked slowly around the magic room fourteen times before he, too, disappeared. Finally, the son who was to be Henry III of France was seen in the mirror, circling the room fifteen times. Each turn of the room was said to signify the duration of each reign, so Catherine now knew that Francis was not to live long.

How True Are the Anecdotes?

First, the story of the white and the black pig, when I read it, seemed somewhat familiar. After searching through many of my references, I found another very similar story told of a different prophet in another country and another time. In late-19th-century Sicily, Gregorio Nuncio Adolfo Pallantrini, whose great career as a prophet had been forecast by yet another seer with the unlikely name of Carucu Farucu, is said to have startled his father by warning him that he would be injured by a black cock that they observed running about the estate. Already aware of his son's prophetic abilities, so the story goes, the father ordered the bird killed and prepared for consumption by the servants. He also ordered a white cock to be prepared for his own table.

Again, before dinner, Gregorio warned his father, who shrugged off his words, confident that the black cock was unable to harm him. During the evening meal, however, the father began to choke violently and had to be relieved of a bone which had become lodged in his throat. Recovering, he was told by his son that he had been eating the black, not the white, cock. The cook, immediately questioned, admitted that a cat had stolen the white bird and that to conceal that fact, she had served the black one at the master's table.

The similarity of the two stories makes one wonder whether this is a standard tale told about all prophets, as soon as they attain enough fame.

(This same Pallantrini built his home on the slopes of Mount Aetna, went quite insane, and perished in the September 18, 1938, eruption of that volcano, an event which he apparently did not foresee.)

In the case of the séance story, I discovered that historian Nicolas Pasquier related an account of exactly the same séance, with Catherine present, the magic mirror and imaginary room and the visions of the three sons, and it even took place at the castle at Chaumont. However, Pasquier says that the medium in this case was not Nostradamus, but Cosimo Ruggieri, who is historically recorded to have been resident at Chaumont at that time, thanks to Catherine's need for an astrologer immediately at hand. For Nostradamus to have conducted that séance, or even to have been present he would have had to make a long trip from his home in Salon, an event which he and his chroniclers do not record. Furthermore, no history book I have consulted does so much as hint at any séance Catherine attended, except for the Pasquier account, and that makes Ruggieri the actor; *every one* of the Nostradamians' books that repeat the séance story have Nostradamus as the medium in attendance.

Along with Rasputin, Cagliostro, Paracelsus and many other charlatans of note, Nostradamus swayed not only the public but kings and popes by his words. We would do well to learn all we can from an examination of the life and the methods of the man who was once Michel de Notredame.

CHAPTER THREE

The Secret of Success

There is no consolation in the ambiguous language of the prophets; it leads the mind into confusion, darkness and doubt.
—JAMES ELLIS, 1832–?

The Philosophy of Prophecy

ONE OF THE PRESENT PREOCCUPATIONS of the New Age devotees is the idea that every event and particle in the universe is related to every other one. This notion is referred to as the principle of the Holistic Universe. With this principle operating, cause-and-effect changes radically, and prophecy is quite possible—theoretically. But without resorting to highly rarefied philosophical means, we can show that prophecy is already possible, on a certain level.

It is undeniably true that every event should be predictable. Possible exceptions are those which occur on the level dealt with by quantum physics,* therefore we will consider only grosser events. The parameters (position, quality, relative motion, etc.) of any entity determine what will happen to it *relative to the rest of the universe.* The rub is that we cannot possibly know all of these parameters. Stock market analysts and racetrack handicappers succeed only as well as their knowledge of the variables within their fields, and their guesses are subject to catastrophic error when an assassination, an "inside trader" or a lame horse brings them a surprise.

*Trust me. You don't want to hear *these* arguments.

Smaller "universes" offer greater success to prognosticators when enough data can be gathered. Throw a pair of well-made, durable dice enough times in a properly randomizing fashion, and it will be found that one-sixth of your tosses will add to seven, one-thirty-sixth will yield "snake-eyes" (2), and other possible numbers will appropriately—predictably—turn up in their proper proportions. The larger the number of throws made in such an experiment, the closer your results will be to those prophesied by mathematics. It cannot be predicted what total any *one* proper throw of a fair pair of dice will produce, but it certainly can be predicted what the *likelihood* of any number will be.

If we move into such larger and more complex "universes" as politics, prophecy becomes more difficult by many orders of magnitude. The parameters of just one human being are almost infinitely complex and unknowable; how much more unknowable are the parameters (and the parameters *of the parameters!*) of a voting population and all the variables that will influence its decisions? And politics is just one aspect of world history.

Of course, we tend to ignore what I have just rather simplistically outlined. We perceive the advent of a war or an earthquake as an event that is just sitting, waiting up ahead in time. It seems not too difficult to accept that some persons, claiming to be especially astute or divinely assisted, can "see" the event in position, waiting to occur. This is a notion that simple logic and a little thought will deny.

The professional prophet may very well believe that he or she has genuine abilities. It is very likely, even if that *is* the case, that the prophet has also encountered enough failures to realize that some showmanship is called for in maintaining a reputation. I think we can show, in the case of Nostradamus, that the Seer of Provence was quite aware of that need.

Rules of the Prophecy Game

It is not difficult to discover the secrets of the successful prophets. Author Dr. Eugene Parker did rather well in his brief 1920 summary of our seer's general methods, which does not include all those methods that I will suggest:

[Nostradamus'] method of prophecy is tripartite. Firstly, he takes past events and gives them a figurative garb which renders them unrecognizable, putting them in the future tense. Again, he describes a series of well-chosen probabilities, based on contemporary conditions, and treats them likewise. Thirdly, he makes a series of random shots all of which are unlikely but still possible.

There are time-honored rules for earning a reputation as a prophet, and a few reflections on the career of one of the most highly regarded of today's crop of oracles, Jeane Dixon, will supply us with the general *modus operandi* by which these folks attract and hold their audiences. I will use her procedures to illustrate the strategies involved.

Ms. Dixon's story was told by Ruth Montgomery in a 1965 opus, *A Gift of Prophecy,* a gushy, fawning book loaded with nonfacts that made Dixon look like the most powerful prophet of all time. It is specified that Ms. Dixon's power comes directly from God and that she has been given a divine mission to spread a special message to the world of sinners.

Dixon should have eventually had to rationalize the long list of major predictions printed in that best-selling book that failed, one after the other, to be fulfilled. Her own book, *My Life and Prophecies,* was reviewed by Marcia Seligson in *The New York Times Book Review* of October 19, 1969. Said Ms. Seligson:

> [The book is] basically . . . the harmless rant of a lady who may or may not be a psychic or may or may not be a fruitcake . . . a silly self-serving back-pat consisting of creepy anecdotes.

Here are the major rules for success in prophecy:

Rule Number 1: Make lots *of predictions, and hope that some come true. If they do, point to them with pride. Ignore the others.*

Over a four-year period, researchers examined predictions offered by major psychics working for the *National Enquirer,* the supermarket tabloid. There were 364 predictions, of which a total of *four* were correct. This means that the psychics—all of them top-rated professionals—were 98.9 percent wrong. They are all still in business, except for one who died. Judging from his record, death was probably unexpected.

Even Nostradamus' editor, Jean Brotot, who begged him for fresh material, was dismayed at the wordiness of the work he received. Late in 1557, with the *Centuries* beginning to create a great demand for the author, Brotot complained to him:

I just received, on September 19, two prognostications. I am stupefied at your verbosity! Today the fashion is to use fewer words. I have therefore decided to print only one of them—your choice—while adding to it the useful elements of the other. . . .

Rule Number 2: Be very vague and ambiguous. Definite statements can be wrong, but "possible" items can always be reinterpreted. Use modifiers like these wherever possible:
I feel that . . .
I see a picture of . . .
It might be that . . .
Perhaps . . .
Look for . . .
I'm getting . . .

English author William Fulke wrote in 1560 on the serious political effects of Nostradamus' prophesying on the new government of Elizabeth I. The public of Britain was reading and being influenced by the translated Nostradamus almanacs that were easily available. Elizabeth's administration, tenuously beginning to take hold after the dreadful reign of Bloody Mary, needed every bit of public support it could muster, and the Nostradamus almanacs predicted, among other calamities such as earthquakes and assassinations, a very short reign for the new queen. Fulke pointed out the ambiguous quality of the French seer's works:

What? is it to be kept in sylence, howe slowlye and coldly the people in the last yeare, seduced by the foolyshe prophesye of Nostrodamus [sic] addressed them selfe to sette uppe the true worshippynge of GOD and hys religion, good Lord what tremblynge was there? What feare? What expectation? What horror? . . . But oure craftye Nostradamus, that could wrappe hys prophesyes in such dark wryncles of obsuritye, that no man could pyke out of them, either sence or understandyng certain. Without doubte he hath herde of the oracles of Appollo, whiche the devyll at Delphos, gave out of an ydoll to them that asked counsel, whiche were obscure, double and suche as myght chance bothe waies.

Fulke had castigated "sixe hundred more [prognosticators] of that sort" for the same techniques of deception, but it was Nostradamus who earned his special ire and attention.

Nostradamians like Charles Ward are quick to supply the classic excuse for this vagueness, on behalf of their master. They think it explains away the problem:

As to his obscurity, [Nostradamus] himself admits it as a thing to be cultivated both in the times he lived in and in those that were to follow. No one can truthfully deny that obscurity and prophecy seem to be almost interchangeable and convertible terms. The prophecies in Scripture are of such ambiguity . . . There are those who will hold that prophecies are useless, as they cannot generally be understood until they have been fulfilled.

Ward then proceeds to give his reader one of the classic paradoxes:

It is obvious that many prophecies are of such a nature as that, if they were clearly understood previous to the event, they would prevent their own fulfillment, and so cease to have been prophecies. What they foretold would never have occurred.

We must point out that Nostradamus, in the prose outline contained in his Epistle to King Henry II, which appears just before Century Eight of the *Centuries,* provides one of the very few places where he actually gave many quite specific, detailed prophecies of events that can now be checked out accurately because they are supposed to have already taken place. There is no ambiguity whatsoever in these statements, and the Nostradamians have carefully avoided discussion of this aspect of the prophet's work. As Leoni observes:

It seems that in the huge mass of predictions that can be found in the prose outline [to the Epistle], there is not a single successful prophecy. The dating of two calamities serves to discredit him completely in this work.

The two calamities referred to by Leoni are Nostradamus' predictions of the virtual erasure of the human race in 1732 and the culmination of a long, savage religious persecution in 1792. Note that both events were scheduled to occur well after Nostradamus would have safely entered the grave.

Nostradamus' obscurity earned the outrage of his clients. In a preserved letter from one François Bérard in 1562, the complaint is quite clear:

> I have read what you wrote concerning the ring, but I didn't understand it at all. Could you be more clear?

Rule Number 3: Use a lot of symbolism. Be metaphorical, using images of animals, names, initials. They can be fitted to many situations by the believers.

Author John Hogue suggests, for example, that a clear Nostradamus reference to Neptune actually means England. Of course, he points out, a lion can also mean England, or it can mean royalty in general. Or it can refer to the city of Lyons in France. The wolf can stand for either Italy or for Rome, since Romulus and Remus, the mythological founders of Rome, suckled from a wolf. Also, since invaders like the German Nazis acted like wolves, that might apply, too. Nostradamian James Laver tells his readers that, "the Leopard, of course, means England." And so on. . . .

Rule Number 4: Cover the situation both ways and select the winner as the "real" intent of your statement.

Jeane Dixon, after more than ten years of failed, published prophecies, predicted in 1953 the death of a blue-eyed Democratic U.S. president elected in 1960. In 1956, she reiterated that whoever won the U.S. presidency in 1960 would be a Democrat—an expected result—who would "be assassinated or die in office" but not necessarily in his first term. Then, late in 1960 she predicted that though she saw a young, blue-eyed and brown-haired man as the next president, John Kennedy would not win that election! Obviously, contrary to popular belief, she was not predicting the death of Kennedy, but of some other successful candidate. At one point, she predicted that Richard Nixon would win the position.

Dixon's "assassinated or die" prophecy did not mention the name Kennedy, or even any initials, nor did the city of Dallas or any times or dates receive mention. In this case her guess was probably prompted by the "presidential curse" notion that every president elected at a twenty-year interval (starting with Harrison) would so perish. Ronald Reagan confounded the experts by surviving this dreaded hex, though we may expect that soon some explanation of his exemption will be offered.

In the book *They Foresaw the Future,* by Justine Glass (Putnam, 1969), it is stated that Jeane Dixon predicted that JFK would be shot in the head, on the exactly correct day, and said that the assassin's name would have two syllables, start with an "o" followed by an "s," and end with a "letter that went straight up." Since Ms. Glass also makes what I know to be wildly inaccurate and irresponsible statements concerning the accuracy of the Nostradamus prophecies, I am not surprised to find that she also performs this service for Ms. Dixon.

Just a passing observation: Has anyone ever asked Jeane about her startling 1970 prediction that before 1980 "the two-party system will vanish from the American scene"?

Rule Number 5: Credit God with your success, and blame yourself for any incorrect interpretations of His divine messages. This way, detractors have to fight God.

Jeane Dixon never fails to emphasize this point, preparing her followers for her failures.

Rule Number 6: No matter how often you're wrong, plow ahead. The Believers won't notice your mistakes, and will continue to follow your every word.

Dixon said, among dozens and dozens of other wrong predictions, that U.S. President Richard Nixon would survive the scandalous Watergate affair and would make a political comeback in 1976, that Russia would put the first man on the moon and would move into Iran in 1953 and into Palestine in 1957, that "Red China" would start World War III in 1958 but be admitted to the U.N. in 1959, that Jackie Kennedy would—first—not re-marry, after which she married Onassis, then in 1976 after Onassis died, that she *would* remarry, which she didn't, that Russia would invade Iran in 1960, that Fidel Castro would fall from power in 1961 and be "more than likely dead" in 1966, that Eisenhower would not run in 1956, that Spiro Agnew would be "rising in stature," and that the Viet Nam war would end on August 5, 1966. The list is *very* long, and this is only a minor sampling. Ms. Dixon continues to enjoy a reputation as a successful prophet.

Rule Number 7: Predict catastrophes; they are more easily remembered and more popular by far.

Jeane Dixon has specialized in wars, revolutions, murders, earthquakes and a variety of other tragedies, thrilling her fans. In 1970 she predicted that in the 1980s a comet would hit the earth, causing great havoc—great earthquakes and tidal waves. She said she knew the spot where it would fall, but wouldn't tell. And she wouldn't tell why she wouldn't tell. Similarly, the prophecies of Nostradamus, where they can be deciphered at all, are almost entirely concerned with wars, leaders, diseases, floods, famines, knights, soldiers and royalty, and they copy, in some respects, the cataclysmic style of the Bible.

Earthquakes, as author Charles Cazeau points out, are the very safest of predictions, unless you have to specify where and when. The Earth's crust is constantly in motion, giving rise to thousands of major and minor quakes a year, with a major one every two or three weeks somewhere in the world. In 1989, there were eighty major earthquakes recorded.

Astrology teaches that though there are both beneficial and catastrophic signs and aspects to its basic ingredients, the catastrophic always takes precedent over the propitious. Discussing the "disaster" technique as used by Nostradamus, author Dr. Edgar Leroy has observed:

It is easy to see, even by a quick, superficial reading of the *Centuries* that they owe much of their incredible reputation to their rather catastrophic content. We tend to remember very little, usually, of the happy times of the past; we keep strong and exquisite memories of old misfortunes . . . [Readers] perceive rather clearly—very clearly, considering the jargon used—that yet more miseries and more cataclysms are announced. Of such are the prophecies of Nostradamus. The more they predict trage-dies, the more probable they seem!

Rule Number 8: When predicting after *the fact, but representing that the prophecy* preceded *the event, be wrong just enough to appear uncertain about the exact details; too good a prophecy is suspect.*

We have an excellent recent example of this technique. On March 30, 1981, the media were full of the story about an at-tempted assassination of U.S. president Ronald Reagan by a man named John Hinckley. Just as much attention was focused the next day on a report that Tamara Rand, a professional psy-chic in Los Angeles, had prophesied the event two months previ-ously during a television interview in Las Vegas. Rand had pre-dicted that the assassination attempt would take place during the last week in March and that the name of the would-be assas-sin was "something like Jack Humley," the report said.

The date and the name were close enough, but not perfect. Rand's technique was classic. As was subsequently discovered, the prophecy was seriously faulted. She had made the videotape of her prediction the day *after* the shooting, and had taken care to "miss" the details just sufficiently to give the right flavor to the prophecy. In Chapter 11, we will examine other examples in the Nostradamus repertoire that use this same technique. Tamara Rand did not originate it.

This same rule number eight was known to Jonathan Swift, the satirical English author of *Gulliver's Travels* who dealt a terrible blow to astrology by writing a *Prediction for the Year 1708, by Isaac Bickerstaff, Esq.* While professing belief in the art under his pseudonym, he also pointed out the absurdities it entails, then directed a barb at a well-known and financially successful London astrologer named Partridge. It took the form of an astrological forecast:

My first prediction is but a trifle, yet I mention it to show how ignorant these sottish pretenders to astrology are in their own concerns: it refers to Partridge the almanac-maker. I have consulted the star of his nativity by my own rules, and find he will infallibly die upon the 29th of March next about eleven at night of a raging fever. Therefore I advise him to consider of it and settle his affairs in time.

In Swift's essay, there followed a letter from an unnamed "gentleman" which described the death of astrologer Partridge on the correct day and at *almost* the correct time. The fact that the hour was somewhat off gave credibility to the piece, in accordance with rule number eight.

Vainly, astrologer Partridge protested in the press to his public that he was alive, even having an affidavit published to prove that fact. In response, Swift scolded him for calling the "gentleman" a liar and answered Partridge's arguments seriously, trying to prove he was dead. The repercussions of this delicious hoax were felt for a long time, but as always, astrology survived the attack.

There are many more methods for being successful in the prophet business, but these are the major items one needs to know. Compare the methods of Nostradamus with those being used by the prophets of today to give the impression that they have pronosticatory powers and you will find that they have adhered to the formulas so successfully applied by the Seer of Provence more than four centuries ago. These methods were ancient even then.

Regardless of your methods, it pays to have the right atmosphere in which you can flourish as a prophet. Nostradamus had exactly the milieu he required.

CHAPTER FOUR

The Right Time and the Right Place

*The most civilized people are as near to
barbarism as the most polished steel is to
rust. Nations, like metals, have only a
superficial brilliancy.*

—ANTOINE, COMTE DE RIVAROL,
1753–1801

The Inquisition

THE CIVILIZED WORLD in the 16th century was by our standards a savage, brutal and terrifying place, but the extremes of that day were commonplace to those who were born into it. Persons who chose to wander from whatever tightly circumscribed class they belonged to, who offended established mores, or who aspired to greatness from a weak position, came under sanctions that are unimaginable to us. It is no surprise that offenses against religious laws and customs were especially severely dealt with.

The medieval Inquisition first came into existence in 1231, when Pope Gregory IX commanded this inquiry into the religious preferences and practices of everyone within his authority. In its early years it was mostly active in northern Italy and southern France.

In 1252, Pope Innocent IV authorized the use of torture to

39

encourage extravagant and satisfactory confessions and valuable denouncements of others from the accused. Peter II of Aragon enhanced the effectiveness and novelty of the public trial-plus-sentence procedure known as the *auto-da-fé* (act of the faith) when he introduced public execution by burning alive at the stake. That process was referred to in official documents of the ecclesiastical courts as "relaxation." It was witnessed by high church dignitaries and noble personages, who applied long in advance for passes to attend such events. Executions were frequently delayed so that prominent guests might be accommodated.

Coming into full and terrible effect with the appointment of Thomas Torquemada as Inquisitor General of the Spanish arm of the Inquisition in 1483, this Holy Office became inarguably one of the most horrid inventions of our species, and was not likely to ever be matched until the blind, mindless mass slaughter of the Holocaust.

Michel de Notredame had excellent reasons for fearing the wrath of the Inquisition. To prophesy coming events denied the power of God to change the future. Furthermore, it was accepted that all thoughts, actions and abilities came either from God or from Satan. The art of living as a Christian was the art of sorting out which was which, a process that required ecclesiastic advice. A former Jew was hardly likely to have God-granted powers of prophecy. Such abilities would have to have been diabolical in origin. Witches were regularly brought to trial for prophesying.

Though in France the Inquisition never attained the ferocity it displayed in neighboring Spain, it was only the border between the countries that protected Nostradamus from the distinct possibility of the physical tortures of the ecclesiastical courts. At home, he might suffer disgrace, imprisonment and loss of property if convicted of heresy, but just across the Pyrenees, suffering and death were the rewards for the same transgression.

The Spanish Inquisition claimed an estimated three hundred thousand victims. This arm of the Holy Office was established in 1478 by Pope Sixtus IV. In the Spanish version of the process, the accused went through a macabre trial which they seldom survived. In 1827, Juan Antonio Llorente, former Secretary of the Inquisition in Spain, revealed the horrid truth of the judicial process that was used to place the accused on the bonfire:

> Never has a prisoner of the Inquisition seen either the accusation against himself, or any other. No one was ever permitted to know more of his own cause than he could learn of it by the interrogations and accusations to which he was obliged to reply, and from the extracts of the declarations of the witnesses, which were communicated to him, while not only their names were carefully concealed, and every circumstance relating to time, place, and person, by which he might obtain a clue to discover his denouncers, but even if the depositions contained anything favourable to the defense of the prisoner.

Llorente went on to explain that there were several options open to those who had been convicted and sentenced. To escape the torture which was usually used to extract a final confession—which was felt necessary to justify the execution—miscreants could admit sins they had never even countenanced and win immediate death. The spectacle was made less entertaining for the witnesses when convicted heretics opted for this fireside confession. In some cases, if they wished to escape the horror of being burned alive, they could confess and then submit to strangulation before their bodies were consumed in the bonfire.

In only one manner could death be avoided, and it was a fiendish method whereby the Inquisition perpetuated its own existence and obtained fresh fuel for its fires. By choosing to implicate other innocents and condemning them to the authorities, a victim could, under some circumstances, earn a commutation of his sentence to a long prison term, loss of property and final expatriation—if he survived the prison dungeon.

There was great fear among the French clergy that the ideas of Calvin, Luther and Zwingli were seriously engaging the attention of the faithful. In 1540, when Nostradamus was thirty-seven years old and had already made his first tentative forays into prognostication for certain prominent persons, the *parlement* of Provence passed a major law against heretics—which essentially but not exclusively meant Protestants—and that law was put into effect with great severity in 1545. The first edition of the *Centuries* was printed just ten years later.

Nostradamus was protected by several circumstances. For

one thing, he had the benefit of some very powerful friends. Catherine de Médicis, Queen of France, was his patron. She was not a person that one might offend by questioning the actions of a favorite. Lesser-ranked sycophants reflected Catherine's acceptance of the seer, and also sought him out. Let us take a few moments to examine just how much of an influence Catherine was.

The Royal Family of France

It was well said and is often repeated that "the hand that rocks the cradle is the hand that rules the world." This most extraordinary woman, not at all a beauty by the most charitable of standards, was described by a contemporary as "a beautiful woman when her face is veiled." She played her role in the constant shadow of Diane de Poitiers, Henry II's quite beautiful mistress, who influenced the king heavily in all respects. Catherine was the daughter of Lorenzo II, the ruler of Florence, who was the subject of Niccolò Machiavelli's famous and influential political essay, *The Prince.* She married Henry, Duke of Orléans, who became King Henry II of France, spent twelve years as Queen of France and then functioned as the power-behind-the-throne for her three son-kings of France.

Nostradamus' time in history was a period of unprecedented civil and religious wars and general calamity for France—exactly the kind of atmosphere in which prophets have traditionally flourished. The superstitious Catherine believed in every charlatan who came her way, and many books on the occult sciences written in her time were dedicated to her. One such book, *Mirror of Astrology* by author/friar Francesco Giuntini, featured an overpoweringly effusive six-page dedication to Catherine. In a somewhat different direction, it is said that Catherine even had Nostradamus cast horoscopes for her so that he might determine the fates of her progeny. Fortunately for him, the prophet was not around long enough to witness the decline and collapse of the Valois family that occurred in defiance of the rosy prognostications he gave the queen at that time. He said that all her sons would become kings—a pleasing and not unexpected prediction—and three out of four did, but he failed to say that they would all be king of *France,* meaning that they would have to die in succession. He said nothing about the terrors and other dreadful events of their reigns, nor the fact that Catherine's family line was about to end.

Henry II of France, her husband, was killed in a jousting accident in 1559. (Nostradamians dearly believe that their hero predicted this event in detail, a matter we shall look into later.) At that point, the perpetuation of the Valois line depended upon Catherine's three sons. She was not favored in that respect.

Francis II, the eldest of her sons but mentally and physically feeble, ascended the throne at the age of sixteen and was adroitly mismanaged by his enemies at court. Ever seeking political and familial advantage, Catherine quickly married him to the daughter of King James V of Scotland, Mary Stuart, who was to earn fame as Mary Queen of Scots, later beheaded by Elizabeth I. Francis lived to reign—in name only, since Catherine was regent—for only one highly ineffectual year, dying of tubercular meningitis. Mary kept her date with fate. She left France for England, and left no progeny for France.

The French throne was taken by the next son, Charles IX, then aged only nine. It appears that the most outstanding attribute that this son brought to the position of monarch was a boyhood zeal for lopping the heads off horses at a single blow, a delightful hobby in which he is said to have excelled. During his reign another discovery of Man's ever-curious mind, tobacco, was introduced to France as a popular pastime. It was also promoted as a cure for ulcers and other such ailments. So much for progress under Charles IX.

Of course, Catherine was appointed regent for him as well, ruling for him until he attained his maturity. She asked Nostradamus to prophesy for him, and in the only letter known in which she mentions Nostradamus, we find an account of the event. The original document is in the Bibliothèque Nationale, dated 1564. It says, in part:

> To my godfather, the Milord Conétable . . . and as we were passing through the Salons, we have seen Nostradamus, who has promised to my son, the King [Charles IX], everything good, and also that he shall live as long as you yourself, who he says shall see your ninetieth year ere passing this life.

Here, in this indisputably genuine reference, we have a prediction by Nostradamus that can be checked. The Conétable died three years later, aged seventy-seven years. Charles IX died at age twenty-four in 1574. Nostradamus missed the first guess by sixty-six years and the second guess by thirteen.

Learning from the manipulation Francis had suffered, Catherine stood firmly behind her second child-king, if not on him, and resisted attempts by the powerful and ambitious Bourbon family to wrest the French throne from under him. In effect, even after her regency expired, it was she who ruled France.

Catherine had very serious problems to handle on behalf of her sons. The Protestant party known as the Huguenots (the French Calvinists) had allied themselves politically with the threatening Bourbons, and for their decision paid a dear price. They were persecuted at every opportunity, and for the next forty years they and their supporters continued to die for their chosen religion at the hands of the Catholics. Charles, urged by the queen mother, ordered what became known to history as the St. Bartholomew's Day Massacre, in which some two thousand Huguenots were murdered in one night. When news of this action spread through the country, another estimated ten thousand French Huguenots were slaughtered in dozens of towns and villages across France.

Charles reigned for fourteen years. He was childless. Upon his death at age twenty-four from intestinal tuberculosis, he was automatically replaced by his brother Henry III, an infamous transvestite who scandalized the court by appearing in public dressed in outlandish costumes with his parading *mignons* (effeminate young men) at his side. Chroniclers of the day, particularly those of other national origins and ambassadors reporting to the home office, delighted in describing Henry's latest apparel, often in great detail. His jeweled brocades, platform shoes and comical corsets were caricatured at home and abroad.

Henry hated the job of being king, but not being suited to other lines of work, he floundered about on the throne of France, carrying out what were, even for that age, perfidious murder plots. Between assassinations and kidnappings, he listlessly conducted minor religious wars and somehow managed to survive them all.

Then Catherine died. Henry's guardian angel was no more, and to the satisfaction of many, a dedicated monk promptly assassinated the troublesome monarch. To no one's surprise, Henry, too, left France no heirs to carry on the line, and the

Valois family thereupon vanished from the history books, being replaced by the Bourbons. It was hardly as successful a family history as Nostradamus had predicted to Catherine.

Among her many other historically important accomplishments, this queen of France doubtless served to protect the prophet Nostradamus until his dying day, merely by the fact of her well-known patronage and the several honors that she and her son-kings bestowed upon him.

Friends in High Places

Nostradamus used his royal connections, real or imaginary, to good advantage. In 1561, his reputation already very well established, he was chided by a minor French noble who had astrological pretensions for failing to deliver certain information as promised. He replied:

> You ask me why I have not responded to your innumerable points. Know, first of all, that I have been too busy. It was absolutely necessary for me to answer to the princes. Then, above all, as soon as I saw your envoy on my doorstep, excellent astrologer, even before he greeted me I felt a blockage within myself by reason of his nearness. From now on, if you wish my services, please arrange matters so that this person does not know what you are asking of me. As far as *you* are concerned, who ask me what your ascendant is, it is Virgo. One of you will drink poison. [Written at] Salon.

One can postulate that the messenger asked for a prediction or two along with what his master had requested, and made an unfavorable impression on Nostradamus, perhaps by asking for a straight answer. Here, the prophet provides a no-nonsense answer, but allows his client to decide to which of the two, master or servant, it applies. There is little doubt who is being encouraged to drink the poison.

The View From the Bench

There has been much discussion about whether or not the practice of astrology was actually illegal. François Buget, the bibliophile who came upon some Nostradamus letters briefly in 1862 before they were again lost, cited Article 26 of the laws of Orléans, dated January 31, 1561, claiming that it forbade astrological prophecy. He erred. Though there were numerous other secular laws against witchcraft and sorcery in general, that Orléans law simply prohibited the sale of almanacs without the permission of the bishop, a different matter altogether. Permission was available if the church coffers were sufficiently improved by the applicant, a system not unlike a regular modern licencing procedure.

The View From the Pulpit

There were archbishops and even popes who were fond of consulting astrologers; the line between God and Satan was not as sharply drawn as some thought. Julius II had his coronation in 1503 (the year Nostradamus was born) scheduled by astrology. His successor, Leo X, had medical forecasts done by his astrologers, and the Consistory of Paul III in 1534 was held on a date deemed by astrologers to be propitious.

Such dalliance by ecclesiastics might have been another factor that kept Nostradamus farther from the flames than might have otherwise been the case. In his writings, he frequently brought the reader's—and Rome's—attention to his piety and reminded them that anything he accomplished was by the grace of God, and with His glory in mind. Any expressed interest in blatantly unholy practices such as the magical rites he hinted at in his first two quatrains of the *Centuries*, could have brought him to the immediate unfavorable attention of the courts of the Inquisition.

Had he been examined by those courts, he might well have argued his way out of his difficulty. Well educated and bright, he could have advanced an ecclesiastically sound argument. Legal arguments in that time were very much a matter of definitions. To 16th-century theologians, there were three recognized classes of extraordinary events. "Marvelous" matters were involved with the ordinary world of plants, animals and other objects. "Miraculous" events and articles were the direct result of God's actions, but "Magical" phenomena were placed among diabolical matters. The heavens were close enough that an interpretation of the movements of stars and planets as related to people was acceptable as marvelous and not magical. The reasoning was that God had set the heavens in motion as a miraculous event, thus observation of that system was acceptable and might even be considered a celebration of the miracle. Therefore, it could be argued, astrology might be marvelous, but it was not magical and it did not invade nor threaten God's territory.

We know of one occasion when Nostradamus did appear briefly before minor representatives of the Inquisition and argued himself out of an accusation concerning a remark he'd made some years before that had become known to the authorities. On another occasion, when he was visiting the royal family, he prudently left Paris earlier than planned when another possible inquiry began to mature. He was no fool, and would not have wanted to call upon Catherine for protection when merely leaving town would serve as well.

An Appeal for Magical Assistance

Even clerics were subject to the vengeance of a threatened church if they attempted to step out of line. An anonymous Catholic cleric wrote to Salon in 1560 pleading for assistance from Nostradamus:

> I am struck down by such despair, that you are my only hope. Because I wish to be relieved from my vows, my superiors threaten me with life imprisonment, and don't even want to hear any discussion of an appeal to the Holy See. They fear that at Rome I might obtain my dispensation. In any case, even if I obtained it, I'm sure that they would not hesitate to burn it and throw me in prison forever. Must I expect an even greater misfortune? Am I to be delivered from this prison? Last May 20th of this year 1560, I was 48 years old. I see everywhere in my nativity the evil influence of Saturn. Could you tell me how to escape from all these perils?

There is no record of the response Nostradamus might have offered this unhappy man.

A Very Careful Life-style

Though history tells us that Nostradamus was not a particularly popular citizen of Salon de Provence, he seems to have behaved himself wisely, pursuing a life-style that was, if not exemplary, barely acceptable. He lived in a modest home in the Ferreiroux quarter of the city, on a street which is now named Rue Nostradamus. Most of his home is preserved there as a museum.

(I met an American photographer who had done an extensive photo essay on Nostradamus for a popular magazine. He told me that he found the Nostradamus home quite bereft of anything that would provide his publishers with the kinds of photographs they wanted, so he shopped around for an engraved medallion, a crystal ball and various old manuscripts which could be properly placed to bring interest to his project. When he was preparing to leave, the gentleman in charge of the Musée Nostradamus suggested that the "props" might be left behind. One recent book on Nostradamus, evidently attempting to perpetuate one of the many titillating stories establishing Nostradamus' prophetic abilities, shows a photo of a medallion engraved "1700." One wonders about the source.)

Though some imaginative writers have "improved" their accounts of his life by ascribing to Nostradamus an active interest in various Black Arts, which included necromancy, witchcraft and any sort of Satanic communication, it is doubtful that he pursued such studies, even in secret. The Notredames were only a generation away from their Jewish background, and from time to time their neighbors doubtlessly reminded them, by one means or another, of those doubtful origins. Careful adherence to their adopted faith and eschewment of any association with pagan magic was prudent indeed for the family.

His biographers, including his eldest son, reported that he was "reviled by the common people" of Salon, and "resented" by the authorities there. They were dismayed by his astrological pursuits and the resultant questionable fame he brought to their city. However, when his influential friends arrived in town to seek his advice, the citizens prudently suspended their insults temporarily to take advantage of his celebrity.

The Index of Prohibited Books

Support of the aristocracy was probably responsible for Nostradamus being permitted to have anything published along the line of prophecy. His writings certainly were eligible for official censure by the church, which would seem to ensure their inclusion on the Index. That instrument of the church was a unique and powerful weapon against heresy, and has an interesting history.

In A.D. 496, the last year of his reign, Pope Gelasius I issued the first list of both recommended and prohibited books, the precursor of the Index. The list was meant at that point as a general guide to faithful Roman Catholics, though special exceptions were made whereby high-ranking scholars could read specified texts for very specified purposes. It was not until 1559 that the first official *Index Librorum Prohibitorum* was printed by Pope Paul IV. This was a strong document, in some cases proscribing the entire literary output of certain authors such as Italian astrologer Luca Gaurico.

The new Index was ardently enforced. Its serious aspects became evident when, in the bull of January 5, 1559, *all* permissions for reading prohibited books were revoked, and officials of the Inquisition were instructed to prosecute all who read or possessed such material. Under the new rules, confessors in every church were instructed to ask their penitents if they knew or had heard of any persons possessing, reading or dispersing writings which appeared on the Index, and in particular anything dealing with Lutheran doctrine, which was the major focus of the bull. The confessors were required, on pain of excommunication, to inform the Holy Office directly of any information thus obtained.

No one was exempt. Church officials, bishops, archbishops, patriarchs, cardinals, kings and emperors came under this order, and accusations poured in from all quarters when it was announced that a 1505 edict was not only still in effect, but was now renewed. That edict awarded to the accuser one-fourth of the confiscated property of any convicted sinner. The bonfires of the Inquisition blazed regularly, fueled by new candidates identified by ambitious informers. Simultaneously, church coffers swelled dramatically.

But it was not until 1571, shortly after Nostradamus' death, that the infamous Congregation of the Index was set up by the Vatican. This was a commission which established and then rapidly expanded the list to include many thousands of books and other minor publications that appeared to threaten the authority of the church. Faced with the effects of the Protestant Revolution, the Index now had teeth, and they were sharp.

As this much more serious Index was published, hundreds of printers fled to Switzerland and Germany to escape the wrath of its author, Pope Pius V. He was a fierce soldier of the church who had once served as inquisitor for the district of Como, in Italy, a position from which he had been recalled as a result of his notoriously excessive zeal for stacking bonfires with hapless local heretics. Pius had openly advocated the slaughter of each and every French Huguenot heretic. He eagerly excommunicated Elizabeth I of England for her reversal of Mary I's commitment of her kingdom to the Vatican and her vexing failure to come to heel, but his various plots to also dethrone her were frustrated.

Pius was certainly not averse to expanding the Index, and Nostradamus' *Centuries* would of course have soon come to his attention. The extent of the support given to the French prophet, even after his death, and his popularity among all classes of society, is indicated by the fact that his works were not placed on that forbidden list by Pius V. In fact, they did not appear there until more than two centuries later, in 1781.

(The church did not abandon the Index until 1966. By that time it had become evident that burning people alive for writing, publishing or reading books not supportive of the faith was no longer as popular nor as acceptable as it once had been. Worse, the Index was serving as a convenient guide for enemies of the church to identify writings potentially useful to their needs.)

It was not because Nostradamus' work was not taken seriously that it remained so long off the Index; his effect on the politics of Europe was very noticeable. Though then as now responsible persons recognized his work for the flummery it was, the general public gave weight to his writings and were influenced by the fears he invoked in them.

In spite of its eventual inclusion on the Index, hundreds of copies of the early printings of the *Centuries*, genuine and spurious alike, are still in existence, having managed to escape the ecclesiastical flames.

The Dreadful Secret

In the Bibliothèque Nationale, the French equivalent of the U.S. Library of Congress, there exists a manuscript designated as BN Lat. #8592. It is a collection of fifty-one letters that passed between Nostradamus and his clients, covering the period from 1556 to 1565. Latin copies of the originals, these letters show signs of having been slightly corrected and clarified by his secretaries and his heirs, but they have been carefully certified as genuine and were undoubtedly from his own files. This correspondence provides us with a view of the character of Nostradamus that has hitherto only been suspected.

A meticulous translation of these difficult documents was very recently done by the scholar Jean Dupèbe. The collection was published in Switzerland as *Nostradamus—Lettres Inédites (Nostradamus—Unedited Letters)*, translated into modern French. The history of the manuscript is fascinating. On February 4, 1629, César Nostradamus (the oldest son of Nostradamus, and then seventy-five years of age) wrote to a close friend named Peiresc:

> I am arranging the old papers that I promised you and I will write as well to my nephew [Melchior] De Seva to send me the book of Latin letters so that it can be given over to you.

On March 20 César wrote to De Seva and with a seemingly strange desperation pressed him for the letters:

> I have looked in vain for the book of nativities that I believe you may have, begging you and conjuring you by the power that the right of nature and blood give me over you, that as soon and as faithfully as possible you should give it over into the hands of Monsieur Le Conseilleur de Peiresc.

A week later, obviously relieved of his anxiety, he wrote a very serious letter to Peiresc, who had just received the book:

> I have never received a letter that has pleased me more than the one that your lackey gave to me yesterday . . . there is no news happier to me than to have learned that the manuscript of Latin letters has fallen by happy fortune into such worthy hands as yours. I entreat you then, with a solemn prayer which has the force of an honorable oath, to guard it inviolably, to correct it on

any points that might have some bitterness in them and not to communicate it to Monsieur de Valois, who has such a horror of anything of which he is ignorant, nor to any soul, whoever it may be, because it is mine by inheritance. As such, I give it to you and consign it to your care with confidence. My nephew [De Seva], who is ignorant and ill-advised, does not know, as I do, the obligation that honor and the name of my father (who was a mortal man, and not an angel) and all his people and myself in particular, thus hand to you, as long as the world shall be the world. Under this condition then—that no one shall ever see it—I send it to you and give it to you.

This book of Latin letters went into the library of Peiresc, and was thought to be lost until a bibliophile named François Buget reported it in circulation in 1862. Then it vanished again and after unknown changes of hand was once more brought to light in the hidden recesses of the Bibliothèque Nationale in 1961. It is fortunate that it was effectively immune from casual scrutiny for so long, and César had ample reason to have it carefully hidden away. This manuscript was at the same time both a precious heirloom and a terrible burden for César: precious because it consisted of rare documents that belonged to his father, and a burden because therein his father had revealed himself to be dangerously favorable to Protestantism, despite his public protestations that he was such a zealous Catholic.

A Blatant Duplicity

Nostradamus, for perhaps quite understandable reasons, exhibited his duplicity and a certain opportunism by loudly proclaiming his orthodox piety publicly and more quietly declaring in his letters where his sympathies actually lay. In his predictions for the month of March 1563, he wrote:

I see here great adventures in and for the Church, the church that I call the Holy Catholic and Apostolic Church, by which all such affairs proceed and for which all the world will be pacified. Those who try to destroy the Holy Mass that was set up by Jesus Christ deceive themselves greatly. Those who do it will not last long, unless they think about restoring it and putting it back into its former state, and similarly to extinguish, suffocate and annihilate the other dreams that they have . . .

What followed was a shameless paean to Pius IV, "truly pious in name and in deed."

In his Epistle to Henry II, which introduced his full edition of the *Centuries,* Nostradamus attacked at length the "paganism of the new infidels," and his Ephemeris for 1561 was pointedly consecrated to Pope Pius IV. The next year, he dedicated an almanac to the Pope's cousin, Fabrizio Serbelloni, a Milanese authority who had been specifically charged with suppressing heresy. In the dedication, Nostradamus thanked Serbelloni for delivering the city of Avignon from the "enemies of God." The prophet specified as enemies the "seditious madmen and tyrants of the new sects" and protested that their stated ambitions seemed to "resemble Judaism more than Christianity."

But in his letters to the German Lutheran Lorenz Tubbe, this astrologer from a once-Jewish family was openly heretical, clearly proclaiming his strong Lutheran sympathies. He referred to the Protestants as "Christians" and called the Catholics, whose violence he detested, "Papists." This declaration, without any doubt, would have placed Nostradamus against a stake with a generous supply of kindling had it been intercepted. In this small sampling of letters, we find more than enough evidence to doom him, and César's fright at not having the wandering letters safely accounted for becomes quite understandable; he, too, could have been burned for his father's transgressions.

In spite of this bombshell that Nostradamus had allowed to circulate into the academic world, that environment was the right time and the right place in which he could flourish. And he did.

CHAPTER FIVE

Medicine in the 16th Century

Medicine has been defined to be the art or science of amusing a sick man with frivolous speculations about his disorder, and of tampering ingeniously, till nature either kills or cures him.
—DANIEL DRAKE, M.D., 1785–1852

Astrology in Medical Practice

THOSE RENAISSANCE SCHOLARS who pored over old magical manuscripts became newly aware that savants of the Middle Ages, particularly the early physicians, had admired astrology and applied it to the healing trade. Ingeniously contrived and derived nostrums ranging from early herbal versions of the ubiquitous mustard plaster and the equally perennial mud bath, to contrived concoctions of various substances such as dried flowers, minerals, animal glands and pollen, used along with the ever-popular practice of bleeding patients for almost any complaint, were said to be more efficacious when prescribed for use during certain astrological configurations, and were even believed to be deadly when *not* used in accordance with astrological discipline. Along with the useful and often dangerous or deadly processes were quite effective treatments such as prescribing rest, the ingestion of liquids and certain herbs taken in the form of teas. The rationale for blood-letting was that certain "humors" were contained in the blood of the patient, and would be drained away with the blood. Both incision of a vein and leeches were used to tap off the vital fluid.

Also, new to Nostradamus' era, a variety of nonorganic chemicals containing such metals as lead, mercury, copper and selenium were administered. This innovation had been introduced by Paracelsus, and the effects were often dramatic but fatal; the disease went, but so did the patient. Much more benign, but useless, was the use of "magnetic" passes of the hands or of actual magnets over the body.

Physicians of the 16th century were among those of learning who most readily accepted astrology and attempted to use it in their work. Medical astrology was taught at such prestigious university faculties as Padua and Wittenberg. This attraction of physicians to astrology was largely a natural result of their attempts to relate all natural phenomena to the functioning of the human body. Astrology satisfied this need by assigning different parts of the anatomy to specific planets and signs. Thus Nostradamus, as a physician, came by his attraction to the art quite easily.

Astrology teaches the ancient notion that various organs, areas and appendages of the human body are "ruled" by the zodiacal signs assigned to them. In Egyptian astrology, which also recognized the planets as gods, the human body was divided into thirty-six parts, with a god assigned to each one. Ra, the sun god, was lord of the forehead, the moon was mistress of the brain, and Mercury governed the tongue. Saturn had only the left eye, Jupiter the right. The Greeks enthusiastically adopted all this claptrap and expanded on it, but switched it around. For them, Saturn ruled the right ear and Mars the left (for males only, it was reversed for females) and Venus, the goddess of love, looked after the belly, the genitals and legs, because those portions, they said, were involved in the passions.

All this superstition has persisted into today's occultism. In modern astrology, the heart is the domain of Leo, Virgo governs the intestines, and Cancer is in charge of the breast and stomach. Saturn in the sign Capricorn indicates skin rash or arthritis. Venereal diseases are likely when Jupiter and Saturn appear together in Scorpio. And so on. Some of us are not yet free of medieval notions.

The early church tried to replace these quite imaginary correspondences with its own, by declaring that body parts were instead protected and regulated by various sanctified persons: Saint Appolonia cares for teeth, Saint Erasmus watches over the abdomen, while the throat and lungs are tended by Saint Blaisius. These equally fanciful relationships are still preached to the faithful, and the days dedicated to the respective saints are still set aside for special prayers and ceremonies concerning specific afflictions. However, the more attractive astrological labels have almost replaced the newer religious attributions. Even today, astrologers teach that there is an association of signs and planets with parts of the body, and use that concept in advising their clients, while the Catholic church prescribes prayer directed to appropriate saints who are empowered to provide relief of specific bodily dysfunctions.

As early as A.D. 1153, the University of Montpellier, where Nostradamus was to study, had become a very important center of medical knowledge. That astrology was part of Montpellier's curriculum was recorded by Chaucer in his *Canterbury Tales* description of a student who attended that famous university:

Well could he guess the ascending of the star
Wherein his patient's fortunes settled were.
He knew the course of every malady,
Were it of cold or heat or moist or dry. . . .

It is a puzzling matter of interest, however, that no astrological texts are listed as having been used at Montpellier in that period. Since the Montpellier curriculum emphasized surgical procedures, to which astrological influences were less applicable, astrology may have been a minor subject of that university.

A Successful Physician

Nostradamus graduated from Montpellier at age twenty-six. He quickly earned a reputation as a physician who had successfully treated the plague. Grateful recovered patients showered him with testimonials and soon brought about his financial security. It cannot be denied that the work he did as a physician, while well paid, required determination, dedication, compassion and above all, courage.

From a distance of more than four centuries, we can only guess how successful he was in his specialty of treating plague victims, with or without astrology. The only treatment we know he offered was the traditional mixture of poultices, inhalants and lozenges made from herbs. It would certainly seem that diagnosing and prescribing by means of astrology could have improved only his client's emotional condition—though that alone might have been sufficient to earn him his renown. Medicine in the 16th century was far more of an art than a science, and in many illnesses the physician's major function, then as now, was in comforting the patient and relieving the symptoms, all the while awaiting the natural outcome of the disease. Frequently that outcome was satisfactory, and the reputation of the physician was thereby enhanced.

In that day, horoscopes dictated, or perhaps only indicated, which medications might neutralize or reverse the patient's condition. We must strongly suspect that a conscientious physician—and Nostradamus appears to have been such—would tend to react to and act upon obvious real indications rather than what astrology would suggest to him, thus behaving more like what we recognize today as an orthodox practitioner, no matter what the accepted astrological portents were or how strong the physician/astrologer's belief in the established discipline. We must also suspect that such a physician, willing to employ good common sense, would therefrom enjoy a much better success rate, a better reputation and a better income.

It was a minor miracle that Nostradamus himself survived the plague, exposed as he was to the various vectors of infection. His first family had succumbed *in toto* to that pestilence while he was away from home treating the disease in another city. As a result of that catastrophic event having occurred in his own household, he was castigated by those who would have been his potential patients. That fact, coupled with the loss of his family and his deteriorated personal relationship with his mentor Scaliger, was what drove him out of Agen and into the far reaches of France and Italy, ministering to plague victims.

The Plague

Of course, there is also the question of just what "plague" it was that Nostradamus treated. Known in the 14th century as the Black Death or Le Charbon, *Yersinia pestis* claimed an estimated one-quarter of Europe's population at that time, about 25,000,000 persons. It was essentially a disease of the poor; the rich—including entire city governments—often left their homes and offices boarded up while they sought the countryside, awaiting the abatement of the disease.

The city of London was hit five times by the Black Death between 1593 and 1665, with a total loss of 156,463 lives, according to records. In the 1664–65 outbreak alone, 70,000 persons died in that city, and even before that disaster had fully abated, it was followed within the year by another, the Great Fire, which reduced the city to one-fifth of its former size. The city of London appears to have a powerful will to survive.

Medical practitioners of the 16th century, though by that time well informed by their own observation and by printed accounts from their colleagues on the progress and outcome of the plague, were little better equipped to deal with it than their predecessors had been, two centuries earlier.

Yersinia Pestis—the Nature of the Disease

Plague is a bacterial disease which occurs in three forms. By far the most common form is known as bubonic. This variety is not necessarily fatal, but sufferers exhibit every possible variation of symptom from mere indisposition to violent and painful death. Bubonic plague cannot be spread directly from person to person except under very unusual circumstances; it requires the flea as a vector. However, the pneumonic and septicemic forms of the disease can be directly communicated among humans by airborne means or by contact. These last two forms of the pestilence were, in the 16th century, almost universally fatal. They often still are, unless modern pharmaceutical and therapeutic treatments are promptly applied.

Doctors who rose to prominence in earlier times did so by a combination of learning, experience, good fortune, force of personality, basic common sense and the ability to bring comfort—not necessarily a cure—to the ailing who came to them. Even Ambroise Paré, a contemporary of Nostradamus and considered by many authorities to be the "father of modern surgery," seems to have been acknowledging this fact when he coined a phrase that he used to describe the healing process: "I dressed him; God healed him." That statement might, however, be more a cautious theological one than a brilliant insight.

It is only in the last fifty years that physicians have had an arsenal of specific remedies for a spectrum of diseases, though the medical function is still largely only an assistance to the body's natural defenses and recovery systems. I think it probable that astute physicians of any era have been aware of that fact, though it is not widely advertised in the profession, for obvious reasons.

Another Possibility

It is not unlikely that in a small percentage of cases the disease identified as plague when treated by physicians of Nostradamus' time was actually syphilis. This infection is believed to have been introduced to the rest of Europe by Spanish mercenaries working for King Charles VIII of France at the siege of Naples in 1495. These soldiers had carried it from the New World and efficiently spread it about Europe. Charles' Italian campaign, ranging through most of the country, established the disease in Florence as well, and from there all throughout the continent. It has been with us worldwide ever since.

Syphilis, with its intermittent pattern of seeming to retreat as it switches to more advanced stages, can be very deceptive to the physician. It often seems to have been completely stopped, only to reappear later in a more dreadful form. Any early physician who applied his efforts to a syphilis sufferer at just the right stage in the disease's natural progress would enjoy a substantially improved reputation. This is a factor which aids quacks even today, as they treat a variety of ailments. Though I certainly cannot call Nostradamus a quack in regard to his medical career, and what he treated was probably most often the plague, some of his practice might have involved the venereal disease as well, undifferentiated from *Yersinia*. It is interesting that Nostradamian John Hogue, keeping topical, has recently declared his opinion that many references in the Nostradamus prophecies to "plague" and "pestilence" may actually predict the advent of AIDS.

Medicine as a Science

Medicine is one of the many branches of science. Like most sciences, it began as a series of trial-and-error examinations of the possibilities. Every notion was looked into. The administration of herbal and mineral nostrums, often exceedingly unpleasant and thus believed more potent, but generally useless, became one approach; the ingestion of castor oil is a modern remnant of that phase of medicine. Various disagreeable physical processes which included cold baths and the application of hot irons, were popular in medieval times, and lasted well into the Victorian era; we can recall the mustard plaster in the not distant past. Included with these approaches was a vast repertoire of magical notions.

Eventually, what worked endured, while useless methods tended to be forgotten. Yet there are still some who believe that castor oil, mustard poultices, copper bracelets, powdered beetles, plain water and other quaint treatments are efficacious against sickness. They continue to believe because those who they think have approved these nostrums, and who are believed to have properly validated them, have not applied scientific methods, followed by adequate replication, in their tests. Quacks depend upon such blind trust by their patients, and it is what allows them to survive.

Against all the nonsense are rallied the true physicians, who use logic, tested methods and not a little intuition in serving their patients. But it is perhaps true that those physicians have tended to depend too much upon "heroic" chemical and botanical administration rather than encouraging more the natural healing powers of the living organism. Doctors of Nostradamus' day depended largely on those powers, since they had little else at hand.

The Baby in the Bathwater

Orthodox medicine has undergone many changes, some of them brought about by, surprisingly, the successes of the quacks. Placebo effects and suggestion, invoked by otherwise useless procedures, have become evident to modern medicine as possible tools for its use. In his book *Examining Holistic Medicine*, Dr. James Whorton quotes an 1858 comment by a New York doctor,

Dan King, on the efforts of Hahnemann, the Swiss quack who originated homeopathy, a bizarre discipline that administers to its adherents distilled water that is claimed to retain "vibrations" of substances that were once in contact with it:

> Perhaps Hahnemann did not live wholly in vain. . . . Through the use of his empty and inert means, we have been able to see what the innate powers of the animal organization can accomplish without medical interference. We have been taught to rely more upon these, and less upon art, and have seen the wonderful influence which the mind has over bodily functions. . . . The public may not require physicians less, but will demand less of them in the way of positive medication.

Great physicians have always been exceptional persons, and have deserved whatever rewards they have received. A persistent problem in medical science has been the lack of real understanding between patient and doctor; the patient often expects too much and the doctor frequently fails to inform about the limitations of the available medical service. My analysis above must not be considered a denunciation of the medical profession, early or modern, nor of Nostradamus. Dealing with the marvelous intricacies of the human organism is and always will be a difficult task, one requiring enduring devotion to an often unappreciated labor. I, for one, accept the failings of the medical profession along with its successes.

Medicine was only one aspect of science that was striving to develop in the 16th century. Belief in magic interfered with its success, as we have seen.

When Magic Ruled

*A belief in the powers of certain delusive
arts, particularly astrology, has greatly
retarded the progress of knowledge, by
engrossing the attention of many of the
finest geniuses the world has ever produced.*
—OLINTHUS G. GREGORY, 1774–1841

MOST HISTORY BOOKS will applaud the Renaissance period for
giving birth to true science. However, the person who is credited
with giving us the specifics of arriving at knowledge by inducing
generalities from basic experimentation was Sir Francis Bacon,
a somewhat post-Renaissance scholar. His ideas, though some
had been tentatively suggested earlier by various observers,
were not put actively in effect in an organized way until the 17th
century. Of the ultimate uses of science, Bacon was very pragmatic. In his opinion,

> The real and legitimate goal of science is the endowment of
> human life with new commodities.

With that statement, Bacon recognized that science, as well as
magic, is involved in the goal of trying to gain an advantage over
the expected and the haphazard aspects of daily life, either by
improved knowledge or by systems of control. Magic aims to
obtain either advantage or both. Science seeks only knowledge;
any resulting control is a direct product of that knowledge.

Sir James Frazer, the Scottish anthropologist who produced

the classic *The Golden Bough*, believed that human thought evolved "from magic through religion to science." He drew a line between magic and science:

> The primitive magician . . . knows magic only as a practical thing, and to him it is always an art, never a science, the very idea of science being foreign to his thinking.

Some Definitions

There is a definition of magic which I have always preferred. It says that magic is an attempt by Man to control Nature by the use of spells and incantations. That is a rather limited delineation of the idea, which I will expand to include any and all attempts to change things-as-they-are and/or to obtain knowledge of otherwise hidden matters by enlisting means that respond to invocation, adulation, sacrifice, threat or other coercion applied to certain postulated entities, forces and principles.

What we know as science stands apart from all magic, though as author Arthur C. Clarke has said, "Any sufficiently advanced technology is indistinguishable from magic." Science employs investigation to determine basic facts about the world, and applies rigorous tests to those facts to determine if they can survive. Religion comes somewhere in between, falling short of science but appealing to either neighbor. Religion is *far* closer to magic than to science, and can be defined as a form of magic.

The recognition of science involves acceptance of the sometimes disturbing fact that Nature does not care about Man, that there are no mysterious beings who guide our destiny, and that events are brought about by the operation of discoverable and quite beautiful laws. That beauty may also be terrifying and difficult to accept, but we enjoy no choice in the matter.

We need a working definition of science before we can discuss magic, since all attempts at learning or control fall under one of those two categories. Magic and science do not at any point overlap. The borders are sharp and clear. Anything in the area of learning or control that is not science, is nonscience; it is magic.

Defining science has been the goal of many individuals and disciplines, and that goal has been met with varying success. A charming though somewhat idealistic and, I believe, naive definition was supplied by Albert Einstein. He said that

> The whole of science is nothing more than a refinement of everyday thinking.

If I had an adequate definition of the term "everyday thinking," and I were sure that everyone is capable of it, I might still think that Professor Einstein was being somewhat unrealistic.

James Conant, once president of Harvard University, said that

> Science is the activity of people who work in laboratories and whose discoveries have made possible modern industry and medicine.

I respectfully suggest that with this statement, Dr. Conant fell into the jaws of those who delight in categorizing science as a sort of monolithic, capitalistic religion that serves to eliminate or neutralize any and all spiritual values. Also, I have seen some of the "activity" at some laboratories performed by people working at what they believe is science. They are sometimes mistaken in that belief. If they were not mistaken, the scientific literature would by now have accepted that nonexistent radiations—N-Rays—are given off by deadwood, metal, plants and most other materials, that pure distilled water can "remember" medications that it once encountered, and that gifted individuals can cause metal spoons and keys to bend just by looking at them.

The definition of science offered by physicist R. H. Bube is even more vulnerable:

> Science is knowledge of the natural world obtained by sense interaction with that world.

Then what, I must ask, can we make of hallucinations and simply wrong sensory impressions? Dr. Bube might be expected to report, after seeing illusionists David Copperfield or Harry Blackstone, that a pretty girl can be metamorphosed into a Bengal tiger by covering her with a colorful cloth, or that a human being can be irresponsibly sliced up by a buzzsaw and instantly restored without damage. His "sense interaction" of performances by these master conjurors would certainly lead him to that conclusion, and science would have then validated conjuring as a miracle art.

I believe that American mathematician and philosopher John Kemeny, a former president of Dartmouth who gave us the Basic computer language, had one of the better definitions:

> I shall use the term "science" to be all knowledge collected by means of the scientific method. . . . The scientific method is defined by the cycle of induction, deduction, verification, and by its eternal search for improvement of the theories which are only tentatively held.

The idea he expresses, that science is constantly subject to change, is absolutely essential to any proper definition of the subject.

I shall dare my own delineation. I believe that science is best defined as a careful, disciplined, logical search for knowledge about any and all aspects of the universe, obtained by examination of the best available evidence and always subject to correction and improvement upon the discovery of better evidence.

What's left is magic. And it doesn't work.

The Rediscovery of Magic, and an Important Book

In the 16th century, the lore of ceremonial magic, which had been handed down from generation to generation—when not simply reinvented—became suddenly known to a vastly greater audience as soon as printing became available. Very old hand-copied books and manuscripts, no matter whether valuable or not, were now sought out and set in type as long as there were potential customers for them. Antiquity, as usual, lent value to whatever could be turned into printed words, and scholars scrambled to obtain these newly minted secrets in attempts to improve their own specialties.

As a scholar of some considerable ability, Nostradamus had access to printed material that dealt with occult matters, and such material had excellent pointers that he could use to advantage. In 1455, a manuscript from the cultural center of Florence titled *Corpus Hermeticum* (Hermetic Works) began to circulate among the intellectuals of Europe. The ideas about magic and its application to mankind that were formulated in this book—

believed to have been written between A.D. 250 and 300—had been mentioned even in manuscripts of the late Middle Ages, though knowledge of the written Greek language in which it had been preserved had been lost in those times. Scholars who regained the use of Greek promoted this treasured, arcane knowledge, much of which was astrological, and it became prized as a privileged key to the occult. Printed copies of the *Corpus* spread throughout the civilized world for the next half-century, and appeared in the libraries of the intellectuals just as a major new religious and philosophical influence was being felt in Europe.

The Protestant Revolution fell upon the established church like a pestilence. It was in part a reaction to the obvious corruption of the Papacy under quite worldly leaders more concerned with fleshly and mundane pleasures than with the old, comfortable standards of spirituality, faith and simplicity that the medieval church had supplied. That revolution brought the Inquisition into full force and installed an atmosphere of dread on every level of society, thereby furthering the cause of the reformists rather than strengthening the hold of the Catholic church, by providing further examples of orthodox excesses.

There was an established medieval notion that certain gifted individuals had control of magical—diabolically sponsored— powers and thus could advise lesser mortals concerning the future. Since that idea was still very much evident in the Renaissance, augurs of various sorts plied a lucrative trade in spite of the threat posed by the Inquisition.

The Renaissance itself was productive for the intellectuals— and for future ages—but not necessarily for the ordinary folks of the time, who upon its debut suddenly found themselves without guilds, property rights or a local system of government in which they could fully participate. These common people were hungry for any advantage that the magicians and supernatural knowledge like Nostradamus' prophecies might offer them.

Printing from moveable type was barely five years old in Europe when the *Corpus Hermeticum* began to become known. The contents of the *Corpus* marked it as, purely and simply, a primer on magic. This book told scholars that the old gods were still alive and powerful. The Egyptian god Thoth, personified by an ibis-headed human figure, was known to the Greeks as Hermes Trismegistos (Hermes the Thrice-Greatest) and was regarded as the inventor of writing, among other basic skills. The *Corpus Hermeticum* was a series of writings ascribed to this god. It was a distillation of his wisdom, a collection of what purported to be practical methods of conducting one's life in tune with divine influences.

Magic has always been involved in two basic goals: It defines the rules for living in harmony with Nature and it is an attempt to *control* Nature, usually by means of spells and incantations; the former aim is preferred, the latter is attempted if that fails. If magic consisted only of a search for natural harmony, it would lose much of its attraction by becoming rational and acceptable, and it would run the risk of metamorphosing into science. In the *Corpus* can be found many reasonable approaches to sensible living, unfortunately far outweighed by accompanying superstition.

The major content of the "popular" Hermetic writings in the Hellenistic culture dealt with astrology, the notion that all parts of the universe are interconnected and that phenomena of Nature, specifically the motions of the planets among the stars, affect human behavior and can be interpreted to the benefit of humans. This information was said to be difficult to discover and evaluate, and divine revelation of the secret formulas and rules was sought by those who studied such matters. The newly available *Corpus* manuscript served to inform readers of the importance and popularity enjoyed by astrology in previous ages, and thus made the subject even more attractive.

The study of the healing arts was, in its early stages, not well differentiated from magic. Causes of disease were as mysterious as recoveries, and having no explanation, were believed to be induced miracles. Hermetic theology, aside from its astrological content, looked at the entire universe, including Man, as an animated entity, in a rather more naive fashion than even our modern mystics envision it under the label "holistic." The *Corpus* peopled the skies—the planets and stars—and the earth itself, with endless hordes of demons and other supernatural creatures. Each heavenly body was home to at least one devil, giving out invisible but potent influences that had to be dealt with.

This demonic anthropomorphism was a logical simplification of a complex puzzle, and really not too far from the truth. If we wish to validate this aspect of medieval thought, we can say that the postulated devils that inhabited the body to produce illness turned out to be viruses and bacteria, smaller than the ancients had expected, but living entities, nonetheless. As has often happened, the metaphor proved almost the fact.

Another interesting political aspect of the time made the *Corpus Hermeticum* popular if not just highly recommended: Its content was approved, endorsed and enthusiastically supported by the influential merchant-prince Cosimo de' Medici, certainly the wealthiest man of his day by far and arguably the most powerful, and by his immediate descendants. Particularly if you were a scholar or artist seeking patronage, it was prudent to admire Cosimo's favorite notions. In his position of influence, he supported and elevated numerous famous artists such as Fra Angelico, Lorenzo Ghiberti and Donatello, and he built, among other structures, the library that became known as the Laurenziana. In that library labored his well-paid copyists who preserved written works from all of Christendom and even the Far East, and Cosimo quickly adopted printing to perpetuate these writings.

One of his handpicked scholars was the humanist Marsilio Ficino, a brilliant man who had learned to read ancient Greek. Ficino became intensely interested in astrology through translating Plato and other Greek writers, and about 1460 he brought a copy of the *Corpus Hermeticum* to the Laurenziana and thus to Cosimo's attention. His Latin translation of the book was published in 1471. Though certainly popular for centuries before printing made its practice more easily learned, astrology was, from that point on, very much more of an interest and trendy attraction to all of Europe.

(Cosimo's branch of the Medici family subsequently produced popes and other influential figures, eventually giving the world Lorenzo the Magnificent and finally Caterina de' Medici (Catherine de Médicis), the queen of France who was to become an important patron of Nostradamus.)

The *Corpus* had a powerful influence on thinkers of the day, so much so that its influence can be detected in modern philosophy. It affected Renaissance scholars to the extent that it molded their approach to learning. The book preached a retreat from any attempt to actually understand the universe by solving its puzzles, a mind-set that was not to be abandoned until Francis Bacon and others introduced the beginning ideas of the scientific method.

In the *Corpus,* students were told that the existence of God can be inferred from a casual observance of Nature, but not from a close, intensive scrutiny; that would be challenging God. No attempt to measure or chronicle Nature was encouraged. The senses of Man were denied, the body resented as a prison in which the otherwise free-soaring soul is temporarily trapped. Knowledge was said to be attainable only through introspection.

The *Corpus* was, in effect, a cowardly surrender in the face of every mystery. It taught that death, and thus escape—ascendance—into a perfect world, should be eagerly sought. Every notion, dream or passing idea was to be considered a divine revelation. No one, it said, ever had an original thought, and Renaissance scholars never claimed to have developed any idea, giving credit to inspiration from previous authorities. In the long run, in their way of thinking, all knowledge came from God.

Though we may look to the Renaissance for poetry and music, not much really brave, hard thought took place. This is not to say that great thoughts are not expressed in poetry, but original, independent discoveries had to await the advent of the scientific method. Frequently, the declarations of Renaissance scholars were nothing more than folklore repeated and perhaps hyperbolized. There was no experimentation, and that idea was abhorred. A discussion of how many angels could dance on the head of a pin was far preferable to an experimental test.

Reading the *Corpus,* a modern reader must be impressed with the earnest nature of the authors, who were casually looking for patterns and formulae, trying to make sense of a complex world that defied their understanding and their naive methods of examination. Though their probing was the prelude to the scientific method, it fell just short of it. Very little of the *Corpus Hermeticum* is of any value in describing reality; it serves mainly as an example of convoluted, analogical poking about. The end effect on the modern reader can only be dismay at the squandering of so much time and intellect by so many scholars who, given the advantage of more freedom from tradition in their thinking processes, might have contributed substantially to the maturity of the species.

The Insane as the Possessed

Judge Bouguet of Burgundy in the reign of Henry IV held and enforced a highly colorful and hyperbolic view of the problem of sorcery in Europe, a view which was probably shared by many of those in positions of power. While there is no doubt that the numbers he threw about were totally unrealistic, his obvious panic is indicative of the general attitude of the day, when neurotics and psychotics were branded as victims of Satan rather than of chemical imbalances and functional imperfections. At the dedication of the Abbé d'Acey, he told his audience:

I believe that the sorcerers could form an army equal to that of Xerxes who had one million, eight hundred thousand men. Trois-Echelles, one of those best acquainted with the craft of sorcerers, states that under King Charles IV, France alone had three hundred thousand sorcerers. If this is so, what is the total number if we include other countries and regions of the world? Are we not justified in believing that since those days the number has increased at least by half? I have no doubts of this, since a mere glance at our neighbors will convince us that the land is infested with this unfortunate and damnable vermin. Germany can do nothing but burn them; Switzerland is compelled to do likewise, thus depopulating many of its villages; Lorraine reveals to the visitor thousands and thousands of poles to which the sorcerers are tied; and as for ourselves, who are not exempt from this trouble any more than others are, we are witnessing a number of executions in various parts of the land. Returning to our neighbors, Savoie is not yet free of them, since she sends us daily an infinite number of people possessed by devils who, when conjured up, tell us that they were put into the bodies of these poor people by sorcerers. Add to this the fact that most of those whom we have burned here in Burgundy came originally from Savoie, and what judgment can we form of France? It is difficult to believe that she will ever be purged, given the great number that

she had in the days of Trois-Echelles, let alone other more outly-
ing regions. No, no, the sorcerers reach everywhere by the thousands; they multiply on this earth like the caterpillars in our
gardens. . . . I want them to know that if I had my way, the earth
would be quickly purged because I would wish they could all be
united in one body so that they all could be burned on one fire.

With such unperceptive, unjust and unreasonable persons in
charge of the system of justice, it is a wonder that European
culture survived at all. Yet, despite these travesties of reason, the
unknown continued to attract followers.

The Direct Effect of Astrology

The effect of magical prognostications was felt very strongly all
through the civilized world. An *Almanacke and Prognostication
for 1559* by a popular English astrologer named Vaughan predicted:

> Dessencions, discordes, contencions, stryfe, great manslaughter,
> murmuracions, feares . . . noughty enterprises . . . moche pyllage,
> theftes, robberies, lyes, great noyses, tumultes, comocions . . .
> great mischiefe, hatred and wrath . . . deceite, treason, burnynge,
> adulterye . . . warre, envy, hatred, rancour . . . and finally all kind
> of wickednes.

There seemed almost no chance that Vaughan had failed to
predict every possible evil for that year, and panic was widespread.

Nostradamus, in particular, was widely read in translation
everywhere. Already primed by his almanacs, which had begun
appearing annually in 1550 and were published each year of his
life from then on, the public snapped up copies of the *Centuries*
(more commonly known as *Les Prophéties*) as fast as they
dropped from the press, beginning—reportedly—in 1555.*

That first printing was probably only a few hundred; books
were not mass-market items. But many pirated copies of the
Centuries and the almanacs, in several languages, circulated

---

*It is barely possible that no 1555 edition existed at all, though it has
been accepted by all leading commentators that it did. See Appendix
II for observations on this interesting possibility.

around Europe. In all there were likely many hundreds eventually in circulation during Nostradamus' lifetime.

In England, his impact was enormous, as modern historian Sanford Larkey has recorded in detail. The powerful *Centuries* had been in circulation for three years by the time Elizabeth I took the throne in 1558. But the annual Nostradamus almanacs had been around since 1550, and were believed to be dependable sources of information, even by such leading English scientists as Leonard Digges and Robert Recorde, each of whom produced many valuable contributions to the orthodox science of Elizabeth's England, mainly in the fields of navigation and astronomy.

Other seers (with the exception of Dr. Dee, whom we will meet in Chapter 9) had predicted that Elizabeth would not live a year, and that Mary Stuart would come to the throne. This was a popular notion that was jumped on by many other seers of the day, who fervently hoped it would come true. Particularly in a kingdom undergoing a major crisis, it was obviously dangerous to allow the magicians to have such influence over the public and thus over the monarchy, and strict measures were sought to limit their activities. A Bishop Jewel begged Elizabeth:

> It may please your grace to understand, that this kind of people, I meane witches, and sorcerers, within these fewe last yeres, are marveilously increased within your graces realm. These eyes have seene most evident and manifest markes of their wickedness. . . . Wherefore, your poore subjects most humble petition unto your highnes is, that the lawes touching such malefactours may bee put into execution. For the schole of them is great, their doings horible, their malice intollerable, the examples most miserable. And I pray GOD they never practise further than upon the subject.

The bishop's sermon, he said, was based upon Luke 11:15, which reads:

> The people were astonished, but some of them said, 'It is by Beelzebub prince of devils that he drives the devils out.'

I fail to see the connection, but no doubt Elizabeth saw it clearly. Edward VI, an ill-starred predecessor, had passed legislation against "fonde and fantasticall Prophesies," but that law had now lapsed. Elizabeth soon reinstated it. The new act of 1562 stated that

> divers evill disposed persons, enclyned to the stirring and moving of Factions Seditions and Rebellions within this Realme, have byn the more bolde tattempte the lyke Practice, in fayning imagining inventing and publishing of suche fonde and fantasticall Prophecies.

Heavy penalties were provided for prophets who might incite, suggest or condone any sort of uprising

> or by reason of any Time Yere or Daye name Blodshed or Warre, to thintent thereby to make anye Rebellion Insurrection Dissention losse of Lief or other Disturbance within this Realme.

Dissemination of such material by any means was illegal, and since most prophecy dealt with catastrophes, pretty well all fortune-tellers and astrologers could not publish. As a result of the new law, twenty booksellers were fined that same year for selling a translated Nostradamus prognostication.

English cleric William Fulke, who was to become a leading Puritan activist, attacked astrologer Vaughan and others in his 1560 book, *Antiprognosticon,* which was all the more valuable because it assailed the subject of prophecy from a logical viewpoint, rather than merely suggesting legislation to curb it. The book underwent an interesting change when it was translated from Latin into English. The original named five prophets in its title, but the English version named only one, Nostradamus. As Fulke emphasized, the Nostradamus almanacs and quatrains were the prophecies that were most popularly read, and which brought real terror to England.

The contemporary English translation of Nostradamus' almanac for 1559 contained this on the title page, purporting to be a brief summary of the most important events he had predicted for that year:

FOUR LYNES UPON ALL THE YEARE

Feare, yee, great pillynge, to pass the sea, to
encrease the raygne.

Sectes, holy thinges beyond the sea more
polished.

Pestylence, heat, fyer, the enseygne of the King
of Aquilon.

To erect a signe of victory, the cyty Henripolis.

But note: though Nostradamus here mentions a King of the
North (Aquilon) and a city obviously named after Henry II, he
fails to mention in this very specifically dated item *that Henry*
II will die in that same year, 1559. As we will see up ahead, this
is but one example of Nostradamus having failed to prophesy
the single most important event of that year, particularly in
regard to his own personal situation and geographical location
in France.

Not all English scholars of the day feared the Nostradamus
prophecies. One brave soul, Matthew Parker, was at first hesi-
tant about accepting an offered appointment as Archbishop of
Canterbury, though he eventually took the post. It was rumored
that he was in dread of some mention made in an almanac
prophecy* by Nostradamus concerning that post, but he replied:

> I pray you think not, that the prognostication of Mr. Michael
> Nostredame reigneth in my head. I esteem that fantastical hodge-
> podge not so well as I credit [other similar books] more than I
> regard Sir Tho. Moor's book of *Fortune's Answers upon the*
> *Chance of Three Dice casting.*

Parker is apparently referring to an early mathematical study of
chance involving dice. Moor (More) wrote a number of articles
on such curiosities, though I am unable to trace this particular
work of his.

We will next look into what the astrologers, both modern and
of Nostradamus' day, claim for their art, and why.

*No record of this almanac is known to exist.

CHAPTER SEVEN

Just What Is Astrology?

This is the excellent foppery of the world,
that when we are sick in fortune—often the
surfeit of our own behavior—we make
guilty of our disasters the sun, the moon,
and the stars: as if we were villains by
necessity; fools by heavenly compulsion;
knaves, thieves, and treachers, by spherical
predominance; drunkards, liars, and
adulterers by an enforced obedience of
planetary influence; and all that we are evil
in, by a divine thrusting on. . . .

—SHAKESPEARE: *King Lear*

I WILL DISCUSS THE NATURE of astrology, not only because Nostradamus used it to prepare his predictions, but because the interpreters of his work have often supported their own conclusions by reference to this ancient theory.

A Very Old Notion

The origins of astrology are usually placed in Babylon around 1000 B.C. However, though copious and accurate records of celestial events and cycles are on record from that time, and it is known that the Babylonians searched for and expected to find significant omens in almost every observable aspect of nature, no evidence exists that they believed the stars governed individual destinies. Masses of accounts, tens of thousands of recorded items carefully kept by the Mesopotamians, have been recovered, but only twenty horoscopes have been found, the earliest dated 409 B.C.

Imperial Rome was very heavily influenced by astrology. Wherever ruins of the Empire are found, strong belief in astrology can also be found. Called *chaldaei* by the Romans, astrologers became so powerful that they were expelled from Italy in 139 B.C., and again several times after that date. They persisted, simply because belief cannot be legislated out of existence. The historian Marcellinus wrote four centuries later that hardly anyone in his day disbelieved in the star seers, even those who had no religious convictions:

> It is singular enough that this vain credulity may often be discovered among the profane skeptics, who impiously doubt or deny the existence of a celestial power.

This persistence of belief has continued today in high offices. It is well known that the Reagan White House, through First Lady Nancy Reagan, used the services of an astrologer. For eight years before this fact was revealed to the general reading public by fired Chief of Staff Donald Regan in his book, *For the Record,* I had been astounding my lecture audiences by informing them of this bizarre reality, and I met with general disbelief. The Regan statement helped place his book on the best-seller list.

During a backstage conversation I had in Washington shortly after the publication of the book in May of 1988, Mr. Regan commented to me that he'd been surprised to learn, after dropping the astrology bomb, that his colleagues had known about the matter all along. "It was a topic of conversation among them, and it was sort of a running joke," he said. Was Mrs. Reagan's dependence on her astrologer, San Francisco's Joan Quigley, a real influence on the conduct of affairs at the White House? Regan thinks so. "Mrs. Quigley was the one that determined when the President of the United States would leave to go on a trip, when the best days were for a press conference. . . . When one controls the schedule of the most powerful man on Earth, one has an awful lot of power." Even Reagan's date for the famous visit to the cemetery in Bitburg was arrived at by Mrs. Quigley, who also claims to have instructed Mrs. Reagan to postpone the President's cancer operation for three days in order to allow the planets to assume a more favorable position.

If we add to Mrs. Quigley's top-level influence the more diffused but equally important effect of prophet Jeane Dixon's advice to numerous senators and other ranking politicians she claims as clients, astrology is seen to be a possibly significant factor in the game of politics, ancient as well as modern. And bear in mind that Ronald Reagan, in his autobiography, *Where's the Rest of Me?*, asserted his close personal friendship with Ms. Dixon.

History provides us with hints of the framework upon which astrology hangs. Galileo was one philosopher who saw clearly the need for our species to find patterns and meaning in what is observed. He said,

> [Science] is written in this grand book of the universe, which stands continually open to our gaze. But the book cannot be understood unless we first learn to comprehend the language and read the letters with which it is composed. It is written in the language of mathematics.

One attempt to read this "grand book of the universe" was, logically enough, the study of the sun, moon, stars and planets. At first, before it grew up, it was called astrology. At maturity, it is now known as astronomy.

In the introduction to *The Case for Astrology*, (Coward-McCann, 1970), a book highly supportive of astrology, authors J. G. Toonder (a Dutch astrologer) and J. A. West (an American novelist) begin:

> Vilified by science for three centuries, derided by philosophy, psychology, medicine, the law and every other orthodox branch of modern learning, astrology refuses to die. As we enter the space age it enjoys a popularity unmatched since the decline of Rome.

It is amazing to me that the authors of that statement have failed to see the significance of the last six words. Official and pervasive concern with superstition has attended the twilight of many cultures that fell to those with more realistic attitudes.

Not only the Roman Empire, but the Incan and Mayan Empires had developed an absurd hierarchy of deities who were expected to protect them and failed to do so in the face of reality. Nazi Germany, too, was increasingly weighted with various superstitious impediments before it fell. Advancement from superstition to scientific thinking has marked the progress of Man, and a retreat to magic has heralded his decline.

Nostradamus' announced method of prognostication, besides sheer inspiration, was the casting and analysis of horoscopes. Though he was an astrologer, less than 2 percent of the quatrains in his *Centuries* contain actual authentic astrological references. But other methods might have entered into his attempts at prophecy.

It became fashionable in the 1960s to speculate whether the major occultists might have derived their powers from the use of hallucinogenic substances. As much as one hundred years ago, students of Nostradamus were wondering about the possible role of alcohol and other drugs in his prophetic methods, and unkind suggestions have been made that our hero was merely a raving drunk who somehow managed to get his ramblings into an acceptable poetic form. I find no evidence to support this canard, but purely as a speculative exercise, I will outline a few facts about a substance which was certainly not unknown to Nostradamus, and which just may play a minor part in the drama.

Absinthe was a highly toxic liqueur known to the ancients as far back as Pliny. He called it absinthites. It was made from distillations of wormwood *(Artemisia absinthium)*, referred to in the early pharmacopeia *De Materia Medica* as Wormwood Dioscorides. Its 70 to 80 percent alcohol content was intoxicating enough, but the wormwood flavoring was what did all the damage to the human nervous system, bringing about powerful hallucinations, yearning, disorientation, crushing depression and often total insanity. Its effects brought about the quip, "Absinthe makes the heart grow fonder."

The French poet Baudelaire was known to be fond of the liqueur, and credited it for much of his inspiration, which was intensely macabre and melancholy. Edgar Allan Poe, who was also said to have favored the drink, was an inspiration to Baudelaire. The French writer's early demise was probably assisted by absinthe and opium, both of which he used. Painter Vincent Van Gogh, whose mental disturbances were classic, drank absinthe regularly and was in its grip when he committed suicide near Arles.

I bring up the subject because in 1913, when the substance was formally recognized by the French medical establishment as a deadly influence in that country, a province-by-province survey revealed that the citizens of France in that year alone consumed more than *ten million gallons* of absinthe, and in the area near Arles, consumption was *four times* the national average! There was great alarm, and by 1915 it had been declared an illegal substance, and is no longer distilled, so far as one can tell, anywhere in the world.

This immediate area near Arles includes both St. Rémy and Salon, where Nostradamus was born and lived. We cannot rule out the distinct possibility that such a popular and readily obtainable substance might have played an important part in the visions that came to Michel de Notredame. His use of the drug in no way demeans his character, taking into account the mores and knowledge of the time, but there may be some reflection upon his judgment as a physician.

It has been suggested that he might have been inspired to divination by a very different source, a mystical book by a writer named Iamblichus, titled *De Mysteriis Aegyptiorum*. This was a how-to book on magic spells, containing explicit instructions on how to perform magic.

A curious man like Nostradamus could not have failed to be exposed to that book, which was first published in Venice in 1497 and republished at nearby Lyons in 1549, just one year before he began his career in magic by issuing his yearly almanacs. Even his described method of divination, brass stool and all, are delineated in the volume, as we can easily see by comparing the following quote from *De Mysteriis Aegyptiorum* with the first two Nostradamus quatrains which are mentioned in my first chapter. I will repeat them here:

Sitting by night in my secret study,
Alone, resting upon the stool of brass,
A slight flame, going out of the solitude,
Makes me pronounce what is not to be believed vain.

The wand in hand, set in the middle of the branches,
From the wave I wet both the hem and the foot,
In fear I write, trembling in the sleeves,
Divine splendor: the Divine seated nearby.

For comparison, here are Iamblichus' instructions for entering a prophetic trance:

> The sibyl at Delphi received the god . . . sitting on a brazen seat with four or three feet . . . exposed on two sides to the divine influx, whence she was irradiate with a divine light. . . . the prophetess of Branchus holds in her hand a rod . . . or moistens the hem of her garment with water . . . and by this means is filled with divine illumination, and, having obtained the deity, she prophesies.

This is almost word-for-word the method Nostradamus describes in his two opening quatrains. The Oracle at Delphi was in business for over one thousand years, so the methodology seems well established by tradition.

This mystical, ceremonial approach to divination is also described in one of Nostradamus' letters. In August 1562, when he was fifty-nine years old, he might have been in an unusually strange mood, or perhaps embracing Bacchus, when he wrote to a client named François Bérard:

> After nine consecutive nights, from midnight until about four, my brows crowned with laurel, a blue stone on my finger, here is what I got from the good genie on your ring.* I grabbed a swans-feather pen (he refused three times the goose-quill) and, at his dictation, as if transported in a poetical madness, I burst into the verses that follow.** Then, turned toward our excellent genie, I asked him to teach me, for his faithful Bérard, an alchemist without peer, the means of obtaining elicium and gold and for purifying pyrite. Then, the back of my neck ornamented with branches of laurel, and my forehead bound with a crown of laurel and periwinkle, I beseeched my guardian angel in order to obtain these transmutations, to inspire me with truthful oracles, thanks to the intercession of Jesus Christ, the Virgin Mary and my invincible patron, the archangel Michael. He then appeared to me in a dream, and answered me in these terms . . .

*Perhaps referring to a lost item of jewelry.
**Turgid, allegorical stuff in Latin.

We can picture the elderly, bearded seer, festooned with branches and a crown of flowers, cavorting about a bronze tripod late at night. It is not a pretty picture, and we must wonder how his marriage survived such episodes. I believe that Nostradamus would have made an unsatisfactory neighbor. In any case, it does not appear that Bérard was taught how to obtain gold, or anything else, for that matter. Nostradamus had performed his costume piece for nothing.

Evidence exists that he used other divinatory recipes from magic lore as well. He is reported to have examined moles and birthmarks on his patrons from time to time as a fortune-telling technique, and also to have "scryed" a dish of clear water, two other then-popular techniques of prognostication. The practice of divining by looking into a bowl of water was quite ancient, and is referred to by very early writers.

An Inevitable Conclusion

The notion of astrology almost had to occur to our species. The inexorable movements of the heavens probably captured the attention of the earliest of *Homo sapiens.* Observing the planets as they moved against the scattered stars, the moon's monthly trip along the zodiac, followed by the sun, and the brief flashes of meteorites as they perished in the upper atmosphere, early Man was provided with real evidence of a remote and wonderful sphere which was actually a marvelous celestial clock, in most respects subject to accurate prediction.

This vast demonstration of spinning lights, it was felt, had to have been put in place for the benefit of the observer. And since the celestial show was so predictable, events in human existence should be equally foreseeable.

A basic calendar was the first attempt to keep track of the movements of the heavens. There are twelve complete circuits of the moon each year, with a bit more than eleven days left over. Thus the month (moonth) became a convenient observable period. Weeks were less formalized, being eight (not seven) days long in the early Roman system, in which they were merely labeled A to H.

The sun was the most obviously powerful skyborne entity, heating and lighting the waking hours and directly affecting all beneath it in many different ways. It therefore received the most attention, being appointed to godhood by most early civilizations. Its risings, settings and variations in position above the horizon during the year became important events to record, and it was soon very apparent that those functions were exceedingly regular and dependable, part of the celestial clockwork.

Next in importance was the moon, and the planets followed. In early times, only five planets were known: Mars, Mercury, Jupiter, Venus and Saturn. Just before the birth of Christ, the Romans began observing a seven-day week which named its days after the sun, the moon and those planets listed above, in that same order. The week was not astronomically derived; it was just a convenient work period.

Living in a time-frame now believed to have been designed by the heavens for their convenience, people observed the great dramas that unfolded in the skies. Wind, clouds, rain, thunder and lightning, sunsets and sunrises were grand theater for everyone. It became a play in which Man could not participate, yet he could hope to reflect to some extent the action that took place above his reach. There was obviously a correspondence between the two worlds, celestial and mundane. The theory of that correspondence became astrology.

Another ancient study, alchemy, mainly concerned itself with finding a mystical substance called the Philosopher's Stone. This was referred to in their literature by many different names, among which were Virgin's Milk, Great Master, Dry Water and Shadow of the Sun. If nothing else, alchemists had a colorful sense of humor. This Stone was believed to have the power to heal all ailments and to transmute base metals into gold. The search for the Philosopher's Stone was an early attempt to attain a science, and eventually was transmuted itself and became chemistry when all the nonsense was boiled out of it.

So it was with astrology, which in its early stages was one study, then was divided into two parts. The part that measured and observed the stars and planets matured into a genuine science, astronomy; the part that believed the heavens mirrored Man's destiny—judicial astrology—has remained with us as well.

An Interesting Set of Parallels

Let us compare alchemy with astrology. There are strong parallels between the two. Alchemy displayed abysmal ignorance of the basic ingredients it dealt with, the chemical elements; astrology assigned invisible influences to stars and planets, without any real knowledge of those bodies. Each implied that it *had* been made to work. Each presented endless amounts of philosophical reasoning on how it *should* work. Forced analogies were invented to validate both. The same respected authorities, often in direct conflict with one another, were quoted to prove both fields. Each study was said to require the right attitude and insight on the part of a practitioner to achieve success. Each was always said to be on the edge of imminent breakthroughs that would prove its claims.

(All of these attributes can also be found in modern parapsychology. Though for over a century parapsychologists have been hard at work trying to find hard, replicable evidence of telepathy, precognition, psychokinesis and other claimed "paranormal" powers, the proof eludes them. What changes this study might undergo, when it is freed of its misconceptions, cannot be imagined. It may just become a chapter in a textbook on abnormal psychology.)

Alchemy has all but vanished today, though the discovery of natural transmutation in the "heavy" elements and of artificial transmutation brought about by radioactive bombardment in the laboratory provided transient hope to a number of modern crackpots. Astrology, not having to produce anything but "trends" and "influences" to satisfy its clients, and seldom allowing itself to be humiliated by proper examination, has persisted.

The English Have At Astrology

That astrology is not a science was observed in 1560 by English writer William Fulke, at a time when the Nostradamus prophecies were disturbing the orderly assumption by Elizabeth I of her troubled throne:

> This is common to all sciences, that they may bee demonstrated.
> For although the principles and grounds in every arte, be of such

a nature, that they canne not bee shewed and confyrmed by things more general, and therefore it is said, that they can not be proved, yet by demonstration or induction they maye be so playnly sette before our eies, that no man neede to doubte, but that they are moste true and certain. But by no waie is it possible, that the principles of this arte of Astrologie, may be either demonstrated or proved. Ther is no mean wherby mans witte may atteyne to so great knowledge, ther is no methode, no induction, that can maintayn truth of these propositions, whyche they take for their principles. . . . I mervayle that menne are so mádde, as to looke for warre oute of theyr predictions, knowing that the cause thereof proceedeth not out of the starres, but of the devyll, whyche alwaye labourethe to breake the bonde of unitie and concorde, that shoulde be among christian men.

Note that Fulke considers war not to be the product of differences between men, and that *evil* wars must only occur between Christians. His logic is flawed and poorly expressed, though his conclusions are valuable.

Opinions of an Early Scientist

Both Sir Francis Bacon and Sir Thomas Browne denounced astrologers of their day, but understandably believed in "astrological science," which was mainly concerned with the positions and movements of the planets, thus bringing it closer to what we now know as astronomy. Bacon contributed the suggestion that astrology could be of some use to society by verifying biblical chronology of specific events and by showing that events prophesied by the "real" prophets—those contained in the scriptures—were reflected in astrological configurations (eclipses, occultations, conjunctions, oppositions, etc.) that indicated disasters, those being, as we have mentioned, the favorite subjects of the prognosticators.

The interest of Sir Francis Bacon in the subject of prophecy is reflected in his essay *Of Prophecies.* He said:

The trivial prophecy which I heard when I was a child, and Queen Elizabeth was in the flower of her years, was,

When hempe is spunne
England's done.

Whereby it was generally conceived, that after the princes had reigned which had the principal [capital] letters of that word hempe (which were Henry [VIII], Edward [VI], Mary [I], Philip [II] and Elizabeth [I]), England should come to utter confusion; which thanks be to God, is verified only in the change of the name; for that the king's style is now no more of England, but of Britain.

There are a few problems with this neat idea, as Bacon well knew. Edward never actually "reigned," having ascended the throne at age ten and died at sixteen; his authority was secondary to the regency of his uncle, the Earl of Hertford. Philip (of Spain) was consort only to Mary I; he never ruled, was only briefly resident in England, and could not in any case have succeeded Mary to the throne.

In the Halls of Academe

In part due to demands by the students, in the late Middle Ages the universities of Bologna, Florence, Padua and Paris—among others—had respected chairs of astrology which persisted into the Renaissance. We have not progressed entirely in that respect. To honor the provisions of the founder of California's Stanford University, there exists today a chair of psychical research at that center of learning. Though the faculty is somewhat embarrassed by the fact, and the chair is only occasionally occupied, it still exists.

The Renaissance Mind at Work

It should not be believed that opponents of astrology were unheard in the Renaissance. They were simply not heeded. At almost the same time when Nostradamus was penning his first almanac, a prominent Italian scholar named Francesco Guicciardini was observing:

> How happy are the astrologers! who are believed if they tell one truth to a hundred lies, while other people lose all credit if they tell one lie to a hundred truths.

In 1687, philosopher Antonio Bonatti wrestled with his conviction that though astrology as practiced in his time was such that "hardly any ray of truth appeared in it," nonetheless "something probably truthful and scientific could be discerned." Bonatti's discourse appealed both to logic and to authority in an attempt to rescue whatever might be valuable in the art, yet he admitted that astrology was laughed at by the majority of philosophers. But he noted that among the common people there still was "universal recourse to traveling fortune-tellers and disreputable jugglers."

Flourishing the names of famous authorities like St. Thomas Aquinas,* Cicero, Roman emperors Diocletian and Hadrian, Emperor Frederick, King Mathias of Hungary, and Ptolemy, Bonatti was using the favorite tool of scholastic disputation in the Renaissance, which gave first place in arguments to quotations from recognized experts who often owed their validity only to their antiquity and the large amount of their writings that were available. References to statements by these authorities were often taken out of context and misrepresented the intent of the authors, but the impact of their names was sufficient to bolster the argument.

Bonatti's readers were also supplied with various strange arguments, some of which are still thrown up by modern defenders of astrology along with the names of their own revered authorities. God, Bonatti reasoned, would not have created the stars if they served no purpose for His ultimate creation, Man. The seasons are seen to change as the sun passes through the various signs of the zodiac, thus there is an effect on Man of that passage. However, since not all summers are equally hot nor winters equally cold, the other heavenly bodies—the planets— must account for the differences. Some persons are observed to be "hot," others "cold"; Mars, Mercury and Jupiter, the "hot" planets, must have influenced the former group. The tides are regulated by the moon, therefore they influence Man. The sun "impregnates" the Earth with its rays in the same way that the male invades the womb, thus bringing life to the planet. And so on.

The Renaissance reliance upon authority and the conviction that such a method served to absolutely refute any argument in

*Specifically in his *Summa contra Gentiles* (1259). Aquinas supported the influence of the stars, but denied that *voluntary* acts of humans were thus controlled.

spite of its strength, was perfectly demonstrated by Jakob Schonheintz, a "mathematician and physicist" who in 1502 blasted away at a well-reasoned and devastating critique of astrology by Giovanni Pico simply by quoting contrary opinions from Aquinas, Augustine, Cato, Cicero, Juvenal, Albertus Magnus, Ovid, Pliny, Ptolemy, Savonarola, Seneca, Virgil and, inevitably, the scriptures that might only hint at references to astrology without using the name. There was no attempt by Schonheintz at logical discussion or reasoning to deny Pico's powerful attack, an effort that became one of the first really serious and effective confrontations between astrologers and informed scholars.

It must be said, in fairness, that Pico himself chose—if he had any choice—to begin his own argument by listing authorities. In the Renaissance tradition, which required him to deny any originality in his work (all origins were of God), he showed that he was not the first to be skeptical of astrology by quoting Aristotle, Cicero, Epicurus, Favorinus, Plato, Pythagoras and Seneca— simply because those philosophers never directly mentioned the subject among the very numerous fields they wrote about, and he argued that if astrology had been important it should certainly have attracted their attention.

The Renaissance process of reasoning also depends upon the finding and use of simple analogies. It is a method that can be valid only in limited cases, but appeals strongly to the unsophisticated even when wrongly applied. Professor Wayne Schumaker at Berkeley, writing about the belief in astrology in his book *The Occult Sciences in the Renaissance* (University of California Press, 1972), describes the use of this analogical method of reasoning by a 16th-century author who defended astrology against critics:

> A premodern reader, being led in this way from the known to the unknown [by the use of analogies] and finding no apparent discontinuities between them, might well feel himself enlightened. For unlettered men the reasoning process still consists largely of finding analogies. It had done so, in a noteworthy degree, for Socrates, and it continued to do so. . . .

Even in 1495, Giovanni Pico had warned against the danger of overusing the analogical method:

In this way anything can easily be proved, since nothing exists which it is impossible to imagine by an argument of this kind to have some similarity and dissimilarity with something else.

The Church's Attitude

Belief in astrology and other forms of divination, which waxed and waned over the ages, became very strong again in the 16th century. The church dismissed and condemned such practices because they brought into question the doctrine of free will and implied a predetermined future for everyone that might not be changed, even by prayer. Without free will, sin is impossible. Without sin and the prescribed penalties, the need for the church becomes less clear and less persuasive.

An interesting dilemma that arose for the astrologers involved an exceedingly favorable interpretation, by a prominent practitioner, of the horoscope of Christ. The astrologer, Girolamo Cardan, was a lecturer at the University of Bologna from 1562 to 1570, when his name was suddenly erased from the faculty roll by order of the senate. Cardan had been arrested by officers of the Inquisition for daring to predict in his *De rerum varietate**—safely after the fact—the major events of the life of Christ as described in the Holy Scriptures. An angry Vatican declared that stellar and planetary configurations could not dictate events in the life of the Son of God. Flexibility being a prominent and essential talent of soothsayers, the astrologer countered with a shrewd response: God, he said, had *arranged* for His Son to be born under a special astronomical configuration and had set the planets and stars into specific motions millennia in advance of the birth date so that the exact propitious celestial arrangement would be arrived at in time for the birth. This clever rationalization did not quite meet with church approval. Cardan, then seventy years old, was commanded by Pius V, the pope who supported Charles IX against the Huguenots, to abjure his writings. He did so and spent the remaining five years of his life in retirement in Rome on a small papal pension. His powerful clients and friends in the college of cardinals were

---

*Surprisingly, this publication had been out for *eight years* before it came to the attention of the Inquisition.

undoubtedly responsible for the leniency with which he was treated by the Inquisition.

A difficult defense of astrology for the church to deny arose from a well-known scriptural excerpt: "The heavens declare the glory of God, and the firmament showeth His handiwork." To comply with religious requirements, apologists for astrology argued that they did not claim that the stars absolutely dictated Man's conduct, but they insisted that it was madness to deny that they had any influence at all. The stars, they averred, affected the passions without compelling behavior. Many backed to the position that astrologers should not predict particular events, but only general tendencies. Such a watered-down philosophy would hardly bring fame or wealth to a practitioner, but it was far safer. It avoided head-on conflict with the church, both in regard to territory and doctrine.

A prominent and very influential Christian writer, Origen (A.D. 185–254), tried to rephrase the Hermetic teachings on astrology:

> Just as the power of the human will is not rendered useless because of God's foreknowledge of the acts that will be ours in the future, even so the celestial signs by which we may be initiated into the foretelling of that future are not a declaration of loss of freewill. Occult influences demonstrate a tendency, but do not submit us to blind fate. The sky is like an open book in which are written the signs of the past, present and future . . . it is the book of universal life . . . it presents the series of tests which composes the circle of each individual existence.

One can only wonder if Origen was aware of a rather earlier writer, Confucius (K'ung Fu-tse), who declared that

> Heaven sends down its good or evil symbols, and wise men act accordingly.

The proscription of specific divination in the Reformation by Catholic Rome was absolute, but generalized prophecy was allowed. As late as 1740, Pope Benedict IV reflected a surprisingly lenient attitude:

> The recipients of prophecy may be angels, devils, men, women, children, heathen or gentiles; nor is it necessary that a man

should be gifted with any particular disposition in order to receive the light of prophecy provided his intellect and sense be
adapted for making manifest the things which God reveals to
him.

Implacable authorities can often be placated; if not, they can
be circumvented or coerced into more reasonable attitudes. Enforced and/or politically expedient tolerance, often achieved by
careful consideration and inspired re-evaluation of scriptural
truth by church authorities, is not unheard of in history. In the
16th century, England's Henry VIII had managed quite well to
manipulate and eventually do without the Vatican in order to
simplify his marital state in novel and brutal ways. Heads and
estates had toppled freely to accomplish Henry's needs, and
these mutinous events by the monarch were duly noted at
Rome.

By 1700, most scholars had pretty well decided against the
validity of all kinds of astrology, though the public continued to
embrace the idea. The very first (1771) edition of the *Encyclopaedia Britannica* defined astrology as:

> a conjectural science, which teaches to judge of the effects and
> influences of the stars, and to foretel future events by the situa-
> tion and different aspects of the heavenly bodies. This science has
> long ago become a just subject of contempt and ridicule.

In 1898 the *Nouveau Larousse Illustré* told its readers that

> [Astrology] now has hardly any adherents other than swindlers
> who play on public credulity, and even those are fast disap-
> pearing.

The contributor was himself more than a little prophetic when
he added this precaution:

> From time to time a renewed interest in mysticism or dilettan-
> tism may bring about a revival of astrology, of all kinds of magic,
> and of spiritualism.

Ecclesiastics such as John Calvin—understandably—raged
against any notion that suggested human performance might be
predetermined by the stars. Sin might thus be seen to be much
less evil and less evidently a willful transgression against God.

But Calvin was still a product of his age. In a 1561 treatise he denied judicial astrology, but medical astrology received his approval:

> . . . we must needes confesse that there is a certain convenience [relationship] betwyxte the starres or planets and the dispocion [disposition] of man's body.

Such selective thinking is not rare among philosophers.

In contrast to Calvin's opinion, even medical uses for astrology were denied by William Fulke:

> Sycknesse and healthe depende upon dyvers causes, but nothyng at al upon the course of the starres, for what way soever the starres runne their race, yf there be in the body abundance or defect, or from outward by corruption of the ayre infection it must nedes be sycke: and if none of these bee, though all the starres in heaven with all their oppositions and evil tokens shuld meete in the howse of sicknesse, yet the body should bee whole, and in good healthe.

Catherine de Médicis' Belief in Astrology

Unspoken tolerance of divination became relatively easy for the church to achieve in the 16th century, especially in the face of open endorsement by such powerful personages as Catherine de Médicis, who was the reigning Queen of France when the *Centuries* of Nostradamus appeared as well as being the dark eminence who stood behind the French throne for more than forty-two years through the reigns of four consecutive monarchs. Her influence, which was felt throughout Europe, and her enthusiastic and well-known support—both political and financial—of Nostradamus himself, seems to have effectively tempered any possible ecclesiastic disapproval. The church, already wounded by the defection of Henry VIII's kingdom, was not about to suffer the Médicis displeasure as well. That family controlled much of the wealth of Europe.

Catherine's dedication to astrology was well known to historians, who ascribed much of her behavior to her belief. The 1842 *Encyclopaedia Britannica* noted:

> The French historians tell us, that in the time of Queen Catherine d'Medici, astrology was so much in vogue that the most inconsid-

erable thing was not to be done without consulting the stars. And in the reigns of Henry III. and IV. of France, the predictions of astrologers were the common theme of the court conversation.

Francis Bacon, in his essay *Of Prophecies,* recounted an anecdote about Catherine:

> When I was in France, I heard from one Dr. Pena, that the queen mother, who was given to curious arts, caused the king her husband's nativitie to be calculated, under a false name; and the astrologer gave a judgment, that he should be killed in a duell; at which the queene laughed, thinking her husband to be above challenges and duels; but he was slain, upon a course at tilt, the splinters of the staffe of Montgomery going in at his bevor [throat protector].

The astrologer referred to by Bacon is probably Luca Gaurico (Gauricus), a seer from Florence who had cast Catherine's horoscope when she was an infant and whom she often consulted in later years. Gaurico, born in the kingdom of Naples in 1476, was already well established at the age of twenty-seven when Nostradamus was born. He is said to have cast the horoscope of Giovanni de' Medici and determined that he would become pope, a not unlikely position for a de' Medici. In 1513, Giovanni became Pope Leo X.* Guarico survived the usual dangers of the life of the mountebank and was eventually appointed by Pope Paul III as bishop of Civita-Ducale and Giffoni, a further proof that divination has its unforeseen rewards.

Another astrologer favored by Catherine was Cosimo Ruggieri, whose story we will relate in Chapter 9. Since he lived in Paris, close to the royal court, he was obviously a great competitor to Nostradamus, who did quite well in spite of his geographical separation from the queen.

Astrology—the Foolish Little Daughter

The astrologers—then in the Renaissance as now—trotted out well-rehearsed alibis for the failure of their art. The strongest excuse they produced was, "Astra inclinant, non necessitant." ("The stars impel, but do not compel.") This first appeared in

*Four de' Medicis became popes.

Giambattista della Porta's* book *Coelestis Physiognomiae.* It has
stood well for them over the centuries.

Though the early astrologers were unaware of it, the Ephem-
erides (astronomical tables) they used were demonstrably
wrong, thus their pronouncements had to be flawed, whether or
not their art had merit. Few of them actually observed the night
sky (in any case, the telescope was not yet available) and they
depended for their information upon numerous authorities
who had drawn up tables of planetary movements, most of them
in conflict with one another and mostly quite inaccurate.

There were also widely differing ideas on how such devices as
the twelve "houses" of the horoscope should be delineated, and
failure to properly assign values to them was recognized as fatal
to any attempt at prognostication. Some time was to pass before
the astrologers were to become fully aware of an element in
astronomy of which they had been entirely ignorant: Precession
of the equinoxes was moving the astrological "signs" well
beyond the confines of the astronomical constellations they had
originally been very loosely assigned to when Ptolemy first pro-
pounded the notions upon which astrology was based, in the
2nd century A.D. Even today, astrologers resist admitting that
most persons supposedly born in any anciently derived sign
actually first see light under the auspices of the sign preceding
their assigned one. It is a proud tradition not to change nonsense, no matter how strong the evidence against it. Astrologers
have scrupulously honored that tradition.

As we have seen, not all competent thinkers rejected the ancient art. It is well known that Johannes Kepler and Sir Isaac
Newton, both persons well versed in astronomy who contributed generously to that science, cast horoscopes. Kepler even

---

*This remarkable man, in 1589, described his discovery that a combi-
nation of positive and negative optical lenses would produce both the
telescope and the microscope. He had obviously experimented with
these tools and constructed the instruments. The next year, Zacharias
Janssen, a Dutch spectacle-maker, demonstrated the first compound
microscope, but it was eighteen years later that Hans Lippershey, another Dutch spectacle-maker, announced his invention of the telescope. Perhaps we have wrongly assigned credit for these inventions
to Janssen and Lippershey, when della Porta should be named as the
inventor of both.

tried to develop a fit between astrology (which depends upon a geocentric solar system) and the newly accepted heliocentric (Copernican) system.

Of course it can be argued by skeptics that these two scientists practiced astrology only to earn money, but little has been produced to show that they did not believe the stars and planets were influential to some extent in the affairs of humans and nations. To be fair, we must quote Kepler with a somewhat opposing view which may express the exact reason for his astrological activities:

> Astronomy, the wise mother, astrology the foolish little daughter, selling herself to any and every client willing and able to pay so as to maintain her wise mother alive.

This statement may reflect the fact that Kepler's very first paid position required him to learn the methods of the astrologer Cardan and to use them to cast horoscopes. Consider a comment this same savant made when he announced the discovery of the laws of planetary orbits that highlighted his astronomical career:

> . . . nothing exists and nothing happens in the visible heavens that is not echoed in some hidden manner by the faculties of Earth and Nature: the faculties of the spirit of this world are affected in the same measure as heaven itself.

This reflects two rather basic medieval assumptions, first, that what Kepler saw of the heavens was all that existed, and second, that celestial events are mirrored on earth, both in nature and in magnitude. Neither is correct, but Kepler, despite his real worth as a scientist, was trapped in his mystic personality, unable to shake off a conviction that magic held the solution to all his questions. This is a defect of some modern scholars, who earnestly seek a baby in murky bathwater into which a child has never been introduced.

Tycho Brahe and Pierre Gassendi were two Renaissance scholars who began as astrologers. Though Brahe contributed greatly to astronomy, he also continued in the folly of astrology until a few years before his death. Gassendi examined astrology and very soon gave it up as a false science, devoting himself entirely to legitimate astronomy. However, strangely enough, he never gave up his belief in another superstition, the ability of dowsers to locate water with a forked stick. It was an idea to which he could have equally well and much more easily applied an examination.

One who came close to Inquisitional flames was Galileo Galilei, who was a child when Nostradamus began influencing Europe, but who must have been aware of the prophet's work. Despite his eventual important contributions to science and his bravery in pronouncing them, Galileo was himself an astrologer who must have suffered through a crisis when he calculated a long and happy life for his patron, the Duke of Tuscany, only to have that gentleman die within two weeks of the horoscope's publication. Galileo's penchant for astrology seems to have escaped the attention of his inquisitors, who apparently found the unwelcome existence of Jupiter's moons more threatening to their established notions than the influence of horoscope-casting.

Divination, even to great thinkers, is a seductive concept. It is easy to accept the notion and, in examining its accuracy, to also accept the manner in which it seems to fit experience. That acceptance, however, is the result of a common philosophical error wherein the reasoner accepts the responsibility for fitting the observed facts to the often metaphorical forecast. Any failure effectively to do so is considered to be evidence of a lack of perception and sensitivity. The diviner or the divinatory method is seldom faulted.

The True Believer

No amount of failure can discourage the True Believer. In a fascinating book—*When Prophecy Fails*—which deals with the sociological aspects of a modern religious group that confidently predicted the destruction of the world on a very specific date, and the reactions of the adherents when the disaster failed to materialize, the authors observed:

> A man with a conviction is a hard man to change. Tell him you disagree and he turns away. Show him facts or figures and he questions your sources. Appeal to logic and he fails to see your point.

We have all experienced the futility of trying to change a strong conviction, especially if the convinced person has some investment in his belief. We are familiar with the variety of ingenious defenses with which people protect their convictions, managing to keep them unscathed through the most devastating attacks.

But man's resourcefulness goes beyond simply protecting a belief. Suppose an individual believes something with his whole heart; suppose further that he has a commitment to this belief, that he has taken irrevocable actions because of it; finally, suppose that he is presented with evidence, unequivocal and undeniable evidence, that his belief is wrong: what will happen? The individual will frequently emerge, not only unshaken, but even more convinced of the truth of his beliefs than ever before. Indeed, he may even show a new fervor about convincing and converting other people to his view.

Though this statement may be very difficult for the reader to accept, I can provide further evidence from my own experience. As a professional conjuror, I must be very aware of the exact "moves" and procedures I perform to accomplish my illusions. On more than one occasion I have had very experienced observers describe to me what they believe they saw me perform, and I know that they have misremembered the sequence or the effect. Sometimes I have been able to show them a videotape of the performance in question, only to have them say, on occasion, either that the videotape was doctored, that it was a videotape of a different performance, or that it simply didn't happen that way and their memory of it is more dependable than the videotape record!

It is often that way with evidence presented against such a belief as astrology. Believers will stretch reason to any extent to rationalize failures, changing small points or even large amounts of data to accommodate their beliefs. The theory is never discarded, only the evidence.

The Horoscope

The primary source of information from which astrologers say they generate data on the governing influences of the stars and planets is a chart known as a horoscope. The name is derived from the Greek for "hour-watcher."

The horoscope consists of a map of the heavens, now depicted in circular form but in Nostradamus' day drawn up in a squared style that was used until the end of the 18th century. The horoscope was shown with the Earth at its center, a convention that seems not to have been affected by the discovery made by Copernicus. The twelve *signs* of the zodiac (the band of sky through which the sun, moon and planets appear to travel, relative to the fixed stars) do not agree with the twelve zodiacal *constellations* in the real sky from which they are said to have been derived. In fact, the constellations themselves are imaginary figures very poorly outlined by stars that in most cases have no significant relationship in location to one another other than being lined up from the point of view of our solar system.

The zodiacal signs are shown on the horoscope to be distributed at equal intervals around the perimeter of a circle, and they are all shown the same size—thirty degrees wide—though the constellations on which they are based are of considerably different widths, and they often overlap. The sun, moon and planets are shown against this band of signs as they might have been seen against the zodiac at the moment of birth—if those bodies had actually been there, which they weren't.

These horoscopes are often generated rather carelessly, though the seers insist that, without accurate information about the exact moment of birth and the precise geographical location of that event, a detailed analysis, or interpretation, is not possible. Working out an equation with great skill but with faulty data can give only a useless answer.

About 130 B.C., the Greek philosopher Hipparchus discovered the precession of the equinoxes, thereby revealing that the astrologers had been assigning the wrong sun-signs to their clients, among other errors. The astrologers of his day ignored this fact, as those of today still do. This discovery, along with the Copernican revolution in 1543, should have killed astrology as an academic subject for good.

A Definitive Test of Astrology

As recently as 1985, University of California research physicist Dr. Shawn Carlson conducted a comprehensive test, supported by a Congressional research award, of thirty American and

European astrologers who had, at Carlson's invitation, been carefully chosen by their peers at the American Astrological Association to best represent the trade.

His test used 116 horoscopes. The skilled astrologers agreed in advance that the test as proposed by Carlson would be definitive and fair, and they even contributed suggestions concerning the conduct of the experiment. Their expectation of success was declared in advance by the testees as being a "minimum" of 50 percent, which meant that they would be able to assign horoscopes to the persons who fitted them in half the cases—a rather poor ambition, one would think, for such an ancient and revered "science." In this test they achieved exactly what would have been expected by pure chance—33 percent. They would have obtained that kind of result by throwing dice, or if no astrological influences were acting on the subjects at all.

It was no surprise to longtime observers of these matters that though the astrologers in Carlson's test had agreed—again, in advance—that the procedure was fair, correctly designed and agreeable to them, following the test they rejected the announced results and began to attack the researchers who had conducted it. They did not try to explain why they had failed, nor did they respond to the question that naturally arose: Why, with no evidence to support it, has astrology persisted?

Shawn Carlson believes he has that answer. "A lot of people believe in astrology because they think they have seen it work," he says. He believes that astrologers are considered successful because they "read" the facial expressions, body language and responses of their clients and provide them with words they want to hear. "People believed in astrology for thousands of years," says Carlson, "and no doubt will continue to do so no matter what scientists discover." I must reluctantly agree with that opinion.

On a nationwide test of astrology, conducted this time with only one astrologer and twelve subjects, I was able to show that no amount of confidence can bring about success in such matters. On June 7, 1989, on a two-hour TV special which was aired live in the U.S.A. and Canada and by delayed broadcast in Italy, Australia, Scandinavia, Germany and France, I put seven seers and psychics through their paces with tests designed and supervised by Drs. Ray Hyman and Stanley Krippner, the latter a past president of the Parapsychological Association. All tests were agreed to in advance by the participants, and among the eager contestants was an astrologer who assured me of his expertise and stated that he was one hundred percent sure of his winning.

The astrologer—perhaps lured by a prize of $100,000 offered for his success—told us that he could and would win that prize simply by matching the twelve subjects to their correct birth signs. He was allowed to ask twenty pertinent personality questions of each person involved, and upon completion of the process said he had won. When the decisions were unveiled, it was shown that he had been wrong in *all* of his choices.

In actual operation, the astrologers require the client to identify and relate to the various aspects introduced. The client is asked, indirectly, to fit the prognostication to the facts. Knowing what he or she wants or suspects to be true, the victim naturally interprets what the astrologer says in light of the best possible fit to that expectation, and is very much encouraged to do so. Since "the stars impel, but do not compel," this all appears quite proper.

Reading a celebrity's horoscope is even easier, because knowing the events of that person's life, the astrologer can fit those facts into the aspects of the chart that seem to be indicated by the mythology of the art. Professional American astrologer Jeff Green supplied for a typically overenthusiastic book, *Nostradamus and the Millennium,* a detailed interpretation of a horoscope he generated for the prophet, based upon a birth date of December 14 (old calendar), 1503, at 12:03 P.M. Mr. Green made serious errors in the calculation of the horoscope, but, apparently unaware of these defects and with the advantage of 20/20 hindsight, Green was able to show clearly that the character and prophetic powers of Nostradamus were perfectly described and predicted by his horoscope.

One question should be dealt with here: Does astrology have any value at all? As a science, no. As a cheap pop therapy, probably. Author Richard F. Smith, in his book *Prelude to Science* (1975), which deals with various divinatory systems favored by the ancients, says:

On the positive side, astrology has always been used as a kind of crude, do-it-yourself psychotherapy. It gives people an excuse for thinking about themselves for hours at a time. Whatever their sign, they can compare what it says about them with what their friends say about them and what they think about themselves. In a society that denies ego support to most people, astrology provides it at a very low price.

I believe that Mr. Smith fails to include in that "very low price" a very substantial surcharge. In accepting the contract, the consumer surrenders individual control of destiny and subscribes to the idea that certain persons can provide him with magical methods of survival.

As might be expected, such a popular notion as astrology has been seized upon by religious and political activists. No fundamentalist group denies that psychic or divinatory powers exist. To disavow the methods by which these powers are established as belief systems, they would undermine and bring into question the methods whereby they have established their own dogmas. These groups take one of two attitudes about astrology: Either it is the work of the devil, and thus evil though possibly true, or it is proof of God's wonderful design, and undeniably true. Evangelists Pat Robertson and W.V. Grant, among many, have repeatedly, in print and in their preachings, assailed astrology and other New Age notions with the first argument. However, despite their abhorrence of such magic, both these preachers have expounded on and performed faith healing procedures that are, purely and simply, magical acts. Grant is seen on television weekly by millions performing what he claims are healing gestures and invocations, while Robertson has largely deemphasized that aspect of his ministry.

Politically, J.B.S. Haldane, writing in the *Daily Herald*, expressed both his naive concept of what astrology claims to be able to do and his vain hope that communism would rid mankind of this scourge upon taking over control of human destiny:

If the astrologers and palmists want to convince scientists of the truth of their 'sciences,' they have an easy task. No doubt (if their claims are right) they must have discovered that millions of young men were going to die between 1914 and 1918. So they ought to be able to predict the dates of future wars. When they get a few such dates right I shall take them seriously. But I am not much impressed by a few lucky shots. However that may be, astrologers and palmists are very useful to the cause of capitalism. They help to persuade people that their destinies are outside their control. And, of course, this is true as long as enough people believe it. But if enough people learn how the joint fate of us all can be altered, things begin to happen which mean the end of capitalism as well as of astrology and palmistry.

For his assumption, Haldane can justly be rapped by the astrologers, few of whom would claim that their art could predict a war by examining horoscopes for probable death dates from armed conflict. Such predictions, though expected of the ancient art, are likely to fail spectacularly. His comment was written back in 1938, just before the Holocaust and World War II provided excellent source material for his proposed test. Author Haldane would be chagrined to know that today Soviet Russia and China, both communist societies, are involved in extensive research on psychic subjects, and that their citizens have as much interest in astrology as those in the Western world. Faith healers and astrologers are featured on daily TV programs in the USSR, and in China hospitals have been built dedicated to acupuncture, remote diagnosis, distant healing and the ancient philosophy of Qi Gong.

Perhaps a last scholarly observation on astrology should be left to England's William Fulke, in his contemporaneous attack on Nostradamus' astrological work:

> . . . astrology consisteth either of no principles, or of false, it is loste labour that is spent in thobservation thereof: in vayne it is to credite [the astrologers'] predictions, unjust it is that [astrology] is of the unlerned people reverenced, more worthy to bee buried under the chanell of *Lethe,* the ryver of oblivion, than that she shoulde enjoying the cleare lyght of men, be had in any estimation. But if there be any Prognosticatour that will take uppon hym to defende Astrologie thus battered in pieces, let hym make haste to dooe it, before she utterlye falle to ruyne.

It would shock Fulke to know that astrology is still looked upon, by the "unlerned," as a science and as a truth.

One Client's Tribulations

We can learn a great deal about the actual (rather than the claimed) relationship between an astrologer and his clients by following the letters that were exchanged between Nostradamus and one Lorenz Tubbe, who lived in Bourges, a city about 100 miles south of Paris. Tubbe fancied himself a competent amateur astrologer, and represented Hans Rosenberger, a wealthy merchant and miner from Augsburg, Germany. Rosenberger was surrounded by astrologers, one of them the famous Cyprian Leowitz, but in 1559, despite such wise advisors, his bankruptcy forced him to seek out Nostradamus. From the city of Fieberbrunn in the Tyrol, where his mines were located, Rosenberger dealt with Nostradamus through his agent Tubbe. It is interesting to note that even as early as the 16th century, owners of mines were seeking supernatural assistance, and the mystics of that day were prepared to meet that need, as they are called upon to do even today.

The "post" employed by scholars of the 16th century consisted of a large number of independent professional couriers who traveled over set routes delivering letters and packets. It was a well-established system and was quite dependable except in the winter months, when inclemencies understandably suspended much of the traffic. It should be understood that many activities essentially ceased during the hard winter, when survival itself was often enough of a reward. The courier system, when in operation, was the means whereby academics were able to share their discoveries with one another and request assistance from other authorities in far-off locations.

Since Nostradamus preferred to write his letters in French, a language unknown to Tubbe and his employer, and Nostradamus' handwriting was notoriously (purposely?) illegible, his original letters had to be recopied by Nostradamus' secretary before being sent to the client's agent. Poor Tubbe then had to translate that version into Latin with the assistance of a French-speaking friend, all the while trying to extract some useful meaning from the enigmatic scribblings. Finally, Tubbe retranslated the Latin version into German and transmitted it to Rosenberger. We can easily imagine that there was a great deal lost of the meaning—if any—intended by the prophet.

Beginning in 1559, a number of letters passed between Nostradamus and the agent of this particular client. Apparently he had already attempted to contract for a horoscope to be drawn up for his master in one or more previous letters that we do not have, the first in April. Tubbe writes:

November 24, 1559: I have just learned from your brother that you have been sent for by the Queen and that you are preparing to leave for Paris.* If you have finished the horoscope of the German lord [Rosenberger] would you send it to me without fail before your departure? You can send it to him at Orléans, where he is at this moment. In any case, he is coming to spend the winter here. [Written at] Aix.

Not having had a reply, Tubbe inquired again:

January 1, 1560: Here it is almost two months since I wrote to you concerning the horoscope of a German who owns mines. Could you tell me, in a word, whether you have accepted this commission? You can write care of [Jean] Brotot, at Lyon, rue de Tremassac, the home of Balieux, or here at the home of Dr. Liparin. [Written at] Bourges.

At last, two and a half months later, on March 16, Tubbe obtained the requested material.

I have finally received, with great pleasure, your letter and the horoscope. Alas! Your handwriting and the text gave me problems. Since I don't know French, I had to appeal to French friends, but it's impossible to decipher you! I was only able to recopy the nativity** and your calculations, along with the titles of the forty-two articles. The German lord does not understand French, and his knowledge of Latin is not very good. Could you dictate a Latin translation of your work, and have it written in larger characters? Beauty of style doesn't matter; all that counts is simplicity and fidelity. I'm very sorry to impose on you, but Dr. Liparin approves of this step. You can count on the generosity of my master. I am unable to restrain myself from sending you my nativity, which I had calculated a long time ago according to the method of Regiomontanus . . . to ask you, not to interpret it, but only to write to me one or two aphorisms on marriage and career. [Written at] Bourges.

*There is no record of this repeat royal command for Nostradamus to consult with Catherine, as he did in 1556, and as we shall see, he did not make this trip.

**The term "nativity" means items of birth information such as date, time, geographical location and the planetary configurations thus obtained. Any scholar could supply these, but only an inspired astrologer could provide an interpretation of them.

(It must have annoyed Nostradamus to read Tubbe's comment that "Beauty of style doesn't matter." To the astrologer it mattered a great deal, since his style was designed to conceal the fact that he could not deliver the "simplicity and fidelity" that his client demanded!)

Again having no response to his entreaties, Tubbe wrote:

September 20, 1560: I have addressed to you, these last six months, several letters concerning a nativity that I sent you in April. I asked you to please dictate a Latin translation and to have it written in larger characters. Since I have not received any response, I fear that I might have angered you. But I swear to you that I could not act otherwise. The French people whom I approached, since they did not know astrology, couldn't decipher your work, and as for me, I don't know any French. All the same, I recopied the nativity and I have sent it to my master, indicating to him that you have prepared a commentary of forty chapters. I knew that those concerning the mines would please him, given his misfortunes. When he read my letter and saw the nativity with your phrase in the margin: "Do not abandon your enterprise," he breathed easier, and he waits impatiently for the rest. Would you like for your honorarium coins or a gold-plated silver cup,* as the German nobles have? You can answer me care of Krafft, (but seal your letter well) or care of Dr. Liparin. If you cannot complete the horoscope rapidly, please at least tell me what you would like [in payment]. [Written at] Bourges.

Soon after, Tubbe received two letters from Nostradamus of which we do not have copies. He responded:

December 1, 1560: I have just received with great pleasure two of your letters. I am astonished to read that you have, during the past year, received my own letters so rarely. It's a fact that they treat the mail of intellectuals a lot worse than merchants' mail. My master plans to pay you soon; don't be impatient at the delay, especially in this season. I'm reading your commentary better. I'm going to translate it into Latin, and the Latin into German. I sent my master your letter. I translated for him the entire passage that concerns the mines. I have also asked him to send

---

*It was considered more fashionable to award such a token for these services in place of money. We have it on record that Nostradamus preferred a cup in place of cash.

me the calculations for the following years. Here I have no means by which I can make calculations. . . . [Rosenberger] possesses an important mine, St. George, in the Tyrol. In what direction should he tunnel, and to what depth? As for my horoscope, I thank you for what you tell me about 1561. Could you tell me something about marriage and career? I would love to be able to defend you against all of these ignoramuses who attack you. Forgive me for chattering on this way.

Tubbe was being urged by his client to get results from Nostradamus, but was hampered by the poor quality of the material.

January 20, 1561: I have just finished the translation of your text, but it's so sibylline that I've had tremendous trouble, and the French people here don't know anything about astrology. However, I've not been able to send my translation to Germany; messengers are rare in winter. Don't worry about your payment. I attach the directions that [astrologer] Leowitz prepared for my master. Since I have no means to do further calculations, I will have to write to Germany.* [Written at] Bourges.

Apparently not satisfied with the responses that were being afforded his agent, the German lord Rosenberger decided that he should direct a personal letter to Nostradamus for the purpose of expediting matters. On March 11, 1561, he wrote:

I received with great pleasure my horoscope with your commentary. Surely, of all the astrologers I have consulted, in Italy or in Germany, you are the only one who shows such admirable mastery of astrology. The text that I have in front of me is alone enough to justify your fame and prove your excellence. The events that you predicted there are only, alas, too true. I am following your advice of perseverance and patience.

A short comment here: How could Rosenberger possibly know that the *predicted* events are "only, alas, too true"? Perhaps these are past events that Nostradamus was told of and which he is retroactively "predicting" for his client. Now, following this traditional academic back-rubbing, a glowing but transient tribute

*It seems that Nostradamus expected all the astronomical calculations to be done for him, and he was to supply only the interpretations.

to the abilities of the prophet, Rosenberger continues by stating some complaints:

> Unfortunately, you have mixed the past, the present and the future in your predictions, and I am having a lot of trouble in finding my way. For the calculations from 1561 to 1573 that you are preparing, could you do me the favor of composing them clearly without mixing up periods that way? I send you a medal with my portrait; this is not in place of your payment, but a simple token of my regard. I will pay you by the next courier. It will probably be a gold-plated silver cup decorated with my coat of arms. Would you do me the kindness to calculate the horoscopes of my two sons . . . [he gives the pertinent data, including the proper names of his mother and wife*] Finally, I must confess to you that I do have trouble reading your handwriting, and I would ask you to please prepare a text in Latin, and to have it copied out without abbreviations. [Written at] Fieberbrunn.

Perhaps sensing that Nostradamus was stalling until he had received his compensation from Rosenberger, Tubbe wrote:

> June 7, 1561: You must be waiting for my master's answer with as much impatience as I am awaiting yours. Please believe that these delays are not my fault, but are due, no doubt, to evilwishers. My master, because of his misfortunes, has made many enemies. Yesterday, finally, I received two letters from him for you. The cup has arrived at Lyon. In order to avoid any additional delay (I may have to leave for Germany at the beginning of autumn) I will recommend to you a young German [Weidenkopff] who has just arrived. He is the brother of one of my friends. Since he expects to visit Provence, he will bring you the package. . . . But to me, [the young man's] horoscope seems unfortunate. If you see in it some misfortune, don't hide it from him. Could you give him a receipt [for the package]? In one of your almanacs, you predict for July some misfortune for the inhabitants of Bourges. What will it be? [Written at] Bourges.

There is no record that Nostradamus ever told the Bourgians what calamity they might expect, nor if any calamity ever occurred.

---

*Many prognostications were based upon a sort of numerology derived from these names. Nostradamus employed it frequently, as we shall see.

Nostradamus replied to Tubbe on July 15, 1561. This was about as quickly as could be expected, given the minimum time that a courier would take to travel the considerable distance between Bourges and Salon de Provence. The young German had accomplished his appointed task, according to Nostradamus:

At the end of June I received your letter with the cup, which is very beautiful, with the medal decorated with your master's portrait. It is easy to see that he is suffering from an attack of black bile.* As for his letters, it is you who is translating them from German into Latin; I recognize your style. I have given to Weidenkopff a receipt, in French, in the name of Krafft. I'm really sorry about the misfortunes of your master and his son. My relative has finished copying out the calculations, which I finished a long time ago. I am sending them to you. I'm working very hard on the horoscope of his son but I would first like to have the nativities done by Leowitz. If not, I'll do them in my style. I promise to be clear. For the end of 1556, as for 1557, I foresee terrible events for your master. I foresee as well many unfortunate events for his climacteric year, but my relative does not wish to copy them out. As for the horoscopes, I prefer to write them in French, if necessary in French and in Latin; French is richer than Latin. The messenger of a great prince was just here, summoning me to court. If I go, I will without fail visit you at Bourges. I am disturbed by your master's silence. Should I fear a misfortune, or are he and [Cyprian] Leowitz making fun of my paltry work? That's unthinkable. I'm truly annoyed that my relative does not wish to copy out the calculations for 1573. For the rest, I fear that these calculations might be welcomed more by laughter than by admiration. In any case, I will do what I can.

A short break here to note that in the letter so far, we see good evidence of the seer's incredible presumption, attempts to tease the client, presages of unspecified disasters, grandiose claims of royal favor, professional jealousy and a little childish pique. What follows in this letter to Tubbe is the "smoking gun" that

*Such a preposterous diagnosis, performed by examining a portrait that was at best inaccurate, was not out of line with medical practice of the time.

César Nostradamus wished to both preserve and hide away: written evidence of his father's heresy. The letter continues:

> Here [in Provence] passions that had already been aroused burst into violence between the Papists and the partisans of the true faith. On Holy Friday, a massacre instigated by a fanatical Franciscan was barely avoided. Like many persons suspected of Lutheranism, I was obliged to take refuge for two months at Avignon. Finally, the Count de Tande reestablished the peace. That is the reason for my silence. Please tell your master that if he perseveres, he will recover his prosperity. The rumor is going around that a Turkish fleet was sighted recently off Nice. I fear for Tunis. [Written at] Salon.

Tubbe replied:

> August 9, 1561: I received with great pleasure your letter and your work. I'm glad that Rosenberger's gifts pleased you. You must attribute my master's delay to the difficulties he has had in finding someone he can trust in his disastrous situation. He is awaiting impatiently the commentaries on the calculations you have sent me. He writes that he is sending his mail to Brotot, who seems to him to be an adequate intermediary. He does not have Leowitz's calculations, and I have nothing here with which to do this work. While waiting, he will be pleased to read the commentary that you have just sent me. I'm keeping a little while longer the interpretations of the data, first of all because I don't have a messenger and next because each day I am expecting your arrival.* My host . . . will receive you at his home, free. . . . I'm getting ready to leave here in September . . . [Written at] Bourges.

On September 9, 1561, Nostradamus wrote to Rosenberger and provided us with examples of the incredible practices of reading a client's character and future from facial features and by numerology:

> . . . I added in everything that I could discover in your physiognomy and in the names of your mother and, above all, your wife. . . . [In 1562] You are going to make important discoveries in minerals, which will pay back all your past misfortunes. Don't be

---

*Nostradamus, had he made the announced trip to Paris, would have passed through Bourges.

discouraged. Prosperity is coming; you are going to discover veins of silver. . . .

Tubbe heard from Nostradamus the news that he was not going to Paris to visit Catherine, as he had previously announced:

October 15, 1561: . . . I am not going to court. I am waiting to have finished Charles IX's horoscope. Also, winter is coming, and I hesitate. Brotot died a while ago, and his son Pierre, who succeeded him, does not inspire my confidence. As for Krafft, I see no reason to be suspicious of him, he's OK. In any case, I close up my letter securely, and I place my seal on it. I have done what is necessary with the couriers so that the horoscopes should arrive at their destination, and I have also written Krafft that he should send your letters to Augsburg . . . [Written at] Salon.

One could read into these lines a hint of conspiracy. It seems evident that Nostradamus and the Augsburg nobles were well into activities that involved Lutheran ambitions, and they were more than casually suspicious that their correspondence might be intercepted or read by persons other than the addressee. Tubbe, having now moved from Bourges, wrote to Nostradamus:

November 15, 1561: I am feeling much better than I was at Bourges, where I wore myself out studying law. . . . My students' stepfather . . . sent us to Anvers in order to shelter us from the religious troubles and from the plague, which is threatening. I looked for you in vain in Paris and at court. In my opinion, if the Papists do not make concessions to the Protestants, the situation will result in civil war. The people of Paris, blinded by superstitions, are completely insane. The meeting at Poissy is languishing because of the cardinals. At the first of October, the king [Charles IX] was sick. He appears to me to be wasted and suffering. The House of the Valois is declining while that of the Bourbons is rising. In Belgium there is no trouble, and the Spanish Inquisition is less vigorous. But here are the new tortures: Suspects are thrown into prison and at night, without any other form of trial, they are hurled into a tank of water, hands and feet tied. Thus, nothing seen, nothing known. They say that the queen of England [Elizabeth I] is going to marry the king of Sweden. I will give you more news when I am in Augsburg. I am pleased that

you are examining my horoscope, and I will show you my grati-
tude. Can you consider questions of marriage, children and career? [Written at] Anvers.

Again, poor Tubbe is pleading with Nostradamus to inform him
about his marriage and career, a request he first made nineteen
months earlier and repeated between then and now. If he
awaited the advice of Nostradamus on marriage before entering
on the sea of matrimony, we may suspect that he died a bache-
lor. In these lines, we can see an example of how Nostradamus
was kept informed of gossip in high places.

On January 19, 1562, Tubbe wrote Nostradamus from Augsburg, reporting that Rosenberger's fortunes were not at all improved, in fact he was worse off than ever. He told of an unfortunate person who had moved to Augsburg to escape his creditors.
He said:

> Why not admit it? He is the younger brother of Rosenberger. If
> you agree to do his horoscope, he will pay you twenty crowns.
> . . . he wants to know in general his future, health, longevity,
> success in business, honors, etc., in Latin, simply—just as you
> speak . . .

Then in April of 1562, things suddenly improved for Rosenberger, and Tubbe credited Nostradamus with a successful prediction. However, the other requested horoscopes had not arrived, and he complained about it.

> Have you received the nativities? I have no response. Could you
> look into this, please? I will pay you as promised. Would you like
> another German cup? I ask you only to please reveal sincerely,
> in your judgment, both the good and the bad events, and do it in
> Latin. Don't send the mail to Krafft, but seek out another German
> merchant of Lyon . . . Rosenberger's mines, it appears, are pros-
> pering. . . .

Nostradamus was enraged by the news that Tubbe had given
him in his letter of November 15, which had been considerably
delayed in reaching him. He wrote, on May 13, 1562:

> . . . What you tell me from Anvers has upset me completely. What
> a monstrous barbarity exercised against Christians! We live in an
> abominable period, and the worst is yet to come. How I wish I

would see no more of all this! . . . I prefer [as payment] a silver cup to coins. For yours, it is up to you to decide what you owe me. I speak to you frankly, as you asked me to do. I await, then, Rosenberger's payment and yours. I may add that I have spent every bit of ten ecus on this work. . . . if I don't send [Rosenberger's horoscope] it's because the religious wars prevent me. Here, all the suspects have fled. I alone remain with my family, at the mercy of an insane people. If you wish, I will sum up for you the memorandum that I wrote on the beginning of the wars of religion in Provence.* Last February, the Estates General were held in Provence; they spoke mostly of religious questions. The popular "Hydra" did everything to prevent evangelical preaching, but nevertheless each city had its own ministers there. At Aix, capitol of Provence and the seat of parliament, the cathedral, Saint Sauver, is especially full of ignorant priests. . . . they used gold to buy the services of a nobleman, a certain Flassans. He used the worst kind of violence against the partisans of the Christian religion. The clergy lend a strong hand to this man, who was defending their interests. The crowd named him consul, along with two others of the same stripe. Each night, more violence broke out against the suspects and the most powerful people. The Christians finally decided to defend themselves by sending one of their own, Mutonis, to the king and queen. . . . [an inquiry was made] into the extortions committed, and to reestablish order. . . .

Nostradamus went on to describe a full-scale war waged against Flassans by the rebels of "the true faith" and the eventual defeat of Flassans. He claimed he had predicted this outcome to the victors, though one wonders whether he had performed the Delphic deception of granting each side the win. Peace was restored when the king replaced the governor, and Provence was quiet again. Nostradamus had somehow survived the conflict. The seer closed this letter to Tubbe with a practical twist:

Tell me about things at your end. I will await your letter with payment. [Written at] Salon.

With this letter, the correspondence between Nostradamus and Lorenz Tubbe closes for us. But just one year before his

* This document is unknown.

death, the prophet seemed to give away his deteriorating health and worse temper in a letter to an representative of Emperor Charles V, to whom he had promised horoscopes of the royal sons.

> July 7, 1565: I was coming back from Aix when my daughter gave me your letter. I'm going to keep my promise to D. Rechlinger—a promise made long ago—concerning the princes' horoscopes. I'll hide nothing from you; the work that Rechlinger's horoscope cost me was thirty golden ecus, and the work of my secretary who copied it out, six ecus. From princes I expect better pay, worthy of the sons of an emperor. You are not unaware of the enormous labor that such work demands. You can make this response to Rechlinger, as I am going to do, myself, but in French, since he is culturally French. This is why I write horoscopes in French, rather than in Latin. . . .

The final letter in this collection is a certain indication of Nostradamus' deterioration. It was written December 13, 1565.

> The day after Gaspar Flechamer's visit, the bourgeois patrician of Augsburg, I had, by what mischance I do not know, such a crisis of rheumatism in my hands, that I was not able to make his horoscope for the agreed-on day. But the pains passed from my hands to my right knee, then into my foot. Here it is now twenty-one days that I have not slept. Today I'm breathing a bit easier. Fillol gave me a letter that gives me news about D. Rechlinger and you. I was surprised at your silence, and I imagined that D. Rechlinger was busy translating into German Prince Rudolph's horoscope. This is a man not only knowledgeable, but also quite virtuous, and he has for us, aside from the Emperor, the greatest of devotion. The package that Fillol brought contained a letter from a German lord, Anton Schorer, asking me for his horoscope. . . . his brother, Hieronymous Schorer, had asked from me a lot of work, and I sent it to him at Lyon, written with my own hand. He sent it back to me with disdain, saying that it was barely readable. I had it copied out, and yet he didn't appreciate it. It would be very disagreeable for me if Anton Schorer should be as difficult as his brother. I speak to you in all frankness. . . . As you see, I have given satisfaction to all the world. Everything you write me about Germany interests me, but I see, as from a lookout, great catastrophes menacing our poor France,

and even Italy. The wars of religion are going to break out again. There was seen at Arles, at Lyon and in the Dauphiné, a meteor, which presages great misfortune. It was predicted in our prognostication of 1564.

Meteors fall by the tens of thousands every year. Nostradamus died six months later. Perhaps that "shooting star" he mentioned was his own very personal death-star.

CHAPTER EIGHT

The World War II Quatrains and Their Creators

Though fraud in all other actions be odious, yet in matters of war it is laudable and glorious, and he who overcomes his enemies by stratagem, is as much to be praised as he who overcomes them by force.
—NICCOLÒ MACHIAVELLI, 1469–1527

Propaganda is an inalienable and vital function of the modern state.
—JOSEPH GOEBBELS, NÜRNBERG RALLY, 1934

THE GERMAN NAZI PARTY was brought to power, for better or worse, by the needs and ambitions of the citizens of that country at that time in history. Catering to the expectations of the populace and fulfilling their expectations, the leaders of the Third Reich wooed them until they accepted the general framework of the party by voting them into power. One strong enticement dangled before them was occult involvement.

Symbolism, from the swastika to the Wagnerian librettos, played a huge part in establishing the "destiny" aspects of the Nazis. All sorts of pseudo-scientific claptrap flourished and was encouraged in the educational system. Flat-Earth theories, medical quackery, dowsing with pendulums, racial "superiority" notions (of course!) and strong belief in astrology were promoted as part of the official dogma. Nazi Reichsführer Heinrich Himmler firmly believed in the Cosmic Ice Theory of a party scientist named Hörbiger, who claimed that the moon was covered with a 140-mile-thick layer of ice. Himmler also avidly supported the German "Ariosophist" group that aimed to "cleanse the world of Jewish science" by deporting such persons as Albert Einstein. The scientist sailed for the United States along with his Theory of Relativity that enabled the Allies to develop the atomic bomb.

It was Himmler who directed tests of homeopathic remedies (pure water) to be used on more than one hundred prisoners at Dachau concentration camp. These unfortunates were purposely inoculated with tuberculosis bacteria and a variety of deadly blood infections, then given the experimental medications. Results were disastrous as homeopathy once more failed to cure. In spite of these continued tests of such quackery, homeopathy is still favored as a popular "alternative remedy" in Germany, France and England.

Himmler had designed the *Dezernat Des Ahnenerbes,* a singular course for selected SS officers. This group was concerned with such matters as recording endless physical measurements of specimens of specially slaughtered concentration camp prisoners of the "inferior" races. Within the curriculum of the *Ahnenerbes* was a unique course of study which automatically brought diplomas to all who studied dowsing techniques, trying to use forked sticks, metal rods or pendulums to find buried treasure and other hidden objects. Persistent rumors of a war treasury of Napoleon buried near Dresden at Dippoldiswalde brought a small army of SS men to the area, dowsing sticks twitching. Hundreds of acres were dug up, but nothing was found. Equally elusive was another fabled hoard, that of Attila the Hun, which was believed to be located at Aurolzmünster, in Austria. Despite their diplomas, the SS officers dug up a lot of dirt but nary a pfennig's worth of treasure.

Though much of the pseudo-science was later officially de-emphasized and even forbidden by law simply because it had served its purpose and was now getting in the way, astrology was retained as a popular belief, possibly because some of the Nazi hierarchy, notably Himmler and Rudolph Hess, embraced it. It was a heady feeling to believe that your destiny was written in the stars, and those of the Third Reich were fond of such ideas.

It was also very much in the interest of the Nazis to encourage belief in obscure and doubtful notions, because such acceptance prepared the German public to accept the racial theories that they were being taught, theories which had no more basis in fact than any of the other nonsense. Pseudo-science is apparently more acceptable when it is in plentiful company.

In late 1938, Minister of Propaganda Goebbels ordered the Gestapo to round up prominent German astrologers for consultation. His aim was to consider the possible uses of astrology as a weapon of psychological warfare. A prominent practitioner who showed up in that group was Karl Ernst Krafft.

A Nazi Party Astrologer

Krafft was born in Basle, Switzerland, in 1900. That year of birth, at the beginning of a new century, was something he never tired of mentioning to his fans as if it were of great significance. He was described as a tiny, pale man with black hair and a sinister look.

Apparently his childhood was exceedingly unhappy, and when a supportive younger sister died suddenly, he developed an active interest in the occult. He visited a spirit medium, and though he was unimpressed by the results he obtained, he thereby became aware of the great public interest in such activities. To his family's dismay, especially since he had proven to be an excellent student at the University of Basle, showing great promise in science and mathematics, he became an astrologer.

Krafft published various statistical papers related to astrology and a "Treatise in Astrobiology," full of endless tables and calculations, following a long period of study with an English authority on biometrics. This "science" in itself was apt to bring him to the attention of the Nazis, who were actively seeking proof of their racial superiority through endless assessment of every aspect of human life. They believed that there were pronounced tendencies, to be established by measuring various parameters, that could be assigned to ethnic groups. It has been noted that there exists a pronounced Teutonic fascination with numbers and measurements.

Krafft opened an office in Zurich, casting horoscopes and advising on investments. It was the latter practice that brought the collapse of his business, as his advice proved as bad as the economic depression in 1931. Krafft's own investments, decided by means of his own occult divinations, collapsed as well, and the failure drove him into an asylum.

The efforts of Goebbels to interest the German public in the occult revived an interest in astrology, however, and Krafft emerged from the mental hospital just in time to reap the benefits of this interest. He moved to Germany, and by 1935, his works were beginning to take on new popularity, and the German Ministry of Propaganda endorsed them enthusiastically. In grateful response, Krafft became a Nazi and introduced into his writings and lectures a line of violently anti-Semitic ideas. He fulfilled the position of willing pawn with great success.

By 1937 the astrologer was well established in Nazi circles, and when Goebbels consulted secretly with him and his colleagues, it was to establish a counterintelligence group which became Section VI of the Reichssicherheitshauptamt (Reich Central Security Office) concerned solely with occult warfare. Officially, the Nazis were now condemning such practices as astrology by means of strict laws, largely to avoid the embarrassment that might ensue should other countries discover their interest; under cover, they maintained a group dedicated to those matters.

World War II began. Astrologer Krafft made a sensational prediction on November 2, 1939, before a meeting of the Berlin Astrological Society. He said that between the 7th and 10th of November, an attempt would be made on Hitler's life. On November 8, an explosion nearly took the Führer's life during a celebration of the anniversary of the famous Beer Hall Putsch. Hitler had left the hall just moments before a powerful bomb went off.

Goebbels had ordered that the only two astrological magazines still being printed in Germany, *Stern und Mensch* and *Mensch im All,* should be monitored by his office. Immediately, it was reported to him that Krafft had made the prediction. Outside in the public sphere, the astrologer became famous overnight. Everyone was talking about his wonderful powers.

The Gestapo, not well convinced that supernatural powers had enabled Krafft to know of this upcoming assassination attempt, questioned him at length, and only the intercession of Hitler's deputy, Rudolph Hess, spared the astrologer further terrors. Hess was an ardent follower of every sort of occult claim, especially those related to prophecy and health quackery.

At this point, Krafft became personal astrologer to Hess. He immediately began a reinterpretation of the prophecies of Nostradamus, in which he had always been very interested. To do so, he probably had to conceal the prophet's Jewish origins from the Ministry of Propaganda.

Nostradamus' works were now being brought to the attention of the public for an excellent reason. Since it was easy to obtain from the *Centuries* any needed meaning, Krafft was commissioned in December of 1939 to find good news in there somewhere for the Nazi cause. That was quickly done, and his discoveries were published widely, in French, Dutch, Italian, Rumanian, Swedish and English.

Then Krafft, exultant over his new position and success, was further thrilled to learn that Hitler himself had become interested in his skills. He predicted a glorious victory for Germany in 1943.

Enter British Intelligence

Learning of the Section VI RSHA Group in Germany, the British in September of 1940 got together their own—equally secret— coven of astrologers, calling it their "black group," within the Department of Psychological Warfare. They put Captain Louis de Wohl, a Hungarian-born astrologer, in charge. (James Laver, the Nostradamian, had his horoscope cast by de Wohl at about this time, and marveled over it.) De Wohl, who had arrived in England as a refugee in 1935, was chosen by the British because he said he knew Krafft's techniques of astrological forecasting, and it became his job to anticipate what the Nazi astrologer might advise the warlords of Germany to do.

De Wohl wrote some fake astrological articles for equally fake astrological magazines that contained discouraging predictions for Nazi Germany. These were distributed throughout Europe by various means, the intent being to influence other countries that might offer support to the Nazis. Not ignoring the renewed German interest in Nostradamus either, he also invented a few pro-British/anti-Nazi quatrains in an attempt to neutralize Krafft's work. He created a 124-page book titled *Nostradamus prophezeit den Kriegsverlauf* (Nostradamus predicts the Course of the War), which was printed in huge quantities and dropped over occupied territories in 1943.

Among many other fakeries, his book contained an "improved" version of the Nostradamus quatrain 3-30, which in the original read:

> *Celuy qu'en luitte & fer au faict bellique,*
> *Aura porté plus grand que luy le pris:*
> *De nuict au lict six luy feront la pique,*
> *Nud sans harnois subit sera surprins.*

> *He who in struggle and iron in a deed of war,*
> *Will have taken the prize from one greater than he:*
> *At night, six will carry the grudge to him in bed,*
> *Naked, without armor, he will be surprised.*

All that de Wohl did in his invented quatrain was to substitute "Hister" (the supposed Nostradamus anagram of Hitler's name) for the first word, "Celuy," meaning "He who . . ." This could not have been a sadder attempt at fakery, since any reader could obtain a copy of any edition of the *Centuries* and instantly spot the substitution. But as one finds even today, the Believers prefer to accept what is given to them, rather than looking to original sources.

(This same Quatrain 3-30 is said by the Nostradamians to be a prophecy of the fate of Montgomery, the unfortunate jouster who took the life of Henry II during Nostradamus' time. See Chapter 11 and the discussion of Quatrain 1-35. It is true that Catherine de Médicis had the satisfaction of ordering Montgomery's head off, but only because he had become a Huguenot leader, and he was not naked nor in bed when captured.)

It appears that de Wohl had misrepresented and hyperbolized

his astrological talents to the British. They soon found that he knew little about the subject and they did not retain his services for long.

An interesting question is whether or not either side in this psychological World War II battle had any real belief in astrology. Both sides have officially denied any such weakness, even until today. It would certainly have been lax of them not to consider the possible use of such a belief in the conduct of the war, but we may never know whether anyone other than Krafft and de Wohl had any real belief in the ability of anyone to predict useful information from the stars.

How did Krafft apparently know of the attempt on Hitler's life? We must remember that he enjoyed the company of top Nazi officials, and there is a very strong opinion among many historians that the Beer Hall assassination attempt was staged by the Nazis to gain sympathy for the Führer and to make the English look bad. The fact that Hitler made a *very* short speech that night, and that the man convicted of placing the bomb was secretly murdered by the Gestapo rather than going on trial, tend to support that contention. Krafft, in the position he occupied, might very well have known about the plan.

This possibility is given further support by an event that took place in June of 1941. One of the top-secret German plans was their intention to invade Russia, a signer of a mutual nonaggression pact with Germany. Early in 1941, Krafft predicted a successful invasion of Russia by Germany in the near future. Given Krafft's connections within the Party, this, too, could have been known to him.

Ordered to draw up horoscopes of prominent Allied leaders, Krafft satisfied his employers by producing quite unflattering and discouraging futures for Churchill, Stalin and Roosevelt. He also wrote, free-lance, a book on Nostradamus that interpreted the quatrains so as to indicate a sweeping Nazi victory. It was published in Danish, French and Portuguese.

Then it was learned by the Gestapo that Krafft was telling others a far different story than that he was supplying to the Nazi propaganda machine; he was prophesying eventual doom for the Nazi cause. On the strength of this, the Gestapo prepared to pounce on him.

Just at this time, Rudolf Hess landed in Scotland after fleeing

Germany, and his personal astrologer was now without his powerful protection. The Gestapo once more hauled him in for examination, along with hundreds of other occultists, in their "Aktion Hess." This was a move to explain Hess's flight to the German people. They said it was a result of the advice of the astrologers. The Gestapo blamed Krafft for Hess's flight and locked him up.

He was held at Berlin's Lehrterstrasse Prison. Transferred to Oranianburg concentration camp, he awaited a trial that never took place. He had become an awkward presence, knowing as much as he did. His predicted date for a glorious Nazi victory in the war came and went, and things only got worse for Germany. Scheduled for the gas chambers at Buchenwald, Karl Ernst Krafft died of malnutrition and typhus on January 8, 1945, in a cattle car on the way to his execution.

The faked Nostradamus quatrains, predictably, have survived Krafft, the Nazis and de Wohl. They are still occasionally quoted as proof of the divine abilities of the Seer of Provence, to prove that he had accurately looked ahead through the mists of four centuries and seen a corporal with a funny mustache named Adolf Hitler.

CHAPTER NINE

Contemporary Seers

Contemporaries appreciate the man rather than the merit; but posterity will regard the merit rather than the man.
—CHARLES C. COLTON, 1780–1832

THERE WERE OTHER MAGICIANS, astrologers and miracle-mongers active in the civilized world while Nostradamus worked his wiles on the House of Valois and the citizens of France. Some of them had, in their own ways, as direct an influence as Nostradamus, and some of them paid dearly for their boldness. But none proved as enduring as the Seer of Salon, having vanished into history as footnotes.

Here are brief biographies of a few of these charismatic characters, who, I believe, will lend a certain coloring to our grasp of the times.

DR. JOHN DEE (1527–1608)

Mathematician, navigator, cartographer, prolific writer, master spy, sorcerer, astrologer and most trusted adviser to Queen Elizabeth I of England, John Dee was one of the most powerful but subtle political influences of his day. He was a tall, thin, mysterious man with a long, pointed beard, a genuinely accomplished scholar who was never reluctant to mix a little attractive claptrap in with his otherwise valuable teachings. It is believed that he was the model for Shakespeare's character Prospero in *The Tempest*.

Dee was born in London in 1527 into a family of moderate means. He was educated at Cambridge University, but the title "Doctor" was not rightly his, since he never attained that exalted state. He was certainly deserving of it. At Cambridge Dee came under the influence of Girardus Mercator, whose cartographical innovations fascinated the brilliant young student.

Captivated by the study of mathematics and astronomy, he dedicated one of his first books to Edward VI of England, who thereupon granted him a handsome pension of one hundred crowns a year. Soon he traveled to Paris, which offered him not only astronomical knowledge but astrological lore, since that city was then, as now, a major center of occult interests. The officials of Paris were sufficiently impressed with him to offer him the position of Royal Mathematician to the French court. Though that was a respected and well-paid position, Dee declined in favor of returning to England.

It was at that time that he began his serious forays into the magical arts, and he soon had the status of a sorcerer, though of shady reputation. He came to the very favorable attention of Queen Mary I (Bloody Mary), who had succeeded short-reigned Edward, and at her command he drew up her horoscope. But it was the attention he paid to the then-Princess Elizabeth, Mary's younger half-sister, that almost ended his career rather early.

Elizabeth was at that time imprisoned by Mary to effectively keep her out of circulation while the queen ruthlessly attempted to officially reinstall the Roman Catholic faith in England by means of torture, decapitation and the stake. A very lucky and cunning prophecy that Dee offered to Elizabeth—obtained, he said, through astrology—put him forever in the favor of the woman who was to be known as the Virgin Queen. He predicted for her a very long life and a very high position in the kingdom, and in both respects he was quite spectacularly correct. Though it enraged Mary, Dee's auspicious prognostication doubtless lent the princess a measure of courage when she most needed it, especially when in 1554 she was summoned by her sister to a stay in the Tower of London. That meant that Mary was likely to call for her head on the slightest whim.

(Lest we attribute to this clever gentleman more than his share of prophetic power for his successful estimate of Elizabeth's future, consider what would have happened had the princess *not* been fortunate enough to survive until Mary's untimely (and some think, unnatural) demise, and thereby assume the throne. Doctor Dee would not have made known his incorrect prediction and no one would be present to remind him about it.)

Mary I was an ill-favored queen in most respects. Her strong compulsion to return England to the influence of the Vatican was unsuspected when she was chosen to succeed Lady Jane Grey, who spent a short nine days on the English throne only to lose her head to the rapacious Mary when she was forcefully supplanted as sovereign. Anxious to give England a proper—Catholic—heir, Mary wed the much younger Philip of Spain and immediately announced her pregnancy, which turned out to be imaginary. That highly embarrassing event was probably what set her off on her spree of butchery that saw over 300 Protestant clergymen burned alive and earned her the nickname by which history identifies her.

Doctor Dee was on record as having predicted that Mary's marriage would be both unhappy and childless (right on both counts, though hardly surprising) and Mary angrily announced that they were not amused. The astrologer was imprisoned for treason—charged with using magic against the life of the queen—and for heresy. Both charges brought him near the Tower block, but fortunately for him, Mary died within a few months, and when Elizabeth took over as monarch-elect, she invited Dee to leave prison still attached to his head and to use it to compute the most auspicious astrological date for her coronation ceremony. From that moment on, he was to enjoy her considerable patronage and trust.

It is interesting to note that when Mary reigned, Dee was suspect as a magician and a probable Protestant, which was to say, a heretic; after Elizabeth ascended the British throne and reversed the religious allegiance of England, he was assailed as a magician and a probable Papist. It seems he had no peace.

Dee was a shrewd politician as well as an otherwise exceedingly clever and accomplished man. Astrology was only the bait that snared him the queen, but once he had her attention, he proved himself capable in so many ways that he became an indispensable member of her court. He drew up geographical and hydrographical charts for Elizabeth's active explorers, and is credited with originating the phrase "the British Empire." The Virgin Queen appointed him to ever more important positions, in spite of a certain amount of disconcertion, both personal and public, over his open association with acknowledged rascals and rumored practitioners of the Black Arts.

John Dee was a strange mixture of charlatan and genuine intellectual. He wrote both a *Treatise of the Rosie Crucean Secrets** and a presentation for methods of finding a northwest passage to China. While he expounded his notions that the letters of the alphabet embodied great powers and that deep mysteries might be solved by a knowledge of superior numbers, he was at the same time laying the groundwork for what we recognize today as the scientific method. He was not at all shy about embracing both worlds. He wrote, "By science man may learn the mysteries of the spirit world." And he probably meant it.

Dee encouraged Elizabeth to greatly expand the British navy, and in common with many other contemporary scholars, he was an early believer in and supporter of, the ideas of Copernicus. Both were wise and far-sighted visions. He also supported, in word and action, the exploration of the new worlds that were capturing the attention of England. By direct order of Elizabeth, none of her appointed seafarers left port before Dee had contributed his valuable cartographical and navigational skills to their efforts. Among these adventurers were Sebastian Cabot, Walter Raleigh, Francis Drake and Martin Frobisher.

Then, in the later years of his life, Dee made two foolish decisions. First, he turned his attention to alchemy. Second, in 1582 he made the acquaintance of one Edward Kelley, a scoundrel who claimed mediumistic and alchemical abilities. Kelley had been in prison, and his ears had been cropped as a penalty for forgery, but this very unsavory background failed to daunt Dee.

Dee's association with Kelley was his downfall. He left England with him in 1583 for a six-year hiatus, at the age of fifty-six. Once on the continent, he immersed himself completely in occult studies and offered to have Kelley make gold for the king

---

*This may have been the work of another occultist. There are conflicting opinions on the authorship.

of Poland and for Emperor Rudolf II in what is now Czechoslovakia. The brilliant scholar abandoned all his truly useful and productive work, seeking the ever-elusive shortcut to wealth and to divine wisdom—always, he felt, through Christian channels—and only found himself betrayed by Kelley and others who fed upon what was left of his fast-fleeing fame and repute.

He returned to an England that had forgotten his contributions, to find himself in disgrace and publicly denounced as a fraud. His home in Mortlake was ransacked by a mob which destroyed his instruments, talismans and many of his magic manuscripts. His colleague Edward Kelley deserted him and was eventually killed trying to escape from prison.

John Dee could have accepted any of the numerous and tempting invitations that he received from kings and emperors, to take up residence at their palaces for fabulous rewards. But, as he himself recorded, he received a visit from the angel Gabriel, who told him, "If thou remainest my servant, and do the works that are righteous, I will put Solomon behind thee, and his riches under thy feet." It was in response to this seemingly uncelestial promise that Dee abandoned his really important work to pursue psychic matters. The bargain was not kept by Gabriel, though respected by Dee.

Upon Elizabeth's death in 1603 at the age of seventy, Dee came nose-to-nose with James VI of Scotland, who now ascended the English throne as James I. Astrologer Dee had rashly predicted the execution of James's mother, Mary, Queen of Scots, and in his position as adviser may even have assisted Elizabeth to arrive at the decision to sign the writ of execution. Dee was stripped of his honors and his income by the vengeful James and sent to live in the countryside incommunicado. He spent the last five years of his life there in extreme poverty until his death in 1608 at the very remarkable age of eighty-one. He is buried at Mortlake between two of Elizabeth's other servants, Holt and Miles.

Some of Dee's magical paraphernalia is still preserved at the British Museum in London, where visitors may see his rose-tinted scrying crystal, engraved gold and wax talisman tablets, wands and formula books. The prize object of the display is a magic black obsidian glass mirror about seven inches in diameter fashioned in Mexico by the Aztec culture. His library of more than 4,000 books on the occult, mathematics and cartography—

the largest collection in Britain at that time—was dispersed soon after his death.

Dee was one of the most important and influential charlatans of history, who spent forty-five years at the feet of the queen who has been called the greatest monarch to ever occupy the British throne.

COSIMO RUGGIERI(?–1615)

This rogue, son of a physician at the court of the Médicis, was brought by Queen Catherine to France from his native Florence. Besides casting horoscopes for the royal court, he became famous for making talismans and wax images that he claimed won the affections of young ladies or caused them to die from longing, depending on which ceremony he chose to apply to the task.

He was a close confidant of Catherine's, who had been warned by him to "beware of St. Germain," and because the Louvre and the Palais de Tournelles—both royal residences—were in the parish of St. Germain, the queen had a personal residence, the Hôtel de Soissons, designed and constructed for her outside the parish by the famous architect Jean Bullant. She often accompanied Ruggieri to the top of the tall tower that was a prominent part of the *hôtel*. That tower, which had been built especially for his astronomical/astrological observations, may still be seen next to the Paris Bourse, adjoining the site of the queen's former home.

The name St. Germain is fairly prominent in France, and Ruggieri's warning to Catherine did not specify anything more than that name. His prophecy might have been made to apply in many different ways. But none of the queen's misfortunes— and there were many—happened to occur at, close to, associated with, before, after or coincident with, any place (street, town, county, park, edifice), person (living or dead), holiday, ceremony or other event named after St. Germaine. *Dommage!*

Catherine, as usual playing for the maximum intrigue, had other interesting uses for the Florentine. She placed him in the employ of Francis, Duke of Alençon, her fourth son, who was a known political malcontent and a constant cause for concern at court. Francis was perpetually smarting under the jibes of the gossips who followed his pursuit of Elizabeth I of England as a bride, and endless jokes circulated about his hopeless quest. Ostensibly in residence at the duke's home as a teacher of Italian, the astrologer was supposed to act as a clandestine agent for the queen, spying on her son to determine his latest peccadillos. Seeing more profit as a double agent, Ruggieri spied instead for the duke, who treated him handsomely.

In 1574, in response to much gossip at court, Ruggieri was arrested on charges of conspiring by sorcery against the king, then Charles IX but with only a few months to live, and the astrologer was put to the torture. He denied the accusations made against him, but was condemned to the galleys. He was rescued from the sentence by several important friends and by the intercession of the queen mother herself, who felt she still had use for this rascal. Taking up residence in a chateau in Nantes, Ruggieri was again arrested in 1598 on rumors that in his drawing room he had a wax figure of the new king, Henry IV, which he daily pierced with a long needle, trying by this means to bring about the death of the monarch.

He was reminded by the judge that he had already been accused and examined under torture concerning the former event, which smacked of Satanic involvement. Ruggieri put up a bold front and began making great claims of predictive and supernatural powers, however saying that his abilities were entirely Christian in nature. He claimed that the Ruggieri who had been arrested for the conspiracy against Charles was actually a Florentine gardener of the same name and related how Catherine, on the eve of the St. Bartholomew's Day Massacre, had ordered him to cast horoscopes for the Prince of Condé, a prominent Protestant leader, and the King of Navarre (soon to be Henry IV of France), and that certainly such service to the kingdom deserved a reward, not censure and condemnation. Catherine was safely dead and not available for verification of this story, and Henry believed him, actually granting him a pension.

This clever charlatan wrote a number of almanacs and other minor publications, dying in 1615 an avowed atheist, much to the dismay of his friends and the horror of the public. The outcry against his failure to embrace religion was so strong that a book appeared, *The Appalling Story of Two Magicians Strangled by the Devil in Paris During Holy Week.* Ruggieri was one of the unfortunate subjects, the other being a *sorcier* named César, who apparently survived his encounter and was detained in the Bastille.

MOTHER SHIPTON (1488–1561)

Though it is difficult to determine whether this English prophet actually existed as she is represented in folklore, writings seriously ascribed to her are being reproduced even today. No reference to her prior to 1641 is in existence, so that what follows is not well supported by documents.

There are several claimants to her title. One lived in Oxfordshire near Wychwood Forest, but since nothing survives in writing from her or from any of the others except a Yorkshire claimant, it is the latter woman who has won the title. From her, we have much in print.

Mother Shipton is supposed to have been born in a cave at Dropping Well, Knaresborough, Yorkshire, in 1488 and the present town owes its tourist trade to that fact. She was Ursula Southill (or Sowthiel, or Southiel), the incredibly ugly daughter of Agatha Southill, known locally herself as a powerful witch. John Tyrrel, a biographer who had some undisclosed source of information, said in his 1740 book, *Past, Present and to come: or, Mother Shipton's Yorkshire prophecy:*

> Her Stature was larger than common, her Body crooked, her Face frightful; but her Understanding extraordinary.

About 1512, a wealthy builder from York, Tobias Shipton, married Ursula. One can only wonder why, unless Ursula had unsuspected and unadvertised charms. Perhaps he was attracted by her extraordinary Understanding.

She soon attained considerable notoriety throughout England as The Northern Prophetess, and because of her unfortunate appearance and reputed powers, was widely rumored to be the child of Satan. Tyrrel recounted the story that the Lord of the Underworld had met Ursula's mother in a field when she was only sixteen and promised her that if she would "comply with his Desires" he would "preserve her above the Reach of Want." It is an offer many young ladies have accepted, and Agatha "readily condescended." Alas, "At length the Embraces of her infernal Gallant produced a pregnancy," and at the ensuing birth,

> such a terrible Storm of Thunder and Lightning appear'd, that Houses were beat down, Trees shatter'd, and the very Features of the Child were so warp'd and distorted, that it appear'd the very Master-Piece of Deformity.

Apparently it was a difficult delivery.

The English court of Henry VIII, deeply concerned with astrology and prophecy, figured largely in Mother Shipton's prognostications, which received ample public attention and were printed in pamphlets for wide distribution. Though copies of these pamphlets and booklets still exist, most of what can be found today are sheer forgeries. Many meteorological and astrological almanacs published as late as the 19th century used Mother Shipton's name freely in the same manner that the magical name of Nostradamus has been used on similar publications. I have in my library an 1838 book which gives an idea of the overblown claims made for such tomes. It is titled:

THE
NEW UNIVERSAL
DREAM-BOOK;
OR THE
DREAMER'S SURE GUIDE
TO THE
HIDDEN MYSTERIES OF FUTURITY:
TO WHICH ARE ADDED,
SEVERAL REMARKABLE DREAMS
AND
UNDENIABLE PROOFS
OF THE
REAL IMPORTANCE OF INTERPRETING DREAMS.
BY MOTHER SHIPTON.

I also have an 1870 reprint copy of a 1686 book, attributed to Edwin Pearson, *The Strange and Wonderful History of Mother Shipton.* Because of its similarity to another book, *Life and Death of Mother Shipton,* I suspect that this biography was probably actually written by Richard Head, who also wrote *The English Rogue,* a racy account of his experiences with various tricksters, cheats and rascals of his day. Head was himself rather a rascal.

Many localized prophecies were invented to use the Shipton name to advantage. In my library is a first edition of the 1740 Tyrrel book, *Past, Present and to come: or, Mother Shipton's Yorkshire prophecy.* In that slim volume is quoted what might well have been issued as a genuinely pre-event prediction:

> Time shall happen A Ship shall sail upon the River *Thames,* till it reach the City of *London,* the Master shall weep, and cry out, Ah! What a flourishing City was this when I left it! Unequalled throughout the World! But now scarce a House is left to entertain us with a Flagon.

Obviously, the prophecy has all of recorded time in which to be fulfilled, since no date is given or even suggested. War, earthquake, fire or the advent of Prohibition could all produce the cited effect, and no cause is specified. In fact, no calamity of a physical nature is inferred. Also, the "House" seems here to refer to a place of business that would be involved in providing a Flagon to visiting sailors. Nonetheless, despite the very large possibilities of interpretation and application of this prophecy, eager Shipton fans have declared that this is an accurate prophecy of the Great Fire of London, which is also said to have been foretold by Nostradamus and other seers. (See Chapter 11.)

A perfect example of what author John Sladek in *The New Apocrypha* (Stein and Day, 1973) calls an "unquestionably true" Shipton "prediction" is:

> *Eighteen hundred and thirty-five,*
> *Which of us shall be alive?*
> *Many a king shall end his reign*
> *Many a knave his end shall gain.*

One can hardly argue with this question and the two statements.

In 1862, a publisher named Charles Hindley produced a liberally augmented and quite false version of Head's *Life and Death of Mother Shipton,* which sold in great quantities. He disclosed his misconduct only after panic set in concerning certain imminent worldwide catastrophes predicted in this publication. Hindley's documented confession did nothing to dampen enthusiasm among believers, who continue to pore over the verses seeking secrets of the future. His and others' inventions on behalf of Mother Shipton continue to be published today.

The famous seeress died at age seventy-three in 1561, and is buried at Clifton, just outside the city of York. On her memorial is carved:

Here lies she who never ly'd
Whose skill so often has been try'd
Her prophecies shall still survive
And ever keep her name alive.

This is said to be the only such tribute to a witch in all of England, since the usual memorial is nothing more than a cairn of stones to mark the spot where such a person was hanged or burned.

PARACELSUS (1493–1541)

He was grandly named Theophrastus Philippus Aureolus Bombast von Hohenheim, a Swiss scholar/physician/mystic who called himself Paracelsus (para Celsus, greater than Celsus). He was born to educated parents in Switzerland, and was admitted to the University of Basle at age sixteen.

His life's work took him to Croatia, France, Germany, Greece, Italy, Poland, Portugal, Russia, Scandinavia, Spain and Turkey. His philosophy was a curious mixture of mystical notions and hard thinking. He added a few facts to chemical knowledge, made some of the earliest attempts to organize medical information, and was among the first to use nonherbal chemicals to treat disorders, but by most measures he was a superstitious, uninformed, argumentative, offensive braggart who alienated everyone with whom he came in contact.

True to his calling as a physician of that day, he insisted upon applying his knowledge of astrological aspects to all healing processes. On a more realistic bent, he laid the basis for an understanding of psychologically based illness by teaching that negative attitudes and stress can invoke certain problems, while a positive attitude is more conducive to avoidance of those conditions and/or recovery. That glimmering of the basic idea of psychological/psychosomatic causes and effects, widely accepted today, was expressed by Paracelsus thus: "A powerful will may cure, where a doubt will end in failure." Rather over-simplified, but with value.

Paracelsus favored the use of magnets in curing patients, and was in that respect the inspiration for Antoine Mesmer, the French mountebank who, 200 years later, discovered the principles of what we now call hypnosis, or suggestion. Mesmer at first believed that magnets were necessary for his induction of the "trance" state, but soon found that what became known as Mesmerism worked just as well without such aid.

The mines of Tyrol attracted Paracelsus, and he studied and recorded methods of discovering and recovering metals from the earth. In that time, diviners (dowsers) used their forked sticks, pendulums and other devices to find not only water, but metallic ores. Then, as now, any success they enjoyed was due either to their knowledge of geology or just dumb luck.

A natural wanderer and vagabond, this scholar managed to lose every friend he ever made, and his superiority complex soon earned him a terrible reputation. That reputation was well earned, as indicated in the preface to one of his books. He wrote:

> In this midcentury, monarchy of all the arts pertains to me, Theophrastus Paracelsus, prince of philosophy and medicine. For to this am I chosen by God that I may extinguish all fantasies of all far-fetched, false and putative works and presumptuous words, be they of Aristotle, Galen, Avicenna, Mesue, or any of their adherents.

This statement castigated just about every authority respected at that time in the medical field, and exalted the author as the sole master of his art. Paracelsus had obviously not been a Dale Carnegie student. As a result of this attitude, though he taught at various centers of learning, he stayed at each for only short periods of time before his superiors and his students decided they'd had enough of him.

He tried to change even the primitive notions of what made up the basic elements of the Renaissance universe. He disallowed the four elements of fire, earth, water and air, replacing them with sulphur, mercury and salt. However, even in this matter he seems to not have ever made up his mind. A sampling of his prescribed treatments yields one for sore eyes. Labeled *zebethum occidentale,* it was nothing more than dried and finely powdered human excrement, blown into the eyes of the unfortunate patient.*

In 1536 he published his *Prognosticatio,* a book of thirty-two illustrations that very much resemble the well-known Tarot cards. He claimed that the line drawings were magical, and wrote accompanying captions for them which he said were prophecies. Allegorical and symbolic in nature, these drawings and texts are as enigmatic as the Nostradamus writings, and may well have inspired the French seer in his style, since they were available to him well before he even produced his first almanac. This work of Paracelsus was referred to by his great admirer, another mystic named Eliphas Lévi, as "the most astounding monument and indisputable proof of the reality and existence of the gift of natural prophecy."

It appears that mystics earn peer approval easily.

There were of course scores of other seers, sorcerers and mountebanks who shared the stage of 16th-century Europe with Nostradamus, but the sampling given here will show that he had peers who in their own ways survived the process of elimination whereby historians exalt or discard personalities. They were siblings whose parents were Gullibility and Ignorance.

*His Royal Highness Prince Charles of the United Kingdom, who is at this writing also the president of the British Medical Association, has urged British physicians to return to the precepts of Paracelsus. Charles is also a believer in UFOs, telepathy and precognition. I trust he will never have sore eyes.

CHAPTER TEN

The Nostradamians

*Interpreters of prophecy during the last few
centuries have been, most of them, childish
and nonsensical; the fact is, when fancy is
their guide men wander as in a maze; they
see, like children gazing into the fire, not
what is really before them, but what is in
their own heads*
—CHARLES H. SPURGEON, 1834–1892

The Believers

HISTORICAL RESEARCH consists of fitting together many scraps
of information into a greater shadow of the reality we seek. That
silhouette is often soft-edged and is cast upon an uneven surface, a ghost that answers our questions faintly and sometimes
in lost idioms. The greater the quantity of information we have,
the better and the more independently reported that data is, the
clearer and more three-dimensional is the shadow we can sum-
mon from former times.

In spite of great care exercised by cautious researchers, historical misconceptions become established and are difficult to correct. I recall, in the 1960s, seeing a New York State Regent's
Examination in science that identified Galileo as the inventor of
the astronomical telescope. Similarly, most people believe that
Thomas Edison invented the electric light bulb, Christopher
Columbus was the first to discover the New World, printing was

invented in Germany, Nicolas Copernicus originated the idea of a heliocentric solar system, and that all the amendments to the U.S. Constitution originated from Americans (most of them were the "rights of Englishmen" that the British had spent five centuries extracting from various of their monarchs).

Nostradamus, too, has been embraced by non-history. Any number of newspaper and magazine accounts, television documentaries, reference books and textbooks assert the legitimacy of his prophetic powers as if they had never come under serious questioning. Much of this inaccuracy is the result of research that consists merely of reading highly colored accounts and accepting them.

When we seek to know the actual history of Nostradamus, a man who cast obstacles in the way of investigators and who employed smoke and mirrors to create illusions about himself and his work, we cannot easily accept much of what is presented to us, especially if the sources have an admitted interest in promoting belief in the prophet's claims.

There exists in society a very special class of persons that I have always referred to as the Believers. These are folks who have chosen to accept a certain religion, philosophy, theory, idea or notion and cling to that belief regardless of any evidence that might, for anyone else, bring it into doubt. They are the ones who encourage and support the fanatics and the frauds of any given age. No amount of evidence, no matter how strong, will bring them any enlightenment. They are the sheep who beg to be fleeced and butchered, and who will battle fiercely to preserve their right to be victimized.

The Flimflam Game

The expression "con man"—it could just as well be "con person"—has a specific derivation and meaning. Expanded, it is "confidence man," and it applies to one who invokes in a victim a feeling of trust, a conviction that he may be depended upon to be honest, fair, kindly, helpful and generally beneficial through some sort of investment in which the victim becomes willingly involved. That investment can be financial, emotional or philosophical, and seldom proves profitable to the investor, despite earnest representations made by the operator. Society treats the con man as a somewhat colorful but harmless rogue—a very dangerous attitude. Con artists are thieves, pure and simple, vicious practitioners of a heartless process that hurts and even kills their victims.

In its simplest definition, the "con game" consists of taking valuables under false pretenses and getting away with it. But there is more to the game than that, for the operator. There is always the danger that the victims might seek redress, and the consummate con artist builds a protection against that possibility, designing his game so that the victim's greed, dishonesty or gullibility will become evident if the game is revealed. Victims seldom wish that to happen, and usually take their losses in silence.

Any police bunco division can supply an inquirer with examples of current cons that are being worked despite the fact that they have been widely exposed, repeatedly, in the media. Tourists in New York City, London, Amsterdam and most other sophisticated centers worldwide still engage in useless battles of wits with the "3-card-monte" artists who set up instant shop on a carton and begin "tossing the boards" and asking the sheep to wager upon the location of "the lady" (the queen) after a few fast moves. No one but the "board-tosser" ever wins, but the sheep continue to elbow one another aside to lay down and lose their money.

The 3-card-monte is an excellent example of the con game. In a well-run operation, at least one of the bystanders is actually a "stick" or stooge who will bend a corner on the card that is to be found while the operator is apparently momentarily distracted, perhaps by a sudden fit of coughing. The stick then suggests to the victim that he lay down a large bet, since he now knows the correct card. The victim is, in effect, being asked to cheat the operator. If he is willing, and places his bet on the card, he is surprised to discover that somehow the bent card has become one of the others, and he has lost his wager. If he now suspects that he has been cheated, he cannot complain without admitting that he was himself attempting to cheat.

In the case of many of the Nostradamians, as in many religious movements, the leaders are themselves former victims who have so much of an emotional investment in their illusions that they cannot afford to abandon them, and will bend the corners of facts, theories and realities to maintain them. They are con men who have been conned.

The case of the Millerites in the 1840s (they are now known as the Seventh-Day Adventists) is an excellent illustration of this point. Though their guru, William Miller, repeatedly promised them that the world was about to end and gave several specific dates (see Appendix IV), followers rationalized his repeated failures and went on believing in him, as tens of thousands of people still do. They worked hard at convincing others of the validity of their guru's theories and philosophy.

On another level, the U.S. Patent Office handles an endless succession of inventors who still produce perpetual-motion machines that don't work, but no number of idle flywheels will convince these zealots of their folly; dozens of these patent applications flow in every year. In ashrams all over the world, hopping devotees of the Maharishi Mahesh Yogi will never abandon their goal of blissful levitation of their bodies by mind power, despite bruises and sprains aplenty suffered as they bounce about on gym mats like demented (though smiling) frogs, trying to get airborne. Absolutely nothing will discourage them.

A Very Selective Madness

The Nostradamians constitute a special subset of the Believers. They are the ones who interpret or accept interpretations of the prophetic utterances of Michel de Notredame. They are more often than not also vitamin C poppers and anti-fluoridationists who attend psychic spoon-bending parties for advanced cultural and educational purposes and purchase lucky numbers through the mail.

One very basic principle of logic is called parsimony. I referred to it earlier. It says that simple explanations, rather than complex ones that require grand assumptions and convoluted reasoning, are most often correct. This is a principle studiously avoided and denounced by the Nostradamians. They prefer to believe that Nostradamus had prophetic powers, and to support that preference they "bend over backwards," often to the point of severe dislocation and/or fracture.

The many eager active interpreters of the Nostradamus works

are, I believe, worth considerable study by a student of abnormal psychology. Happily bypassing any and all arguments against their notions, they freely move in and out of their looking-glass world with shining eyes and determined steps. Their fixation is amusing to some and distressing to others, but it is an example of the same kind of obsession that often obstructs the pursuit of valuable knowledge and wastes developing minds that might have been the Curies and Einsteins of a generation.

Widely published anecdotal accounts about the great successes of Nostradamus must be taken with a huge grain of salt. Most were written well after his death by authors not unwilling to enhance their accounts. I have had some personal experience with similar stories about the life of another colorful, real personality, magician Harry Houdini. His actual exploits were numerous and very newsworthy, but when editors sought a new "angle" on The Elusive American, they instructed their writers to invent new episodes in his career. If an invention proved to be attractive enough, it easily became part of the legend, indistinguishable from the facts unless examined closely. Of course stories that were invented postmortem were much safer. So it is with Nostradamus.

Charming and seemingly convincing episodes appear from various authors, but cannot be properly considered as evidence. Any acceptable evidence must come from verified printed material that Nostradamus produced, and the only inarguably genuine material is in the quatrains, presages, dedications, almanacs and letters, though even some of them can be shown to be spurious and many others are highly suspect. We will examine here how the Nostradamians have accepted and treated this material.

Some "authorities," such as Erika Cheetham, are not discussed here simply because their work is not properly enough researched. Cheetham has French king Louis XV as the *son* of the "Sun King," she appoints Philippe Egalité, the Duke of Orléans, as the *brother* of Louis XVI (he was not related), and she startles us with the assertion that Henry IV was a member of the Valois line (hardly!). She mixes up astrological signs and characteristics as well as history in any fashion that serves to prove her points. Her books on Nostradamus are among those most widely available and read today, but she cannot be taken seriously. Any critical treatment of her work would take an entire volume just to correct errors.

A Modern Example: John Hogue

A glossy, attractive and popular 1987 book titled *Nostradamus and the Millennium* (Doubleday), by John Hogue, naively declares that the French seer's quatrains are "still defying explanation," which is a little like saying that Mr. Hogue is still trying to figure out what happened to those Watergate tapes.

He chooses to follow the seductive path down which most Nostradamus researchers have happily stumbled. Freely—better, frivolously—assigning mystical value to quite ordinary words and phrases and distorting the more veiled references penned by Nostradamus until they groan from the ordeal, he liberally turns sand castles into the palaces of Camelot. As an example of what I find to be incomprehensible reasoning that he employs, note this statement:

> . . . we might translate anagrams for a future anti-christ foreseen emerging from the Middle East in this way: *Mabus—Abu Abbas* where the first 'A' and the last 'S' are dropped.

Yes, we *might* translate them that way, but it's not likely. Just what does that sentence *mean?*

As with the great majority of Nostradamus books, his is a rehash of what has been done, with a few new and hilarious observations, in one of which he discovers Libyan leader Muammar Khadafy* represented in several of the quatrains.

That discovery will bear attention here. Hogue bases it on 10-96, which reads:

Religion du nom des mers vaincra,
Contre la secte fils Adaluncatif,
Secte obstinee deploree craindra,
Des deux blessez par Aleph & Aleph.

The religion of the name of the seas will win,
Against the sect of the son of Adaluncatif,
The obstinate deplored sect will be afraid
Of the two who are wounded by A & A.

*Hogue uses the spelling Khaddafi.

Author Hogue somehow obtains this incredible translation from 10-96:

A colonel will plot through ambition.
He will cease the greatest part of the
  army against his
Prince through a false invention . . .
Religion named after the sea will win out
Against the sect of the son Adaluncatif:
The obstinate, deplored sect will be afraid
Of the two wounded Aleph and Aleph (Alif).

I'd give a big bag of silver dollars to know how the "colonel" got in there, let alone how he is going to "cease" the "army." Adding to this wonderment, the author gets his Khadafy correspondence from the word "Adaluncatif" by rearranging it to form "Cadafi Luna" and saying that: Cadafi Luna = Khadafy Moon = Khadafy of the Crescent = Islam.

Yes, I know that we get "Cadafi Luna*t*," not "Cadafi Luna," from the strange Nostradamus word, but Mr. Hogue apparently doesn't, so he sails happily on. . . .

Consider this: There are many current Romanized versions of the name of the Libyan leader. We have Khadaffi, Khadafy, Khaddafi and Qaddafi. Nostradamian Hogue presents us with his new version—Cadafi—since none of the others will work for him.

Hogue even snatches from Newton the discovery of the Law of Gravity, declaring that Nostradamus anticipated this fact, and he denies Kepler the distinction of finding the ellipticity of the planetary orbits, Nostradamus having known of it all along. Of course, not one bit of proof is offered by the author for these claims, but Nostradamians are not known to be finicky about such niceties.

As a pharmacist, John Hogue would be a failure, if we are to judge from another of his original discoveries re Nostradamus, this one concerning his transcendental skill as a physician. In his book *Excellent et Moult utile Opuscule à touts necessaire qui desirent auoir cognoissance de plusiers exquises Receptes,* Nostradamus printed a recipe for what he believed to be a preventative for the plague. Hogue describes the seer "plucking roses by the hundreds" before sunrise and taking them back to his home where he would "dry and crush the petals into a fine powder" which he then blended with a herbal mixture which consisted of several plants, including cloves. This concoction was made into lozenges that Hogue says Nostradamus called "rose pills."

> He admonished his patients to keep these pills under their tongues at all times without swallowing them . . . [careful diet and exercise] helped most of his patients respond to the rose pills' strong doses of vitamin C. These 'rose pills' successfully cured the cities of Aix and Salon.

This text reveals the author's naive belief that megadoses of vitamin C can prevent and cure disease (a popular New Age idea left over from the 60s), and that Nostradamus had anticipated this wonderful discovery by more than four centuries. Let us examine his notion.

First, vitamin C, though a necessary daily requirement for good health, does not work the way the health faddists believe. The megadose idea, so vigorously promoted by Nobel laureate Linus Pauling, has long ago ceased enjoying any validity, and is now known to be a potentially harmful practice.

Second, anything Nostradamus was doing with his "rose pills" would have no effect on the plague. The disease has been discussed in Chapter 5.

Third, there is no vitamin C content whatsoever in rose petals. Any vitamin C is contained only in the rose "hip," which is the mature berry of the plant which develops well after the flowers are gone.

Fourth, even if this vitamin source *had* been used, it has other drawbacks as well. It is exceedingly unstable, changing soon after exposure to air. Health food stores that offer "vitamin C from rose hips" are usually selling a mixture of about 10 percent rose hips (essentially bereft of any usable vitamin C) and 90 percent synthetic ascorbic acid (the chemical name for vitamin C).

Fifth, even if Nostradamus were using rose hips, which he wasn't, the vitamin C content is so small that it would require a lozenge *the size of a baseball* to supply his patient with twenty-five milligrams of the substance, which is less than half of the MDR (minimum daily requirement) of the vitamin, and just *one percent* of the dose required by quack medicine to produce the

Frontispiece from an early edition of Nostradamus' work.

The coat of arms of the Nostradamus family.

DANS CETTE MAISON
VECVT ET MOVRVT
MICHEL NOSTRADAMVS
ASTROPHILE
MEDECIN ORDINAIRE DV ROI
AVTEVR DES "ALMANACHS" ET
DES IMMORTELLES "CENTVRIES"
MDIII   MDLXVI

Marble plaque above the entrance to the Nostradamus home in Salon de Provence.

The entrance to the Nostradamus home in Salon de Provence.

RÉSIDENCE de MICHEL NOSTRADAMUS au XVIᵉᵐᵉ SIÈCLE
= QUARTIER FERREIROUX SALON =   Cheinet 1966

A representation by André Cheinet of the Nostradamus home as it probably looked during his lifetime. The view is from inside the courtyard, now closed in. M. Cheinet has put an observatory on the roof.

*An early poster represent-
ing Nostradamus in full astrological garb, though we
have no evidence that he
ever used that costume.*

*A commemorative bust of
Nostradamus atop a foun-
tain in the town of Salon
de Provence. He wears the
traditional four-cornered
hat that marks him as a
physician.*

"Les Antiques," Roman ruins near St. Rémy de Provence. "Le Mausole" is to the left and "L'Arc" to the right.

From the ruins of Glanum, we see Mt. Gaussier and on the left, the hole in the mountain mentioned in Quatrain 5-57.

"Le trou" of Quatrain 5-57. Through this hole in Mt. Gaussier, we see the town of St. Rémy de Provence, birthplace of Nostradamus.

Frontispiece and title page of the 1672 London edition of the Centuries of Nostradamus *by Theophilus de Garencières.*

THE TRUE

PROPHECIES

OR

PROGNOSTICATIONS

OF

Michael Noſtradamus,

PHYSICIAN

TO

Henry II. Francis II. and Charles IX,

KINGS of FRANCE,

And one of the beſt
ASTRONOMERS that ever were.

A
WORK full of Curiosity and Learning.

Tranſlated and Commented by *THEOPHILVS de
GARENCIERES,* Doctor in Physick Colleg. Lond.

LONDON,

Printed by *Thomas Rateliffe,* and *Nathaniel Thompſon,* and are to be
ſold by *John Martin,* at the *Bell* in St. *Pauls Church-yard,* Henry *Mortlack* at the
White Hart in *weſtminſter-Hall, Thomas Collins,* at the *Middle-Temple Gate, Edward Thomas,* at the *Adam* and *Eve* in *Little Britain, Samuel Lownds* over againſt
Exeter-houſe in the *Strand, Rob. Boûter,* againſt the South-door of the *Exchange, Jos. Edwin,*
at the *Three Roſes* in *Ludgate-ſtreet, Moſes Pits* at the *White Hart* in *Little Britain,* 1672.

The infamous Henry III of France.

The remains of Michael Nostradamus lie behind this slab in a church wall in Salon de Provence.

claimed miraculous beneficial effects! A Nostradamus patient would be hard put to place one of these, let alone a hundred of them, under his tongue.

Sixth, Nostradamus himself theorized that the plague was communicated through the air, a popular theory at that time. Actually, two less common forms of plague can be communicated that way, but Nostradamus' prophylactic idea would not have been effective in any case. He designed his lozenges to "sweeten the breath" and thus, he thought, block infection. Certainly, all of the ingredients in the lozenges, especially the rose petals, aromatic calamus, Florentine iris and cloves—all highly scented plants—would have the sweetening effect, but little more medicinal value of any kind.

Also remember that these lozenges were intended by Nostradamus to be prophylactic in function, not curative—as claimed by the author of *Nostradamus and the Millennium.*

The artist in Hogue's book portrays the various plants specified by Nostradamus as ingredients in his rose lozenges. The illustrations are wrong, all but one. He has mistaken the *lign aloes* bush for the *aloe* plant (no relation), uses a full-color, detailed representation of a Passion Flower for what he then labels "Rosehip" (which is not a plant but a fruit) and follows that with a picture of a stalk that looks like Mistletoe but is supposed to be "Green Cyprus." If what is meant in this case is Cyprus Cedar, the illustration is quite wrong, and if "Cypress" is meant, it is equally wrong. He got the illustration for the Cloves plant right, apparently photocopying the illustration straight from an early issue of the *Encyclopaedia Britannica.*

Though it is not a significant factor in his analysis of the powers of Nostradamus that Hogue's book was incorrect in the illustrations of these plants, it is a good example of typically careless work and of how a little basic research can prove or disprove the case. To add to his botanical bloopers, he surmises that "For his trances Nostradamus may have experimented with mind-expanding herbs such as nutmeg." I have not been able to discover any claims that nutmeg has this effect, and it most certainly cannot be described as a herb.

John Hogue's brave try at making Nostradamus into Superdoctor fails on all counts. His attempt to reveal the prophetic powers of the French wizard by using an astrological analysis flounders as well. As mentioned earlier, even the horoscope generated by astrologer Jeff Green for the Hogue book is faulty. The planet Neptune appears in two positions in his zodiac. One position of Neptune—which Green places in the sign Pisces— should have been the planet Uranus. And Pluto, the planet said to most affect psychic/intuitive powers, is badly misplaced in the horoscope.

Mostly, author Hogue copies the interpretations of the popular writers, but also produces a few whoppers that appear to be his very own. His power of distorting words and twisting anagrams out of shape in highly imaginative ways has seldom been surpassed. In this regard, he is the equal of the very best of the Nostradamians.

Finally, the Hogue book displays two illustrations, one in full color, of Nostradamus smugly clutching a telescope. I have refused to allow Hogue to credit the Seer of Provence with the discovery of gravity and of elliptical planetary orbits, and I also deny him the invention of the telescope, which was not known until Nostradamus had been in the tomb for more than forty years. Author Hogue might have spent a few hours on high school science before expounding on matters far beyond his expertise, unless his intention was to present a romantic novel rather than a factual account of the life and work of an historical personality. Because his book can be found prominently displayed in most bookstores and is frequently referred to by the Believers, I have taken this time and space to analyze Hogue's work.

A Century Ago It Was Worse: Charles Ward

In 1891, writer/Nostradamian Charles A. Ward, described in a biographical dictionary as a "noted British scholar and historian," wrote a very long book, *Oracles of Nostradamus,* in which he expressed this warning, obviously directed at those he considered to be incompetent writers on the subject:

> Without special study you cannot understand [Nostradamus] . . . I hope, however, when this book comes to be read by the competent few, it will be seen that there exists far more than a mere name to be dealt with here. . . . Science, so called, must enlarge its narrow categories. . . .

We have already met author Ward when discussing a Nostradamus quatrain which refers to Elizabeth I of England. His very inventive techniques were shown there.

Ward disparages another Nostradamian, Theophilus de Garencières. Author of the first English edition of the *Centuries,* Garencières failed to use his imagination creatively enough to satisfy Ward, since he accepted that in at least some cases Nostradamus might have actually meant exactly what he said. This is a dangerous lapse for any Believer, who should always assume profundity at the cost of good common sense in order to produce needed evidence. Garencières is taken to task by Ward for his "naive" comment about one quatrain in which Nostradamus quite clearly speaks of an earthquake and a fallen person. Said Garencières of this quatrain,

The words and sense are plain, and I cannot believe that there is any great mystery hidden under these words.

Ward warns incompetent readers of Garencières that

Words put a slight upon men's minds to think they understand what they see written; from this it is clear that you may understand the words, and yet comprehend nothing from understanding them.

As for an interpretation of the quatrain in question, 1-57, Ward ignores the actual words of the verse and obtains a political revolution, a fleeing populace and the dead French king, Louis XVI, from the four lines, but no earthquake. Le Pelletier agrees with this view. From the very same quatrain, prominent Nostradamian Henry C. Roberts extracts a "clear and forthright prediction" of the attack on Pearl Harbor and the Japanese Coprosperity Sphere. Again, no earthquake and this time, not even a "fallen person." To further confuse us, a minor Nostradamian named Cazeau finds the rise of Adolf Hitler in this verse. I cannot imagine three more dissimilar sets of events than those derived by Ward, Roberts and Cazeau, yet they are all convinced of the strength of their respective interpretations. Perhaps Roberts' version should receive most respect from us, since in a radio interview with me many years ago, he declared that he believed himself to be the actual reincarnation of Michel de Notredame. And all of this was before such intellectual giants as Shirley MacLaine brought us the advantages of "trance-channeling."

Ward, who seems never to learn at all, then lists another Nostradamus quatrain that he happily, without any sense of the paradox involved, admits fits two totally different and real historical events. He says of this one,

> The circumstances of [the two actual events] are so much alike in many respects that it is not surprising that such a description as this . . . should fit both . . . almost equally well.

Ward describes Nostradamus' *Centuries* in these words:

> . . . the work must for one reason or other [after Ward's interpretations] stand out as the most wonderful book of its kind that was ever written or printed in this world.

Even for a Nostradamian, this seems a rather strong statement. The Seer of Provence might well both smile and blush at this gushy endorsement of his poetry. Ward continues:

> [The *Centuries*] has now to go forth and take its chance, good or evil, of notice or of neglect amongst the mass of printed matter, largely rubbish, that deluges our life.

How true, though Ward seems not to have a good handle on the word "rubbish." And this is a Nostradamian who has the audacity to complain,

> It is painful to see how men manipulate these things to suit their theories.

I heartily agree.

Author Ward is particularly titillated by Presage number 141, printed two years *after* Nostradamus' death, but probably legitimate. In this prediction, it appears that the seer foresaw his own demise. Unlike most of his work, the language in this, the *last of all the presages and the last known writing of Nostradamus,* is very clear and unambiguous:

> *Du retour d'Ambassade, don de Roi, mis au lieu*
> *Plus n'en fera: sera allé à DIEU:*
> *Parents plus proches, amis, frères du sang,*
> *Trouvé tout mort près du lit et du banc.*

On his return from the Embassy, the King's gift, put in
  place
He will do no more of it: he will be gone to GOD:
Close relatives, friends, brothers by blood,
Found entirely dead near the bed and bench.

Ward says that this verse should be accepted, not *because it is accurate*, but because

> the fact that Nostradamus assigns no date for his death, in this presage, goes to establish its authenticity, one would incline to say. For supposing it to have been foisted in, after his death, surely a fabricator of the marvellous would first of all have made it to show *trois vingts et trois bis* [three twenties and three more, or 63], and twisted that into some colourable shape.

Ward is saying that a clever forger would have used a typically Nostradamian obscurity to get the number sixty-three—the seer's age at his death—into this quatrain. It seems not to occur to Ward that perhaps Nostradamus did not know at what age he would die.

Other simple but hideous facts interfere with Ward's acceptance of Nostradamus' final words in print as an accurate prediction of his own death. The prophet had not made any "return from the Embassy," nor had he just received any "King's gift." He was very sick, bedridden and certainly expecting his demise.

Though he could not have been unaware of it, Ward also chose to ignore, in his gleeful embrace of this Nostradamus *coup*, the fact that Nostradamus *did* assign a date to this presage, and thus to his own death! It was in an almanac designated *by the prophet himself* to apply to a quite specific and clearly stated date: November of 1567. That was seventeen months *after* he actually died. *Encore, dommage!*

We see that again, in one of his rare specifically dated prophecies, this time on a matter of great personal import about which he in particular should have had not only accurate physical but also psychical knowledge, Nostradamus was wrong.

It is amazing to observe Ward, a dedicated Believer, being confronted with unacceptable errors which he fails to account for and actually solving aspects of the cunning methodology whereby he has been personally deceived, yet failing to apply that same reasoning to all the other evidence that he accepts! In every respect, Ward fulfills the definition of our True Believer and receives unqualified certification as a typical Nostradamian.

The First Translation Into English: Garencières

Theophilus de Garencières has been mentioned several times. He wrote the 1672 first English translation of Nostradamus, titled *THE TRUE PROPHECIES OR PROGNOSTICATIONS OF Michael Nostradamus, PHYSICIAN TO Henry II. Francis II. and Charles IX, KINGS Of FRANCE, And one of the best ASTRONO-MERS that ever were.* I consider him to be the least offensive of the Nostradamians, though even I can improve upon his poor translations from French.

As a source of Nostradamus' words Garencières unknowingly used a fake 1568 edition that was actually printed in 1649, less than twenty years before he began his work. This printing was also the source used in his 1867 book by Anatole le Pelletier, another famous Nostradamian, and contains the false quatrains 7-42 and 7-43, added by some unknown forger in an attempt to discredit Cardinal Jules Mazarin, who had succeeded Cardinal Richelieu as prime minister of France in 1643. The brilliant, willful cardinal was widely resented for his heavy taxation of the French, and he had many enemies. Inventing prophecies that told of his downfall was a clever method of convincing the public that Fate itself was against the cardinal.

The Mazarin quatrains are so good, so accurate, that they are transparently fake to any observer of these matters. The first of the two, in Garencières' translation, reads:

Quand Innocent *tiendra le lieu de* Pierre,
Le Nizaram Sicilian *se verra,*
En grands honneurs, mais apres il cherra,
Dans le bourbier d'une Civile guerre.

When Innocent *shall hold the place of* Peter,
The Sicilian Nizaram *shall see himself*
In great honors, but after that he shall fall
Into the dirt of a Civil war.

That the deception was a success is shown by the naive acceptance and commentary of Garencières:

Nothing can be more plain and true than this Prophecie, and those that deny it, may also deny the light of the Sun, but to make it more evident, we will examine it verse by verse.

He then pointed out that the pope in Mazarin's time was named Innocent (X), that Nizaram is a perfect anagram for Mazarin, that Mazarin was born in Sicily, that Mazarin did attain great honors, and that a civil war did take place. In other words, he swallowed the bait and the hook completely. But this interpreter added immeasurably to his defects when he concluded:

> . . . can anything be more plain, and yet when I read this forty years ago, I took it to be ridiculous.

Really? If Garencières recalled reading this quatrain forty years earlier (in 1632), his memory must have been quite remarkable, *especially since the verse was not written until 1649!* Here we have a perfect example of a very small lie providing very heavy proof of authenticity to the unwary. This remark of Garencières about his having read 7-42 in his youth, previous to Mazarin's ascendancy, seems relatively harmless. Yet it serves to legitimize the quatrain, and adds to the confusion about our subject.

Even today, writers who fail to look into this subject carefully enough continue to fall for the Mazarin hoax. In a widely sold book published in England, *Natural & Supernatural,* author Brian Inglis declared that, to him, quatrains 7-42 and 7-43 "defied rational explanation." Perhaps, for Mr. Inglis, they did.

I think Garencières was a man overwhelmed by his task, fearing to offend established authorities in the field but intent upon producing the first French/English edition of the *Centuries.* This he did, for better or worse. Author Edgar Leoni has referred to this translation as "a very superficial and careless work." Everett Bleiler says Garencières provides students with "very bad text and translations."

An Author With an Obsession: Edgar Leoni

Leoni was himself described to me by a critic of Nostradamus as a "madman." I find myself agreeing with that assessment as I get more involved with the subject at hand. For a man to spend so many years and effort to produce a comprehensive 823-page volume on Nostradamus, he *must* be somewhat mad, though only in the kindest sense of the word, and certainly no more than I myself, in my own pursuit of the subject.

Leoni does not come under the category of True Believer, however. His valuable work, *Nostradamus: Life and Literature* (1961), now titled *Nostradamus and His Prophecies*, was accepted as his thesis for a BA at Harvard. Working as a translator and cryptographer for the U.S. Army certainly was no handicap to Leoni in producing his opus, which is thoroughly cross-indexed in every imaginable way. Planetary configurations, dates, place names, proper names and many other categories are listed and assigned to specific quatrains. His book is indispensable as an information source on the subject. And all this was done by a man who calls himself a "dedicated amateur."

There is one major point where I differ with Edgar Leoni. Dr. Eugene Parker of Cambridge, who was not at all fond of Nostradamus, said in his doctoral dissertation (1920) that in his opinion the French sage was a deliberate fraud. Concerning that opinion, Leoni wrote:

> It is a very tempting [idea], and it further leaves our hero on top with the last laugh. However, it is much too farfetched to be acceptable . . . that Nostradamus could have fooled his 'disciple' [Jean-Aimé de] Chavigny, his son [César], various notables of Salon, the rulers of France and Savoy, several ambassadors and scores of other people with this gigantic 'joke' of his is quite ridiculous.

I shudder at the naiveté of author Leoni. Charlatans have always been able to deceive politicians, relatives, close associates, royalty and other "notables" because those persons usually have no expertise with which they can differentiate between popular fraud and genuine phenomena, yet passionately believe themselves above being deceived. There was, within recent memory, a conjuror who managed to have several scientific papers written about his claimed ability to bend spoons by mental power alone. At one time, a few PhDs and lesser intellects believed sincerely that the spoon trick was a real miracle, for the very same reasons that the savants of Nostradamus' day believed in his powers, as some still do today.

It is surprising that author Leoni was not more convinced of the huge hoax that was perpetrated by Nostradamus. He quotes many examples of very harsh criticism of the prophet's methods, among them this cogent 1882 comment by Jean Gimon, an historian of Salon:

> The style of the *Centuries* is so multiform and nebulous that each may, with a little effort and good will, find in them what he seeks. Like airy vapors, they assume, as they unroll, the figures which the spectator's imagination lends them, and this fact assures this sibylline work of an immense and eternal success with those who are devotees of the marvelous.

Taking no advocacy position, Leoni's work is by all standards the most complete, in-depth cataloging study that will probably ever be done on Nostradamus, and though I am grateful for the references it supplies, I feel it is a pity that a subject so unlikely to add to our really useful knowledge of our world attracted this man's attention to such an extent.

The Casual Scholar: James Laver

With an impressive list of scholarly credits and literary production as his authority, English writer James Laver set out to look into the Nostradamus enigma just prior to World War II. His own account of how he uncovered the wonders of prophecy as shown by our subject, besides providing us with a hint of Laver's tendency to discover meaning and "synchronicity" in events, also brings a pang of envy to any serious book collector who has yet to experience the ecstacy of The Buy of a Lifetime:

> . . . I was engaged in that most fascinating of all occupations of the hour of idleness, strolling along the *quais* in Paris and pausing from time to time to turn over the *bouquins* in the booksellers' stalls perched so precariously on the edge of the Seine. In one of these, somewhere on the Quai St. Michel, on the south bank of the river, I came across a somewhat battered little book bound in frayed yellow leather. It was Bareste's edition of Nostradamus.
> '*Combien, Madame?*'
> The proprietress of the stall glanced from me to the book and back again. Obviously the price was a matter which depended as much upon the look of the prospective purchaser as on the appearance of the wares. Neither in this instance was in 'mint condition': no *jeunesse dorée,* no 'top edges gilt'. Calculations of

lightning rapidity went on in the brain beneath that screwed back hair and after barely a second, the sibyl spoke.

'Quinze francs, monsieur.'

With my prize in my pocket, for the volume is a small one, I made my way along the *quai,* past the Louvre and the Pont Neuf, until I reached, opposite *l'abside de Nôtre Dame* (an appropriate spot for a first perusal of Nostradamus) the little restaurant of the *Cloche d'Or . . .*

The bookstalls on the Paris *quais* have undergone considerable evolution, *malheureusement,* and are not now the sources of such treasures that they once were. While I am jealous of his serendipitous stumbling onto this great prize, I am more amused at Laver's finding enchantment in the almost unavoidable coincidence of the Quai St. Michel, the apse of Nôtre Dame and the title of the book he holds. That fascination with coincidence, often poorly drawn, was to be carried into his techniques of researching the Nostradamus puzzle.

All through his book, *Nostradamus, or The Future Foretold* (1942), the author offers evidence of his self-deception. He rejects unfortunate interpretations and translations of the material and he reaches far beyond reason to create his relationships. He even says that he finds it difficult to believe that Nostradamus was popular before his prophecies began to "come true," when it is very evident from reputable historical accounts of diverse origins that the prophet was very well known and sought-after in his own day.

Of an obscure set of lines in one quatrain which he has translated to fit an event, Laver comments

Other readings might be given, but the sense is clear enough.

"Other readings" than the one he chose would not serve his purpose, so he easily rejects them. He finds it remarkable that Nostradamus said, in Quatrain 6-63, that

Seven years will she be weeping in grief
Then with great good fortune, long life for the kingdom

and that this applies so well to Catherine de Médicis, whose court was in official mourning for her husband for almost exactly seven years. (Actually Catherine was in personal mourning until her dying day.)

"It is not so often Nostradamus speaks so clearly," says Laver. Really? It seems not to have occurred to him that Catherine, a devoted follower of occult advice, especially that of Nostradamus, might very well have chosen to fulfill that first line of a verse that she might easily have taken as a reference to her life, as an act of compliance with fate, especially if she believed that the second line would thereby be accomplished. It was not to be so, for Catherine was presiding over the last act of a tempestuous drama known as The Rule of the House of Valois, a fact that Laver ignores.

Laver delights in seeking out obscure relationships between scraps of widely separated quatrains. Of one of these efforts, he says

> Once more, we have a quatrain obscure, and even misleading, when taken by itself, but adding to the cumulative effect.

He is able to accept a quatrain if it says something plainly and it seems to work. If it obviously *doesn't* work, he *makes* it work, since he is convinced that Nostradamus must work, somehow. Laver's rules allow a quatrain to be taken by itself as an entity or to be divided into two sets of lines for separate handling. Two quatrains can be split up and recombined to supply the needed significance, or any line may be discarded and disregarded if that suits better.

There is an excuse offered for everything. When he found a reference to be sufficiently vague, Laver exulted that "Nostradamus loved these learned circumlocutions." In another example, he explained that

> Unfortunately, [the quatrains] are even more than usually marked by that pedantic punning in which Nostradamus took such delight.

Yet another obscurity, this time with names, brought the comment that "[Nostradamus] had a passion for nicknames."

Now in all fairness, it must be said that writers of Nostradamus' day did indeed tend to vie with one another for cuteness. Involved classical/mythological references were often invoked in a sort of see-how-clever-and-well-educated-I-am competition. Puns were often used, as well as other witty tools of literary dexterity. Indeed, the meaning of quite important texts could be smothered beneath such precious dilettantism. I believe that Nostradamus used this fact and relied upon his strange, obscure style to suggest greater meaning than he ever put into his work. James Laver is only one person who fell for the ruse.

Concerning one example which provides a very romantic, titillating correlation which even he admits fits poorly, Laver comments,

> . . . if [this] quatrain does not really refer to the Duc de Berry at all, the reader will probably regret it as much as anybody.

This, as if, for his reader, truth is not to be preferred to fiction-painted-as-truth. A book that presents itself as an historical account cannot be a plaything. Verity is too valuable to juggle with.

In his book, author Laver designates interpreters as "commentators," as if the Nostradamus material is clear enough to merely receive comments rather than inventive presumptions, tortuous rewriting and free amplification. But he provides us with glaring examples of hyperbole and innovation by his own hand. The line, "Au mois troisième se levant le Soleil," which easily translates as, "At the third month, the sun rising," Laver sees as, "The hundred days are past! The hour is nigh!" This helps satisfy his idea that the verse from which this is selected refers to the period between Napoleon Bonaparte's Elba exile and his eventual abdication. (Though history texts refer to this period in 1815 as The Hundred Days, it was actually one hundred and nine days between the time Napoleon landed in France and the day he was defeated at Waterloo. A casual observation, nothing more.) The fact that Napoleon returned from Elba on March 1—the *third month!*—is enough for Laver to associate the prophecy with this event. Unfortunately for his fantasy, the "hundred days" *began* on March 1, they were not "past."

Laver handles particularly difficult rationalizations of the more obscure Nostradamus material by advising that "the impatient sceptic is advised to skip them altogether." After discussing two of them, he declines to do any more, fearing that their inclusion "would have served only to weary and confuse the reader." One suspects that perhaps Laver is either making fun of his self-deception or hinting at a joke he is playing on his readers. I fear neither possibility is real.

At the close of his book, James Laver postulates the three major objections that skeptics might offer to his acceptance of

Nostradamus as a prophet, then offers to explain them away. He is setting up three straw men rather than a Trojan horse. First, he says, doubters might say that all the books containing these quatrains are forgeries printed after the fact. This is a preposterous premise which no serious critic would entertain, though certain spurious printings and misdated editions do exist. Nostradamus did write and publish the vast majority of the work ascribed to him, and he was a real, historical character.

Second, says Laver, it can be claimed that

> . . . commentators have been overingenious . . . that some of the quatrains are so obscure and ambiguous that they might be, and have been, forced to do duty for different events, cannot be disputed.

That is one of the few statements in his book with which I can agree, and he himself provides excellent proof of it. But searching such a large mass of material and managing to fit some of it, with difficulty, to events that have taken place or will take place, is no way to conduct research. That way, one can find Mickey Mouse in the Bible, and Kermit the Frog on the moon.

For his third straw man, hanging his claim on the Nostradamus line "Senat de Londres mettront à mort leur Roy" (The senate of London will put their King to death), Laver points out that occasionally Nostradamus was absolutely right. We will discuss this fact in Chapter 11, when we discuss ten selected examples.

Finally, in a ludicrous stab at bringing scientific support to his premise, author Laver appeals to his readers that since telepathy and clairvoyance have been proven real, powers of prophecy as ascribed to Nostradamus should not be doubted. He is quite wrong in this supposition. In the fifty years since he wrote his book, science has learned much more about how easily some persons, many of them scientists themselves, can quite innocently deceive themselves in such matters. It goes with the territory.

La Méthode Rigoureuse

I believe that Jean-Charles de Fontbrune (a pseudonym for M. Pigeard de Gurbert, a French pharmaceutical executive) as a Nostradamian can be eliminated with one shot. He described his books on Nostradamus as based upon "a rigorous method-ology" he and his father Max had developed. I will merely quote his brilliant mathematics as an example of this method-ology.

Troubled by the fact that Nostradamus specified that his prophecies ran to the year 3797, de Fontbrune employed some arithmetic soft-shoe that is dazzling in its absurdity. I will quote directly from *Nostradamus 2: Into the Twenty-First Century* (1984), a book of which the title itself is interesting, since the author says everything ends in 1999! It was written by Font-brune Jr., who took over his father's work without making it too clear that he is the second generation of this enterprise. De Fontbrune had to somehow produce the number 1999 out of 3797. Here, in the words of de Fontbrune himself, is his venture into arithmetic:

> In his Letter to César, Nostradamus wrote: 'I have composed books of prophecies, each containing one hundred astronomical quatrains, which I wanted to condense somewhat obscurely. The work is comprised of prophecies from today to the year 3797. This may perturb some, when they see such a long span. . . .'
>
> Most commentators have taken the date 3797 quite literally. I was not content to do so because one must always bear in mind that Nostradamus 'condensed,' deliberately obscured or codified his texts—by his own admission. Nostradamus dropped a sly, even humorous, hint when he stated that some people might be put off by such a distant date, i.e. 3797. Why should he have written that, had not this figure concealed some sort of trap for the interpreter?
>
> But there is an even more obvious clue here. There was no need to give this 'date' and then add 'from today to,' for it is surely self-evident that since his letter is dated 1 March 1555, and he is talking of prophecy, his quatrains cannot refer to any earlier date. This tautology is untypical, for Nostradamus' style is con-cise [*sic!*].
>
> The phrase 'from today to the year 3797' must therefore be looked at carefully, as though it were strictly mathematical: when in mathematics one says 'from point A to point B,' it indi-cates a straight line, and Nostradamus is indicating between point 1555 and point 3797 a precise segment of time. The value of this segment of time is calculated by subtracting the former from the latter, and the result is 2,242 years.

This should be carried over to the biblical chronology given in the Letter to Henri, Second King of France,* i.e. 4,757 years from Adam to Christ. If one adds to these 4,757 years 2,000 years A.D., the result is 6,757—which does not make up the full seven millennia. I believe this is the reason why Nostradamus 'fabricated' this extra segment of time—in order to cover the 242 years required to reach the year 7000** according to global chronology (6,999 − 6,757 = 242). By adding this segment of 2,242 years to the biblical reckoning one obtains 4,757 + 2,242 = 6,999 (i.e. 1999 A.D.), a date clearly specified in [Quatrain 10-72***].

What the text is trying to tell us boils down to this: De Fontbrune *fils* was away from school when arithmetic was taught. He has thrown in the figure 2,000 for no reason whatsoever except that it is needed: it is 1,999 + 1. By fussing about a bit and missing a year or two (he arbitrarily changes 7,000 to 6,999), he subtracts all the numbers except 1,999, which he believes was miraculously produced, then holds it aloft in triumph! I am merely trying to be *rigoureuse*, Monsieur de Fontbrune!

And really, how can de Fontbrune say that 6,999 = 1,999?

The de Fontbrune book in which this strange exercise in futility first appeared in France *(Nostradamus: Historian and Prophet)* sold 700,000 copies in the first eighteen months. A weekly French publication, *Paris Match,* commented upon the publication of the book:

> Fear is becoming a market. One hundred days after having brought Mitterrand to power, our citizens are paying [$20] a copy [for the book] to shudder in horror.

---

*He means "Henri Second, King of France," though this incorrect punctuation may be a misunderstanding by the translator. This book is an English version of *Nostradamus, Historien et Prophète* (1980), in which the phrase appears as "Henry Roy de France second" without any punctuation. This latter version agrees exactly with the strange rendering in my copy of the *Centuries.*

**The figure 7,000, which was accepted by all the New Testament writers, is derived from the Book of Enoch. How this becomes "global chronology," I cannot guess.

***See Appendix IV, End-of-the-World Prophecies.

A later opinion poll of France conducted by the magazine revealed that three-quarters of the French public knew about the book, and one-quarter of them believed its message. This would indicate that one-quarter of the French also have no knowledge of arithmetic.

All in all, the Nostradamians are a strange group, nursing a marionette in hopes that it will come to life. They defend, in spite of the futility of their dedication, the basic notion that Michel de Notredame had the power of prophecy. They cannot be dissuaded nor discouraged, and their inventiveness is something to marvel at. They have expended a mountain of candles, barrels of ink and countless years of their lives trying to breath life into their puppet, who without their careful manipulations is a pile of painted wood, paper and strings. It is comic. It is sad.

I will allow the prophet a response to all this criticism. In place of Quatrain 6-100 in the 1568 Rigaud edition of the *Centuries* appears this admonition in medieval Latin:

Legis cantio contra ineptos criticos.

Quos legent hosce versus, maturè censunto,
Profanum vulgus & inscium ne attrectato:
Omnesq; Astrologi Blenni, Barbari procul sunto,
Qui aliter facit, is rite sacer esto.

Translated:

Incantation Against Inept Critics.

Let those who read this verse consider it profoundly,
Let the profane and ignorant herd keep away:
And far away all Astrologers, Idiots and Barbarians,
May he who does otherwise be subject to the sacred rite.

Many of us who have failed to be enchanted by M. de Notredame might do well to expect the sacred rite, whatever that might be.

CHAPTER ELEVEN

The Ten Quatrains

*Reason can never permit the mind to reject
a greater evidence to embrace what is less
evident, nor allow it to entertain probability
in opposition to knowledge and certainty.*
—JOHN LOCKE, 1632–1704

NOSTRADAMUS FIRST COMMANDED my attention because of his perennial popularity. As I looked into his life, I became impressed with his ingenuity and his fling at immortality. I recognized his worth as a physician and as a poet, his perseverance and courage. He was a person of considerable ability who would have succeeded in any age.

In this chapter we will examine ten Nostradamus quatrains suggested by leading Nostradamians, those most often thrown up by the Believers as positive, irrefutable evidence of prophetic powers. The chapter will be rather long, but only of necessity.

The Power of the Press

Access to printed books was perhaps the single most important development to affect intellectual progress in the 16th century. Though pictures had been block-printed as early as A.D. 770 by the Japanese, and the printing of individual pages of text impressed from carved wooden blocks had been accomplished by the Chinese long before their invention of movable type, the adoption of that idea by Gutenberg finally made the printed word accessible to a far greater number of persons, though only the rich enjoyed the actual possession of books, and for some time those were almost exclusively religious tomes of varying quality and value.

Equally as important was access to the printing process itself that allowed contemporary authors to now more easily set down and disseminate their new thoughts without the inevitable dilution or distortion introduced by the process of copying and recopying generations of handwritten words.

The use of movable type and the thus-improved access to printed knowledge barely predated Nostradamus' appearance in history, coming to France in 1470, fifteen years after the first known book from the Gutenberg press and thirty-three years before the birth of the prophet. Excitement at the new availability of books for education was very high among the middle and upper classes of French society. Eventually, of course, a means of instant celebrity through publication became obvious to the ambitious, and a man of erudition and ability such as Nostradamus naturally took advantage of that opportunity.

As a physician, the primary professional skill for which he was trained, the man who was to become known as the single best-known astrologer and prognosticator of all time first published his recipes and a few medical writings of only moderate worth and then in 1550 made his debut as a mystic with the first of his annual astrological almanacs. Copies of his almanacs still survive, the earliest dated 1557.

A physician such as Nostradamus performed a variety of functions. He not only prescribed medicines, but he was his own pharmacist as well. He was expected to know how to compound his own remedies from plant sources—all gathered at the correct phase of the moon—and from varied animal parts as well; the witches of *Macbeth* called for "eye of newt and toe of frog" with some authority. Even today, powdered pearls and cockroaches, black rhinoceros horn and tiger penis form an active part of the traditional pharmacopeia of China.

Nostradamus also advised on cosmetics, beauty aids and deodorants for Renaissance ladies, who as a rule bathed only twice a year and wore the same underclothes for months on end. It may be easily believed that this was a brisk trade.

Those same heavily scented ladies came to him for culinary advice, too. Physicians applied their herbal knowledge to matters of the palate and put together aromatic spices for their clients.

In all likelihood the great popular success that was accorded Nostradamus' prophetic pamphlets encouraged him to begin production of the *Centuries,* the work that was to so impressively survive him. Though he continued his medical practice, eventually becoming, by appointment, physician-in-ordinary to Henry II, Francis II and Charles IX of France, his career as a soothsayer effectively took most of his attention and earned most of his money from that time on.

No book on the seer would be in any way complete without examining the evidence upon which his fame is based. I have selected ten of the prophecies that, in the opinion of the True Believers, present the best evidence for Nostradamus' abilities.

Edgar Leoni quotes an interesting observation that was made by English Jesuit Father Herbert Thurston in 1915. Father Thurston was concerned with the impact that he believed Nostradamus' writings were having on the conduct of World War I, and to minimize the effect on the war effort, he tried to explain just how people were self-deceived when interpreting the quatrains:

> Undoubtedly the unrivalled success of Nostradamus' oracles is due to the fact that, avoiding all orderly arrangement, either chronological or topographical, and refraining almost entirely from categorical statements, it is impossible ever to say that a particular prognostic has missed the mark. . . . Nostradamus provided an ingenious system of divination in which the misses can never be recorded and only the hits come to the surface. For the reputation of the would-be prophet, such conditions are naturally ideal.

While appreciating his opinion, I must beg to differ somewhat with Father Thurston. *Many* very glaring misses of Nostradamus have been recorded, and prognostications that he made clearly and that were in some cases actually dated are seen to be very wrong.

Mr. Bleiler has pointed out the interesting fact that the form of the Nostradamus quatrains—known as *vers commun**—often reveals discrepancies because of the poor "fit" managed by spurious or altered verses. Both Bleiler and Leoni attribute prodigious wit, poetic quality and sophistication to Nostradamus that I am unable to find. In doing so, they just may be surrendering to the same tendency shown by the interpreters to find meaning where none was intended.

There are a great number of very specialized "rules" applied to handling interpretations of the Nostradamus writings, rules developed by the Nostradamians to allow great latitude in assigning—and creating—correlations between historical fact and prophecy. Probably some of these usages and devices were actually used, but others seem unlikely in the extreme. It is particularly important to note that these gimmicks are invoked when needed, but ignored when not called for. For example, when Nostradamus names the city of Narbonne, a center well known to him and mentioned twelve times in his writings, the interpreters have accepted that he is actually referring to the city in some instances, but they assign another function to the name (proper personal name or rank) when necessary to wring meaning from the verse in which it appears. The French word "noir," meaning "black" in English, is most often presumed to be an almost-anagram (see the rule for creating anagrams up ahead) for the French word "roi" (in English, "king"); in some instances it is simply accepted as "black" because it fits better. The Provençal spelling would have been "roy."

Once they establish—to their satisfaction—that a certain usage or rule makes the prophecy work, the Nostradamians invoke it again and again for any subsequent situation that even

---

*Four lines of ten syllables each, with a strong pause after the fourth syllable of each line. As an example:

Nostradamus, in his four-sided hat,
Told his strange tale in a kind of ping-pong.
Hinting at this, making guesses at that,
Too bad for him, but his forecasts were wrong.

—ADAM JERSIN

remotely resembles the one in which the artifice was established. De Fontbrune clearly expressed the way he did his own research:

> The reader will discover, through the translation of each quatrain, how I have proceeded in order to squeeze the text to the maximum, considering that the only 'key' possible is philological.

The aim is to discover some supposed clever, obscure clue or hint that Nostradamus placed in his verses for future generations of scholars to discover. The fact that the quatrains may have expressed notions about quite ordinary matters in a quite ordinary fashion seems repugnant to these learned folks.

They use the theory they are trying to prove, to prove the theory they are trying to prove. They accept modern usage and spellings ("Nostradamus could see the future, couldn't he?") when those serve the need, but fall back on Latin, Old French, Provençal and Greek when they are needed. *I* cannot accept that Nostradamus knew modern English or French.

Nostradamian Stewart Robb came upon a quatrain which he believes predicts a specific event. The verse says, "Near Saint Memire," but the event he wishes to connect with it didn't happen there. Robb is so convinced his hero has prophetic powers that he actually states

> The rebellion that overthrew him was centered around the Cloister of St. Meri, so Nostradamus either heard the name imperfectly or was anagrammatizing it.

Here are a few of the arbitrary but very useful rules we must be aware of:

(1) Anagrams may be used. An anagram, according to the Oxford English Dictionary, is "A transposition of the letters of a word, name or phrase, whereby a new word or phrase is formed." The Nostradamians, however, allow one, two or more letters to be added, changed, or dropped. Thus, Hadrie can become Henrie, Henry, Harry or a number of other words or names.

(2) Punctuation, we are told, may be inserted where absent,

or changed when present, since Nostradamus often failed to use it or to use it correctly.

(3) Symbolic references, using animals, mythical creatures or other words to represent the "intended" thing are said to be quite common in Nostradamus' work. (See Chapter 3, under Rule Number 3, for several examples of this usage.)

(4) Quatrains may be used as self-contained units, in sets of two lines, as single lines, in pairs, or any way needed. Parts of quatrains may also be combined.

(5) Names of persons or places, we are told, can be "hidden" in common words. As an example, the French word "Pasteur" ("pastor," in English) can actually mean Louis Pasteur.

(6) Foreign derivations—from *any* language—are embraced. We can easily accept Latin sources, since Nostradamus and other writers of his day used the language. They also delighted in demonstrating their erudition by dropping in classical names and allegorical references as well as obscure foreign words.

(7) Validations for "discoveries" are obtained through *other* "discoveries." This is, quite simply, circular reasoning.

There are five usages of which we may approve:

(1) Synecdoche (Hogue calls it "synedoche"), the use of a part to represent the whole, is applied. An example would be using "Washington" to represent "the United States of America," or "bread" for "food."

(2) The use of ancient, classical names for cities and countries, rather than the then-current names.

(3) The use of "u" for "v," "y" for "i," "i" for "j," etc. These are quite legitimate.

(4) The frequent absence of written accents, because orthography was not well established. In early French the verb "être" was written "estre," the letter "s"—rather than an accent—indicating a vowel inflection.

(5) Ellipsis is allowable, in which obvious words understood to belong in the text are left out.

I will use a classification method of my own for the quatrains. It was admittedly inspired by another similar system in a book on another very doubtful subject. There are six kinds of verses found in Nostradamus:

Quatrains of the First Kind (Q1K) are those that were made for the safely far future. Since they have all of recorded time in which to be fulfilled, they will very probably come true, or have already come true, within certain limits.

Quatrains of the Second Kind (Q2K) are those that were apt to be fulfilled very soon after they were written. The events were very likely to occur because of historical circumstances then known to Nostradamus.

Quatrains of the Third Kind (Q3K) are those that were absolutely sure to be successful prophecies because they were written *after* the event, sometimes immediately after. They are what Leoni calls "retroactive prophecies."

Quatrains of the Fourth Kind (Q4K) are those that are not handled here at all. Because they are such garbled, mystical nonsense, semantically and logically, they cannot be properly examined.

Quatrains of the Fifth Kind (Q5K) are those that describe quite ordinary events and circumstances in Nostradamus' time, with a bit of a likely story dropped in. They involve matters with which he was familiar, and which would be recognized by his contemporaries. In many cases they are not even attempts at prophecy, being rather editorial commentaries or folk tales.

Quatrains of the Wrong Kind (QWK) are those that were and are simply wrong. Events proved them untrue, either during Nostradamus' lifetime or subsequently.

Ten Excellent Examples

I will list the ten quatrains. They are:

(1)   1–35   The Gilded Cage—The Death of Henry II

(2)   5–57   The Invention and Use of the Montgolfier Balloon

(3)   2–51   The Great Fire of London

(4)   9–20   The Flight and Capture of Louis XVI and Marie Antoinette at Varennes

(5)   9–34   The Flight and Capture of Louis XVI and the Queen at Varennes and the Attack of the 500 on the Tuileries

(6)   9–49   The Execution of Charles I of England

Here, then, are examinations of ten pieces of the evidence most used to prove that Nostradamus had prophetic ability. These quatrains are constantly dragged out before us as indisputable proof of his powers, so we will explore them in some detail.

(#1) THE GILDED CAGE —
THE DEATH OF HENRY II
1-35

Le lyon jeune le vieux surmontera,
En champ bellique par singulier duelle:
Dans caige d'or les yeux luy creuera,
Deux classes vne, puis mourir, mort cruelle.

The young lion will overcome the old one,
On the field of battle in single combat:
He will burst his eyes in a cage of gold,
Two fleets one, then to die, a cruel death.

(I must add this note: The subject of the third line is the "young lion" who will burst the eyes of the "old lion." The usual translation of the strange word "classes" is "wounds," taken from the Greek word "klasis." That derivation is convenient but unlikely, a much better one being the Latin "classis," meaning "fleet" or "army.")

This is, by all standards, the single most famous of the Nostradamus quatrains, one that in his day officially put him at the forefront of all the seers, and continues in that role even today. Let us examine the historical circumstances of the event that it is said to represent.

In the summer of 1559, the royal court of France held a huge celebration in the streets of Paris to honor a double marriage, one of Henry II's daughter Elizabeth to Philip II of Spain and the other of Henry's sister Marguerite to the Duke of Savoy. In the Rue St. Antoine, a traditional full-scale tournament was staged, with jousting by honored nobles and by the king himself. All was festive until sunset of the last day, the first of July.

Henry had distinguished himself in the jousting, and in these last hours of the celebration, he rode against Gabriel de Lorges, Comte de Montgomery. Having failed to unseat him in the approved manner, the king insisted upon another try. Bound to honor the request, the count gave Henry another chance, but due to his miscalculation, Mongomery's lance shattered as the two met in the course and a splinter entered the helmet of his royal opponent, pierced the skull above his right eye and penetrated his brain.* Henry fell, mortally wounded.

For ten days he lingered on in delirium, suffering the best that his physicians could offer him, and at last he died. The kingdom immediately began examining prophecies to discover whether this momentous event had been foreseen by any of the seers.

The curious already had one prediction to ponder over. Claude l'Aubespine, a member of Henry II's court, is quoted in an 1835 book, *Archives Curieuses de la France,* as saying that on February 5, 1556, almost a year after the publication of the *Centuries,* a letter had arrived in Paris from the famous Italian astrologer Luca Gaurico in which, among other things, was a horoscope which, l'Aubespine said, warned Henry to

> avoid all single combat in an enclosed place, especially near his forty-first year, for in that period of his life he was menaced by a wound in the head which might rapidly result in blindness or even in death.

I find this peculiar. The prediction is so good it is suspicious. Henry met his death in what might be described as "single combat," if we accept jousting as combat, though not in "an enclosed space." It was in his forty-first year, and the fatal wound was in the head. We must not forget, however, that this quoted information was taken from what is said to be an 18th-century copy of an original letter—which is not now available—and we have to consider the possibility that the document just may have been invented to enhance the art of prophecy. Such a procedure is not unheard of in the prediction business.

But let us look back to 1552, seven years before the fatal tournament. In a prediction sent to the Duke of Ferrara at that date, the same Gaurico had predicted (in a document presently

---

*Francis Bacon, however, reported that Henry was wounded in the throat, the splinter having entered at the bevor, or throat protector.

available from the French archives, and not from a later copy) "a most happy and green old age" for Henry, but also "some impediment from horses and tears flowing from the left eye." The second part of this prophecy is not unlikely to become fact, since in Renaissance France all men of noble birth spent much time in the saddle and falling out of it, and Henry II was renowned not only as an enthusiastic and reckless sportsman, but particularly as a horseman. Between wars, kings of that time had little else to do.

Clearly, Gaurico saw a long life for Henry II, not an agonizing death at forty-one. The more specific warning quoted by l'Aubespine—not represented as a prophecy but easily taken as such—might well be a highly embellished version of the Ferrara communication, produced after the event. Even more interesting is the fact that the original Latin is faulty, though in a probable translation* it also says that Henry will be

> master of other kings, . . . [and will] reach the pinnacle of affairs and arrive at a vigorous and happy old age before he dies. . . . he will acquire the utmost dominion over those cities subject to the Ram. If he survives his 56th, 63rd and 64th birthdays, he will be brought to the 12th day, 10th month of his 69th year over an auspicious and unobstructed path.

Note that the additional items concerning Henry's predicted "happy old age" are ignored in most accounts that quote the Gaurico letter.

Great Expectations

That Nostradamus also expected Henry II to go on living for a long time cannot be doubted. In his introduction to the second section of the *Centuries* that comprises books eight to ten, Nostradamus provided a lengthy Epistle to Henry II (dated March 14, 1557), that can induce advanced caries merely from a quick reading. Try this opening on your teeth:

> Ever since my long-clouded face first presented itself before the infinite deity of your majesty, O most Christian and most victori-

---

*Kindly provided to me by the Reverend Canisius F. Connors, O.F.M., a specialist in Latin of that period, who pointed out several errors in the usage.

ous king, I have remained perpetually dazzled by that sight, not ceasing to honor and worship appropriately that date when I presented myself. . . . I was seized with this singular desire to be transported suddenly from my long-beclouded obscurity to the illuminating presence of the first Monarch of the Universe. . . .

Ad nauseam . . .

In the Epistle, the prophet predicts great things for Henry, who in actuality was to die immediately after the first probable appearance and circulation of this Epistle in manuscript form, and well before it appeared in print. This obvious and glaring example of a major failure for Nostradamus has been an embarrassment for the Nostradamians ever since, though they have—of necessity—come up with many ingenious excuses to get around it.

The opening words of the Epistle are:

A L'INVICTISSIME,
TRES-PVISSANT, ET
tres-chrestien Henry Roy de France
second; Michel Nostradamus son
tres humble, tres-obeissant serui-
teur & subject, victoire & felicité.

TO THE MOST INVINCIBLE,
MOST POWERFUL, AND
most Christian Henry King of France
the second; Michel Nostradamus his
most humble, most obedient
servant and subject, [wishes] victory and happiness.

Note that the monarch died little more than two years later, a fact that does not speak well for invincibility.

Though the addressed monarch in the opening is without any doubt the one and only Henry II, King of France, the ruling monarch at the time Nostradamus wrote this fawning Epistle, one interpreter, showing his Royalist leanings, decided that the reference was actually to some messianic Second King who would arrive to save France from the Republicans. Some interpreters have averred that this dedication was actually a "red herring" produced by Nostradamus as further proof of his cleverness, since in their judgment it turns out to be a wordplay that actually means Henry *V!* Others, since no Henry V of France ever appeared, or seems now likely to appear, have tried to

assign this title to the Napoleons and other French leaders up
to Charles De Gaulle. These Royalist Nostradamians look about
until they find someone they would like to see head up a resur-
rected French monarchy and designate him as the coming
Henry V.

One of the faithful, Sylveste Moreau, abandoned all such attempts in 1603 and printed his own edition of Nostradamus that
is essentially complete except that Henry's name is *omitted* in
the Epistle section. Even the most devoted Nostradamians felt
this was a bit much, and the Moreau edition is not held in high
esteem.

Aside from the Epistle and Quatrain 1-35, several of the Nostradamus quatrains quite obviously refer to a substantial future
for Henry. Often this is done by using the acceptable anagram
Chyren (for Henryc, from the Latin Henricus) and reference to
his family crest, which contained a crescent moon.

EVIDENCE FROM THE QUATRAIN

The Nostradamians celebrate hugely over the coincidences between Quatrain 1-35 and history, but closer examination of the
quatrain itself throws a dark cloud over their bacchanal. Consider the first line:

The young lion will overcome the old one.

Though Montgomery *was* younger than Henry, the difference
was not at all significant, only a few years. Certainly the difference is not one of "young" versus "old." The French kings used
the fleur-de-lis in their heraldic devices, and the fighting cock
was their animal symbol, not the lion. It would have been very
strange to refer to a French king, or any other member of the
court, as a "lion." The French, as a matter of record, have never
used a lion as a symbol of the monarchy, that use being almost
entirely reserved to Britain, Spain, Belgium, Holland and Sri
Lanka, along with a few German provinces, though there are no
lions in any of these countries, nor have there ever been.

Line two reads:

On the field of battle in single combat.

It is important to note that the event at which Henry was killed was not a duel nor was he "on the field of battle" at all. It was a formal jousting contest in which serious injury was not expected to take place. It was, in fact, a serious *faux pas* to draw blood at these events.

The third line is full of good symbols:

[The young lion] will burst [the old lion's] eyes
in a cage of gold.

James Laver and others assert that Henry's visor was gilded. Still others, to make this line work, claim that it was made of gold. There exists *no evidence whatsoever* that either statement is true, and in fact it is very unlikely to be true. Just take a walk through the remarkable collection of body armor in the Tower of London and you will see that wherever gold appears on the armor, it is in ornamental lines and heraldic devices. No actual piece of armor would *ever* be made of gold, since that metal is soft and of little protective value.

Nowhere is there any indication that Henry II's eyes were "burst." The wound occurred *above* the right eye (remember that Gaurico warned Henry about his *left* eye).

Finally, line four says:

Two fleets one, then to die, a cruel death.

What the reference to "fleets" is, I do not know, since we know of no union of fleets that satisfies the circumstances. Were I a Nostradamian, I would search around for something like the Greek word previously found, and choose it to make the line work better with the word "wounds." Even then I would be out of luck, since there was but one wound which carried off Henry. I cannot afford that indulgence.

Henry II's end was, indeed, "a cruel death." But these are the *only* few words that connect his demise with this quatrain, and there is an abundance of evidence that denies any connection whatsoever.

Let me leave this suggestion with the reader. It originated from author Louis Schlosser: Move across the English Channel to Britain. Consider the fact that Henry VIII of England, whose symbol was very definitely the lion, at age forty-four, locked up Sir Thomas More (aged fifty-eight) in a very special royal prison (a golden cage?) the Tower of London. This was the result of a protracted battle of wills between the two for control of the religious leadership of England. There were two "classes" in battle here, the Holy Roman Church and the royal insurgency of Henry. Henry won the day, and after a farce of a trial, More was put to a cruel death, decapitation. The event was an affront to Catholic and Protestant alike, and it occurred twenty years before Nostradamus penned 1-35. Just a suggestion, nothing more!

A gentleman named F. Buget, in his *Étude sur Nostradamus et ses Commentateurs* of 1863, concluded about Quatrain 1-35,

> There is not, then, as far as I can see, a single word in this quatrain which is applicable to the unhappy end of this prince [Henry II].

(#2) THE INVENTION AND USE OF THE MONTGOLFIER BALLOON
5-57

One of the two most compelling of the nearly 1,000 Nostradamus quatrains is this one, number 5-57. It belongs in category Q5K. I will quote from the 1672 Theophilus de Garencières edition of *The True Prophecies or Prognostications of Michael Nostradamus,* and I reproduce here an accompanying photographic copy of the actual quatrain, followed by Garencières' translation into English and his interpretation. The italicization, capitalization and spelling are his:

LVII.
Iſtra du mont Gaulſier & Auentin,
Qui par le trou aduertira l'armée:
Entre deux rocs ſera prins le butin,
De Se x t. manſol faillir la renommee.

Istra du Mont Gaulsier & Aventine,
Qui par le trou advertira l'Armée,
Entre deux Rocs sera prins le butin,
De Sext. Mansol *faillir la renommée.*

One shall go out of the Mountains Gaulsier *and* Aventine,
Who through a hole shall give notice to the Army,
Between two Rocks the booty shall be taken,
Of Sext. Mansol *shall lose his renown.*

The Mountains of *Gaulsier* and *Aventine* are two of the seven Mountains of *Rome*, out of which, it seems, one shall go out to give notice to the Army without, and the Booty of the *Pope*, called *Sextus*, shall be taken. But what he meaneth by *Mansol*, I am ignorant.

(Garencières is wrong in saying that both Gaulsier and Aventine are part of the famous Seven Hills of Rome. Gaulsier is a name unknown in Italy. None of the hills is named anything that sounds like Gaulsier, but one is named Aventine.)

Now let us examine an account by Vlaicu Ionescu, a Nostradamian described by his publishers as having

dedicated more than forty years of his life to the study of the work of Nostradamus. He is unanimously recognized as the leading authority on the text of 'The Centuries and Predictions.'

One would expect accuracy, scholarship and logic from such a "leading authority." One would be disappointed. Ionescu is the author of a heavy volume titled *Nostradamus, l'Histoire Secrète du Monde* (Nostradamus, the Secret History of the World), in which he says a good deal about this quatrain.

His transcription of 5-57 is faulty in a few respects. He substitutes

de	for	du
GAULFIER	for	Gaulsier
AVENTIN	for	Aventine
SEXT	for	Sext.

He has excellent reasons for these changes. His use of SEXT does, however, agree with the 1568 Rigaud edition which I have accepted as the *editio princeps*, except that he leaves out the period following the word, a very important omission, as we will see. Ionescu's slightly revised version suits his purpose much better. He obtains from his rendering the following translation:

The day when there will be a French army warned by a man placed under the hole of a certain machine named Montgolfière, and in which Rome also makes war, the holy see will renounce at the same time the two rocks that support it. The glory of a pope, the sixth of the name, will be lost.

(Stewart Robb, another Nostradamian who adores this quatrain, ignores all accents and makes other omissions and changes in the original French, thus increasing the "fit" of the verse to certain historical facts. Robb is a Nostradamian who is never unwilling to improve upon improvements.)

In a couple of effortless steps, author Ionescu then liberally amplifies his translation of Quatrain 5-57 to this:

At the time when the newly-invented balloon will make it possible to put a man high up in a basket attached below the opening, to survey the position of the Austrians at the Battle of Fleurus and to inform the French army about it, and when the Republic will be at war with the Italians, the treaty of Tolentino (February 19, 1797) will take Avignon from the pope, and the battle of Venaissin in France and Italy will take the provinces of Bologna, Ferrara and Romagna. Soon after (February 10, 1798), the splendor of the ruling pope, Pius VI, will be eclipsed, when he is dragged as a prisoner out of his estates. He will die at Valence, in a foreign land.

There follows a long, involved "cabalistique" discussion showing how this dedicated researcher can turn:

ISTRA DU MONT GAULFIER ET AVENTIN
into:
ÉTIENNe De MONTGAULFIER AéRo-STaTI AVUs

which he translates as:
Étienne de Montgaulfier, l'ancêtre de l'Aérostat
(Étienne de Montgolfier, the ancestor of the hot-air balloon)

"Étienne" is the name of the younger of the two inventor brothers whom we will meet in a moment. No explanation is given, in the procedure above—or is usually sought—for the extra letters a,e,e,é,o and s, all of which he has dropped in to make this ridiculous "anagram" work, besides discarding an accent on another letter. Those extra letters are shown in lower case in Ionescu's invention, above.

The use of the word "ancestor" is ludicrous, since a person cannot be the ancestor of a machine. And note that Ionescu now chooses to use the correct "du" of the original printing of the verse, rather than the "de" he changed it to. To further insult common sense, he tells his readers that one can also find the word "vent" (wind) in the word "A-vent-in," and he says that since Nostradamus obviously meant "Mont. Aventin" (Ionescu has freely added a period, indicating an abbreviation), he was really saying, "montage à-vent-in" (carrying up by means of wind) which, he tells his readers, exactly describes how the balloon works.

A Novel Invention With an Important Application

Before we further examine Ionescu's inventive translation, we must look at a few historical facts. In June of 1783, two sons of a family of wealthy papermakers named Montgolfier, from a small town near Lyon in the south of France, constructed and flew a hot-air balloon for the first time. That one was unmanned. Today, such a device is known in France as "une montgolfière," taking its name from the brothers who first filled that linen bag with hot air and made it fly. The similarity between the words in the first line of Quatrain 5-57 and the name of the brothers is the feature upon which Ionescu—among others—bases his entire analysis.

(I will not argue whether the difference between Mont Gaulsier (or Gaulfier) and Montgolfier is significant. I will grant the interpreters their adjustment of the words, since I have to make a small adjustment myself. It will consist of changing Gaulsier to Gaussier, as you will soon see. One favor deserves another.)

Back to 1783. A manned flight of a balloon followed within four months of the debut of the invention, and soon after that hydrogen-filled bags were also constructed and flown successfully. The original was a device that differed little from the ones in use today by those who enjoy such expensive hobbies, except that the early version heated its air from a fire of straw and wool. All of Europe was intoxicated with the fact that Man had finally been released from imprisonment on the surface of the planet, and the celebrities of the day were those who had risen above their fellows in the swaying baskets that spun beneath the barely controlled bags of hot air. But even with the numerous refinements to the invention that quickly followed one upon another, the *montgolfière* remained for the first few years as a novelty and nothing much more.

Since the day the balloon was first flown, the great revolution had taken place in France, followed by the French Revolutionary Wars in which the country was attempting to expand in several directions. A young general from Corsica named Bonaparte was beginning to come to the serious attention of the new republic, and he was eager to implement any technology to update his army. His interest was aroused by this novel device, and before long the revolutionary government had established a school to teach military balloon use. One of the first really practical uses of the balloon came on June 26, 1794, when the Battle of Fleurus was won, some historians say, largely because of the use of a tethered reconnaissance balloon used to observe the Austrian troops during the French invasion of part of what is now Belgium.

Now, back to the quatrain. Let us see how accurately it describes, as Ionescu claims, the use of the hot-air reconnaissance balloon at the Battle of Fleurus. To heat the air, a fire was built in a metal bowl suspended beneath the hole in the bottom of the large bag. The lighter hot air rose to displace the denser cooling air already inside the bag, and it was thus kept aloft. An occupant of the basket below therefore could rightly be said to be "under the hole." Certainly, that brave soldier who ascended to view the advancing Austrians and report to his superiors below "warned" "a French army." And the hot-air balloon, in France, *is* called a "montgolfière." This sounds like an excellent match between the prediction and the event.

Some Printing Errors

Ionescu's error of "Gaulfier" for "Gaulsier" is understandable. Many other editions and interpreters of Nostradamus used this spelling, too. In early printing, including all editions of Nostradamus up to and well beyond the 1672 Garencières (the first English edition), the letters "s" (except when it is the last letter in a word) and "f" are printed respectively as ſ and f

The only difference is in the crossbar, which extends both to the left and right of the vertical in the "f," but only to the left in the "s." Printers in early times were often semiliterate, and transpositions of these two letters, along with inversions ("n" for "u" and "d" for "p") occur occasionally in their work. Nostradamian Erika Cheetham, in *The Final Prophecies of Nostradamus,* allows every "s" to appear as "f" in the French versions of the quatrains. Thif if difficult to underftand.

Some early editions of Nostradamus had "Gaulfier" in Quatrain 5-57, and that suited the eager interpreters much better than the correct spelling, which is "Gaulsier." How we know that is the correct spelling, I will come to shortly.

In early editions of Nostradamus (including the 1568 Rigaud), the word "Sext" in Quatrain 5-57 is printed in upper case with a period following it—"SEXT." Ionescu's version of this word, aside from the period, is correct. But he changed "du" to "de" before the word "mont." Why? At risk of subjecting my reader to an elementary lesson in French, I will explain. Any reader reasonably conversant with the language may skip the next paragraph.

An article, in French, must agree in gender with the noun that follows it. For the definite article (Eng. = "the") "la" is used for a singular feminine noun beginning with a consonant, "le" for a masculine. The French word for "from" and also the possessive "of," is "de." When used before a singular feminine noun, the form "de la" is used, but what would be "de le" contracts to "du" when used before a singular masculine noun beginning with a consonant. Thus, "of the girl" is "de la femme," and "of the boy" is "du garçon." However, the article is not used when a *proper* noun follows the "of." When one wishes to say, "the soldier from (or "of") Paris," it is "le soldat de Paris." End of lesson.

Now, if the masculine noun "mont" in Quatrain 5-57 means "mountain" or the noun "mount" as it usually does in French, it would require "du." But Ionescu *wants* "mont" to be part of the word "montgolfière," which is a *feminine* noun, and would call for "de la" rather than "du." So he has substituted "de" for "du," and depends upon the fact that the use of "de" without the "la" before a *proper noun* like "Montgolfier" is quite acceptable. Thus, he implies that Nostradamus meant the word to be a name (and thus the French word for balloon) rather than the simple noun "mont." It is a cunning semantic trick.

The deception continues. The word "mansol" magically becomes, in Ionescu's brazen treatment, "man. sol." There is no reason given for this transformation; it simply suits his purpose, so he does it. He gets this from a fancied contraction of "manus solus" which he says means "man alone." (James Laver gives us "manens solus" as "the man who lives alone.") Ionescu claims that this, in turn, means "celibate," and therefore signifies "pope." However, even if "mansol" *did* mean "pope," the interpreters have a serious problem here, because the most dependable versions of the *Centuries,* notably the Bareste reprint of the 1555 edition, have this word as "mausol." The "mansol" spelling is incorrect, probably a result of a typesetter's error, inverting the "u." The error even appears in the 1568 Rigaud edition.

A Scene From Nostradamus' Youth

But there is a much better reason for choosing "mausol" over "mansol." Take a short visit with me to the ancient town of St. Rémy de Provence, where the hero of our story, the eminent astrologer/physician/poet Nostradamus, was born. Our visit may convince you that in this quatrain, Nostradamus was relating nothing more than an episode from his boyhood, creating a Q5K.

St. Rémy is today one of the leftover jewels of medieval Provence, known then as now for its remarkably beautiful old olive groves surrounding the city. Walking those ancient narrow streets, I tried to overlook the ubiquitous Cinzano posters, the swarms of buzzing Renault 4's and the forest of television antennae to imagine how young Michel de Notredame had experienced his birthplace. Very much the same faces probably looked down upon him from the deep, narrow windows overlooking the worn cobblestones, nodding, smiling and wondering with curious ferocity about the purpose of this visitor. I imagined that the subdued, excited chatter that was exchanged across the streets after I passed by had also echoed after Michel in his time.

Even when Nostradamus made his home here, St. Rémy had a long and rich history. Modern street maps reveal the outlines of the ancient walled town that was substantially added to by the invaders of Gaul. One of the major Roman highways ran north-and-south through the town, and it became an important center of trade. The Romans extended the limits of the city as far as the much older city of Glanum, the ruins of which still exist about a mile south of the center of the present city. Glanum (referred to on some maps as Cité des Glaniques) itself was built upon the remains of a yet older Greek trading center that was destroyed in A.D. 480, and tourists today wander through the extensive foundations and toppled pillars that were once a symbol of Rome's power in Gaul.

The modern city of St. Rémy is peppered with reminders of its most famous native son, who lived there for the first sixteen years of his life. Cafés, fountains, streets, hotels and numerous landmarks bear the Nostradamus name. His birthplace, an unimposing house in the Rue des Bàrri*—the part of it that still survives—is now carefully preserved. A popular festival is held every year in St. Rémy to celebrate the fame of the astrologer, providing an excellent opportunity for "New Age" devotees and mountebanks of every sort to hawk their crystals, charms, potions, horoscopes and booklets in much the way that medieval humbugs probably did in these same streets.

Very close to Glanum stand two monuments that figure prominently in this present discussion. They are known as Les Antiques. These enigmatic artifacts were already fourteen centuries old when young Michel de Notredame and his friends played among them. One of Les Antiques was once thought (erroneously) to be the mausoleum of a Roman named Sextus. In fact, in the introduction to his very first book, *Excellent et moult utile Opuscule*, Nostradamus identifies himself as "Sextropheae Natus Gallia," or "native of the area where the mausoleum of Sextus can be found." The seer was very much aware of Les Antiques, and they were a familiar part of his early life.

When Nostradamus and his young friends looked up at the

*Formerly Rue de l'Hôpital.

"mausoleum," an impressive tower with an inscription running around the top, they might have made out the very badly eroded dedication which is now believed to read:

SEX.L.M.IVLIEI.C.F.PARENTIBVS SVEIS*

and from the ground level, as I have seen for myself, that first word stands out rather clearly as "SEX."—to the unaided eye. The rest is pretty well indecipherable. I believe, for reasons to be explained, that Nostradamus obtained the word "sext" from this source. His use of "SEXT." rather than simply "SEX." seems strange, since he was careful enough to use the period which actually follows the word incised on the monument. It may be that his memory of the exact word, seen by him some thirty-six years previously and perhaps not again since that time, was faulty. Add to that the misconception that the monument was dedicated to a man named Sextus (which might be abbreviated as Sext.) and his error is still more forgiveable.

Finding this small word cannot, of course, justify its identification with the quatrain. But stay with me. Folks in St. Rémy told me about the former opinion that the great tower was always thought to be a Roman tomb, until modern investigation showed it was merely a memorial, albeit an impressive one. But the locals have always called it "Le Mausole," and it is thus represented on maps. The name is apparently derived from "mausolée," which is current French for the Latin (and English) "mausoleum."

I found evidence of the antiquity of that name when, at the suggestion of some *habitants,* I hiked over to a building I could just see from the foot of Le Mausole. It is the ruin of an old medieval cloister, and the still-habitable part is the asylum—still in use as such—where painter Vincent Van Gogh spent his last days in 1889 before moving briefly to the nearby town of Arles, where he died by his own hand. Since at least the 12th century, this cloister has been known as St. Pol de Mausole. "Pol" is the old Provençal version of the name "Paul."

I stood at the base of Le Mausole, and by turning a half-circle

---

*One expansion, given to me in St. Rémy by the local museum, is: SEX(tus) L(ucius) M(arcus) IVLIEI C(aii) F(ilii) PARENTIBVS SVEIS. This could be simplified as Sextus Lucius Marcus Julius Caius Filii Parentibus Sueis.

I could see the prominent and very jagged range of mountains known as Les Alpilles that lies just south of St. Rémy. The old Roman road passes beneath an imposing peak known in song and poetry as the Lion of Arles, from a promontory which looks, in silhouette, remarkably like a crouched feline. Van Gogh even painted it in his work "Champ de blé aux Alpilles" (Wheatfield in the Alpilles), but it is properly named on modern maps as Mont Gaussier. A local official at the museum told me that it had been called "Gaulsier" at one time, but he offered no source for this statement. However, old maps of Nostradamus' time which I consulted at the Marseille Library and the New York City Public Library do show this mountain named both Gausserius and Galserius.

Nostradamus seems to have taken for his use some intermediate version of these names, or the variant may be one of the not infrequent typographical errors in his works, errors often perpetuated in following editions. Also, remember that spelling was not at all consistent in his time, and startling variations are found.

Detailed modern maps show another bit of evidence that supports my conclusions about this quatrain. Mont Gaussier and the peak next to it are marked as "Les Deux Rochers" (The Two Rocks). This is a good correspondence with the "deux Rocs" of the quatrain. The lesser peak has yet another distinction. It is listed on those maps as "Le Rocher des Deux Trous" (The Rock of Two Holes), and from where I stood near Le Mausole, I was astonished to see, very distinctly, that there were indeed two very large holes in the side of that prominence with blue sky showing through clearly. Of course I had to visit the spot.

Arriving there with some difficulty, I found that the Nostradamus quatrain had suddenly become much clearer to me. Standing in the larger of the two holes, I looked down, not only on the entire town of St. Rémy de Provence, but on Le Mausole and the ruins of Glanum as well. To my left was a trail leading down to the Roman road approaching from the south. A position standing by that hole in the mountain was the absolutely ideal place from which a posted sentry could alert the Roman garrison at Glanum to anyone approaching on that road, lighting a fire or signaling by other means.

There are moments in such investigations that are only well

described as "delicious." One can almost *taste* the satisfaction of a solved mystery. I knew that I was standing where Nostradamus himself had often stood, his adolescent imagination filled with the ancient wonders that might have been witnessed from this exciting spot. I feel that he could not have resisted setting down on paper that very moment in time. When he wrote his book of prophecies thirty-six years later, I think that he relived that part of his boyhood while scratching out Quatrain 5-57. He re-created for his readers his fantasy of someone running from the sentry post by the hole atop The Two Rocks to give warning to the army garrison below, and added that the fame of the ancient mausoleum bearing the word "SEX" would fade away—as the inscription was doing, even in his time.

Where "Aventin" fits into the story, I have been unable to determine with any confidence. Since—to my knowledge—the name shows up in history only as one of the Seven Hills of Rome, it might have served young Nostradamus as a symbol of the long-dead Romans who once held sway there. Provence, in his youth, had just adopted a rudimentary constitution based, as were all its laws, on the Roman code. Rome and the Romans were models for the young student. On Mount Aventine, in Italy, are the ruins of a major temple to the goddess Diana. *If* we could find a hill near St. Rémy where there was also once a temple to the same deity, it could be the metaphor Nostradamus was hinting at. Up ahead, I will attempt to titillate your imagination with yet another possible connection.

A Second Visit to St. Rémy

But now I must add to these comments on Quatrain 5-57 a few on 4-27, because there are some old friends to be found there. Garencières says 4-27 reads:

Salon, Mansol, Tarascon, de Sex, *Larc,*
Ou est debout encor la Pyramide,
Viendront livrer le Priuce Denemark,
*Rachat honny au Temple d'*Artemide,

Salon, Mansol, Tarascon, Desex, *the arche,*
Where to this day standeth the Pyramis,
Shall come to deliver the Prince of Denmark,
A shameful ransom shall be paid in the Temple of Artemis,

The final comma in the last line is obviously a printing error, as are the inverted "n" in "Prince" and the "u" in "Mausol" (again!) in the French. There are other errors. I disagree, also, with this translation. I'll not take your time with a detailed analysis of this quatrain, except to point out that here we find:

(a) Salon, where Nostradamus lived as an adult and when he wrote the quatrain, seventeen miles from St. Rémy

(b) Le Mausole, the monument one mile from St. Rémy

(c) Tarascon, a town nine miles from St. Rémy

It all sounds very much like old home week, doesn't it? But wait. There's more. "Sex" rears its ugly head again, and in the *editio princeps* it is spelled in upper case with the period: "SEX." And what's this "Larc"? From the 1568 Benoist Rigaud edition of Nostradamus, we know this is an error for "L'arc," meaning "The Arch." Though Garencières believes this arch is one located far north of St. Rémy, I think not. There are several Roman arches to choose from in Gaul, and one of them fits the bill rather spectacularly.

I neglected to tell you that the other member of Les Antiques is a beautiful Roman arch that stands less than sixty feet away from Le Mausole. It was erected by Julius Caesar to commemorate his victory at the battle of Vercingetorix, so named after the Gallic chieftain he vanquished in 52 B.C. Considering the association of the other landmarks, we can conclude that this is the arch Nostradamus refers to in Quatrain 4-27.

As for that pyramid, it's not the Cheops variety at all. It's a local rock quarry worked in former days by the Romans to build Glanum, among other structures. It is still visited by tourists in the St. Rémy area who follow road signs pointing to "la Pyramide." When I walked into it, it was obvious, from its huge slab walls and solid tomblike appearance, how it had come by that romantic designation. The proprietor told us that it had "always" been called by that name.

We are left to puzzle only over the identity of "Artemide," since no prince of Denmark, so far as we know, was ever held ransom anywhere near St. Rémy de Provence, and that part of the quatrain appears to be the prediction section. Artemide is French for Artemis, the original Greek goddess of the hunt who was called Diana by the Romans. Could a temple dedicated to

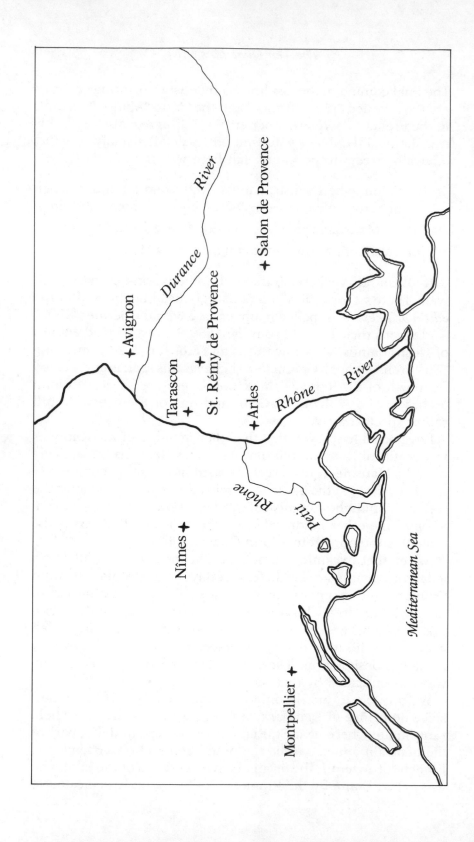

Artemis/Diana once have stood on a hill near St. Rémy? There was one at Nîmes, and, as an amusement, if we draw a line from Salon to St. Rémy (seventeen miles) then to Tarascon (nine miles), we can continue to Nîmes (fourteen miles). I find the Diana connection between the two quatrains 5-57 and 4-27 rather strong, especially since Le Mausole and Sex(t) are also part of both those verses. I will allow my reader to wonder over these matters.

We have examined in depth some of the notions written about what some Nostradamians think is one of the most important and convincing of the quatrains of their master prophet. The highly fanciful, detailed and precise interpretations, naming specific dates, places, personalities and events, that Ionescu and other interpreters have given this quatrain, were arrived at only after diligently searching through history for something—anything—that would fit the very wrong, altered, misspelled and misconstrued poetry of Nostradamus. The fit is fashioned by very poor tailors. Such efforts make a mockery of research.

The question must be asked: Is it not more reasonable to accept the simple, likely relationship of fact and poetry that I have described above than the tortuously oblique and inventive process offered by the Nostradamians?

The moment that gave rise to the fifty-seventh quatrain of Century Five might have been a vivid adolescent daydream that young Michel de Notredame had while perched atop Le Rocher des Deux Trous, and he may well have believed it was prophetic, but it certainly had nothing to do with two inventors and their flying contraption, all three of which were almost two centuries away from conception.

(#3) THE GREAT FIRE OF LONDON
2-51

From Rigaud:

Le sang du iuste à Londres fera faulte,
Bruslés par fouldres de vint trois les six:
La dame antique cherra de place haute,
De mesme secte plusieurs seront occis.

The blood of the just shall be wanting in London,
Burnt by thunderbolts of twenty three the Six(es),
The ancient dame shall fall from [her] high place,
Of the same sect many shall be killed.

Death, foreign intrigue, wonders of Nature, a mystery woman and suspicious religious overtones are all here in this quatrain, with its vivid imagery which has titillated generations of Nostradamians. It does tell of an historic event, but the verse itself is a Q3K.

In the spurious edition of *Centuries* that Garencières used, the word "Feu" in place of "fouldres*" in the second line is wrong. It has been used almost universally by the Nostradamians because it suits their Great Fire of London interpretation better; the original, correct word as shown above, means "thunderbolts." Also, the Rigaud edition of the quatrains says, "de vint [vingt] trois les six," not "vingt & trois," as many other editions do, thus showing an appreciable variation introduced into the text.

Here, the Nostradamians would ask us to believe that their hero was writing about an event that was 111 years in his future: In 1666, London was devastated by a fire that destroyed four-fifths of that city. Garencières, for whom the Great Fire was a very recent event (it occurred only six years before his book was published) was an ardent Monarchist. Ever intent upon adding his own charming mysteries to the muddy brew, he postulated that this fiery disaster was a divinely administered expiation for the 1649 execution of Charles I; the unexplained seventeen years of delay in the retribution seems of no importance to his analysis. He also explained that the last half of line two means, "the number of Houses and Buildings that were burnt," rather than the more popular interpretation by almost everyone else that it means 66, therefore somehow giving them 1666. How that date was obtained by him—or by others, for that matter—is difficult to see. Nonetheless, several of the Nostradamians go on to explain that "La dame antique" refers to St. Paul's Cathedral, which was consumed in the fire, along with many other churches, thus the claimed validation of the line, "Of the same sect many shall be killed."

*Modern spelling is "foudre."

Problems with History

I consulted many references here and in England, and so far as I have been able to determine, St. Paul's Cathedral was never called "The Old Lady," as many Nostradamians claim. The word "antique" in Old French meant "old" *or* "eccentric." The latter derivation is similar to that of the English word "antic." Usually, in French, "old lady" would be expressed by, "vieille dame." Though the old pre-fire St. Paul's Cathedral was the highest church then known, there is no "high place" from which it could have fallen. Some fans, recognizing this discrepancy, claim that a statue of the Virgin Mary stood atop St. Paul's, and that it was that figure that Nostradamus was referring to as the Old Lady. Not so. My early edition of the *Encyclopaedia Britannica* provides a clear, detailed line illustration of the old pre-fire cathedral that shows it was severe Gothic in style, with a squared roof area and no external statues at all. Another contrived notion falls from its high place. We are left with only the reference to London to tie this quatrain to the Great Fire in that city.

This quatrain is a Q3K. It refers to an actual event which was taking place as Nostradamus was penning his opus, but a very different event, and certainly *not* the Great Fire of London. Here are the historical facts:

(1) In 1554, the ferociously Catholic queen Bloody Mary (I) of England announced a wholesale cleansing of her kingdom, and in January of 1555, she began executing Protestant heretics in London. Their only crime was the variety of their Christianity and their stubborn refusal to abjure it. Many were prominent churchmen, intellectuals and statesmen.

(2) They were burned at the stake with the "merciful" addition of having bags of gunpowder tied between their legs or around their necks to quicken their passage.* When they eventually expired, it was with a spectacular explosion. The trial, sentenc-

---

*One unfortunate, Bishop Ridley, had an especially horrid exit from life. His brother-in-law, wishing to lessen his suffering by hastening his death, had piled the faggots so high about him that the flames could not reach the gunpowder, and the poor man cried out that he could not burn. His benefactor thereupon opened up the pile of wood, at which point the powder ignited and brought an end to the atrocity.

ing and burning of these unfortunates began January 22, 1555, in neat groups of six.

(3) Queen Mary, haggard, totally obsessed with religion, disappointed in love, ill with dropsy and other assorted diseases repeatedly imagined that she was pregnant by her Spanish husband Philip. The consort was seldom at home and in 1555 left England and Mary for good. She wandered about her palace half-naked while these atrocities were being committed in her name. She died three years later, incoherent and considered quite insane. It was strongly suspected that her exit was hastened.

(4) Over 300 Protestants died this way at that time.

Consider these facts, and compare them line-for-line with Quatrain 2-51 as seen in this much better translation:

(1) The blood of the innocent will be an error at London,

(2) Burned by thunderbolts, of twenty-three, the six(es),

(3) The senile lady will lose her high position,

(4) Many more of the same sect will be slain.

I think my point is plain. Will and Ariel Durant's *Story of Civilization,* from which some of this information was drawn, adds this comment:

> . . . nowhere in contemporary Christendom—not even Spain— were so many men and women burned for their opinions as during [Mary I's reign].

And Nostradamus? The first edition of the *Centuries,* in which this quatrain is printed, is dated May 4, 1555*—more than three months *after* the first set of heretics mounted the faggots in London. I believe that the seer was writing of an event which certainly would have made news in France, and—in view of what we now know about his true religious beliefs—about which he was thus expressing his righteous horror.

---

*See Appendix II. If the author of the document quoted is correct, we have yet more reason to believe that 2-51 is a Q3K.

Some authorities date the 1555 edition of the *Centuries* as March 1, though it is imprinted at the end:

Ce present livre a esté achevé
d'imprimer le IIII. iour de may M.DLV.

(This book was finished printing the fourth day of May 1555.)

The shorter time span—a month or more—would be barely long enough for the news to have reached Nostradamus, even with his informers working out of Paris, but the sentences of the inevitable executions would have been passed some time before the events, since in that day the condemned often spent many months in prison while their wealth was located and acquired by the crown; carefully applied and controlled torture effectively extracted information about concealed assets from the condemned. Thus, either publication date is adequate for the described scenario.

It appears that Nostradamus, in common with other scholars of the day, probably maintained an active "grapevine" with his colleagues. There was a very brisk traffic of couriers hastening along the sea routes and the highways of the continent and Britain, carrying everything from mathematical discoveries to astronomical measurements and observations between interested scholars. This was not a casual, opportunistic process; there were those who made their living as couriers transmitting such information, so much so that a postal system was coming into existence as a result of the demand for this service. Along with that valuable scientific knowledge went current news events, as well, of perhaps equal value. Also, having the approval and support of Catherine, Nostradamus was likely to have her eyes and ears as well, and might hear from Paris much sooner than others not so favored. He would have been in an excellent position to know of quite recent events from faraway places.

(#4) THE FLIGHT AND CAPTURE OF LOUIS
XVI AND MARIE ANTOINETTE AT VARENNES
9-20

De nuit viendra par la forest de Reines,
Deux pars vaultorte Herne la pierre blanche,

Le moine noir en gris dedans Varennes
Esleu cap. cause tempeste feu, sang tranche.

By night will come by the forest of Reines,
Two couples, detour, Herne the white stone,
The black monk in gray inside Varennes
Elected cap. causes tempest fire, blood slice.

Le Pelletier and others have decided that this quatrain predicted the same important event of 1791 described ahead in Quatrain 9-34, though the actual historical details of this well-documented incident, which I will now present, are somewhat different from his version.

A Bad Plan Founders

The French Revolution was well under way. The status of the royal family was being debated, some wanting to keep the king as a figurehead, others not wanting him to keep his head at all. Louis XVI and his queen, Marie Antoinette, along with their two children, were prisoners in the Tuileries Palace. They had decided that they had to flee the city of Paris, which was becoming more threatening to them day by day. Two years into the revolt, there was much agitation to bring the royal couple to trial rather than suffering them to live on at the Tuileries.

The king and queen planned to flee to Montmédy, northeast of Paris, where they were sure of protection because of a large garrison of loyal troops there, and perhaps even an attempt at a counterstroke could be made to regain control of the kingdom. From Montmédy at least they would be able to escape to Belgium if everything else failed; the border was only ten kilometers away at that point. To this end, they ordered a berlin (a luxurious four-wheeled chariot-like carriage drawn by six horses) to be prepared.

This was done, though perhaps too well. Painted green and yellow, and upholstered inside in fine velvet, the carriage was as inconspicuous as a burning bush. It was more than well outfitted for a royal flight. It contained cooking pots and stoves, two chamber pots of tanned leather, sumptuous food and drink and all sorts of spare parts. Though such appointments were not unheard of among the rich, Revolutionary France was apt to notice such a grand vehicle, and to be curious about its passengers.

The royal family (king, queen and two children) were to be in the big berlin with two ladies of the court, followed by a cabriolet (a smaller carriage) with three bodyguards and two ladies-in-waiting. Eleven horses were required for these conveyances alone, and mounted soldiers preceded and followed them.

We may wonder mightily why the family of four could not have simply taken off without the entourage in a simple carriage and passed unnoticed to the border, but the aristocrats of France absolutely required the style which was due them, and they could not live outside of that atmosphere. To them, a shortage of fine caviar was to be feared more than a pestilence. Had that not been the case, the history of France and of Europe might have changed substantially.

The route out of Paris would be via Bondy, Bourget, Châlons-sur-Marne, Pont-de-Somme-Vesle, Sainte-Menehould, Clermont, Varennes, Dun-sur-Meuse, Stenay and finally their goal, Montmédy.

By June 20 they had decided upon their course of action. They left the Tuileries palace, which was guarded by revolutionary troops like a fortress both against entrance and exit, after eleven in the evening. They exited by an unguarded door in the apartments of a M. de Villequier, First Gentleman of the Bedchamber, who had already fled the country. They left Paris in their rather glorious procession, and by dawn were well out of the city, but far behind schedule due to various small delays at checkpoints.

At each town beyond Châlons, they were preceded by a mass of dragoons and their horses were replaced. Naturally, they attracted a great deal of attention, especially since the peasants in those small towns seldom saw prominent travelers passing by, and saw dragoons only when their taxes were unpaid. They had excellent reasons for being attracted to the strangers and their entourage. Louis himself was little help in maintaining security, disembarking at every opportunity to speak with the locals about their crops and other rural matters.

Entering Varennes seeking another change of horses, the royal party was finally stopped by suspicious authorities, exactly twenty-four hours after they had left Paris. They were once again prisoners of the Revolution, and were returned to Paris and their eventual dates with Madame La Guillotine.

A Differing Version

A discussion of this quatrain obtained from the *Encyclopedia of Occultism and Parapsychology* gives these rather remarkable interpretations and rationalizations for the words employed by Nostradamus. The *Encyclopedia* tells us that the word "forest" (forêt, in modern French) stands instead for the Latin "fores," meaning "door." The word "pars" means "part" (in Old French, husband or wife), "vaultorte" is a composite of "vaulx" (valley) and "de torte" (tortuous), "Herne" is an anagram for "reine" (Queen), "moine"—they use "moyne"—is Greek for the French "seul" ("alone"), "noir," rather than being the French word for "black," is an anagram for the French word "roi(n)" ("king"), "cap." equals "Capet" (formal name of the king), and "tranche" ("slice") means "knife."

The total meaning they obtain is: Two married people, the king alone, dressed in gray, and the queen, the white precious stone, will leave one night through the door of the queen, take a tortuous road, and enter into Varennes. The election of Capet will cause storm, fire, bloodshed and decapitation.

Most supporting evidence has been taken from the account of one Mme. Campan, lady-in-waiting to the queen, who gave her story in *Les Mémoires de Marie-Antoinette.* She says that during the royal flight, King Louis XVI wore a gray suit, and the queen was dressed in white. She also says that upon their return to Paris at the hands of the revolutionaries, the queen's hair had turned white from the ordeal. According to her, the attempted furtive escape of the royal couple was effected from the palace through the special exit door of the queen, a means generally unknown to the public. The route of flight was for some unknown reason altered at the last moment by Louis XVI, to lead from Verdun into Varennes.

Despite the fact that it has been a popular belief for centuries, it is a myth that hair can turn white "overnight," as reported by Mme. Campan, the major source of all this information. In fact, Marie Antoinette's hair was ash-blond, not far from white in the first place. The authenticity of Mme. Campan's account must come under further suspicion when we realize that though she was privy to much information on these matters, she did *not* accompany the king and queen on this aborted journey, as claimed by several of the Nostradamians. In her own personal account, she relates that she was in Paris during that episode, and:

> Therefore I won't be able to give any details of the flight of their majesties other than those I heard from the queen and from the other persons who witnessed her return.

Also, it is not at all probable—in fact, it is highly unlikely—that the queen was dressed in white. The rigors of coach travel in those days, especially over back roads at high speed, would most certainly destroy any appearance of a white costume. Travelers in those days wore dark clothing for such purposes, especially if they were attempting to pass by unnoticed, as this pair certainly should have been. They were fleeing for their lives, against specific injunctions not to do so.

(The above paragraph was written at an early stage of the preparation of this manuscript. Since that time I have conducted a diligent search of historical sources to determine the garb worn by Marie Antoinette. All documents produced from evidence of statements of persons who, unlike Mme. Campan, were eyewitnesses to the flight and/or capture at Varennes state that Marie Antoinette wore a *gray* dress with a black cape. She did not wear white.)

Le Pelletier says that because he had been abandoned by his people, the *"monk"* in *gray* caught in *Varennes* is Louis. Marie Antoinette, the *white stone* (dressed in white, with white hair) left the Tuileries by a secret *door* in her chambers *by night.* The party made a *detour* through Varennes through the *forest of Reines,* at the whim of Louis. Louis as an *elected* monarch will cause *fire, blood* and the *slice* of the guillotine.

Let's examine this interpretation. First, the royal party was not one pair or couple, it was three, or just one if we wish to use the designation of a married couple, husband and wife. The numbers just do not agree. The quatrain calls for two couples.

True, Louis was dressed in gray. There was no white stone to be found, certainly not Marie Antoinette, who just does not match the description in any way. The door by which the royal party left—all of them, not just the queen—was all the way at the very opposite end of the palace from the queen's chambers.

True, they left by night. There was no detour made by the royal party, in spite of arguments made by the Nostradamians that Varennes was not on a direct route to Montmédy. That is not true. Leoni even says that, "it is substantially true that the party took a poor route to Montmédy." Nonsense. Reference to any detailed map of the region shows that the most direct route possible by coach, without having to pass through the major city of Verdun and risk discovery, is passing through the minor towns named above, exactly as planned for the royal family in great detail, well in advance, by their would-be rescuer, the Swedish count Axel Fersen, who worshiped Marie Antoinette.

Concerning line four: Louis, following his capture, was designated by the National Assembly as a constitutional monarch of France, rather than the absolute monarch he had formerly been. But "cap." as used here might well be the Old French word, "captal," which meant "chief" or "leader." It suits the Nostradamians to have it mean "Capet," the formal name of the king, because that is necessary to give the meaning they seek. Such a use would not have been unknown to Nostradamus, since all French kings, from the year A.D. 987, were known as descendants of Hugh Capet, the first somewhat formal monarch of an area that was roughly France as we now know it.

But Louis XVI was not "elected," as the word "esleu" ("elu") would indicate. He was placed in that lower position by the revolutionaries to incapacitate him without having to do away with him, since he still had the respect of many citizens, and the time had not quite arrived when it could be acceptable for his head to fall to the guillotine.

There was no forest called the Forêt de Reines (which in any case would have been "des Reines,") nor was it the Forêt de la Reine that the royal entourage passed through: it was the famous forest of Argonne. The Forêt de la Reine is more than fifty miles southeast of this particular town of Varennes. And I cannot see why "noir" has to be seen as an anagram for "roi" when it fits so well and so logically into the one line of the four that makes any sense at all.

No, the flight of four royal personages through the Argonne forest is not at all well described by the Nostradamus Quatrain

9-20. A man dressed in gray, a town named Varennes (there are *twenty-six* of them in France!) and a journey by night—the only correspondences that can be agreed upon—are not enough to invoke this important event in the history of France.

We will deal further with this event in the next quatrain we examine.

(#5) THE FLIGHT AND CAPTURE OF LOUIS XVI & THE QUEEN AT VARENNES AND THE ATTACK OF THE 500 ON THE TUILERIES
9-34

Le part soluz mary sera mittré,
Retour conflict passera sur la thuille:
Par cinq cens un trahyr sera tiltré,
Narbon & Saulce par coutaux avons d'huille.

The single part afflicted will be mitred,
Return conflict will pass over the tile:
By five hundred, treason will be titled,
Narbon and Saulce by knives we have oil.

The premise that Nostradamus was a prophet almost requires that he would be concerned with French history-to-come. In order to support that requirement, believers have searched diligently for anything that seems to indicate events of the French Revolution. Here again, we have the Nostradamians connecting a quatrain with the flight of Louis XVI from Paris.

The above rendition into English is far from satisfactory. The usual translation of, "Par cinq cens" is "By the five hundred." This cannot be, Everett Bleiler points out, because of the required division (caesura) at the end of the fourth syllable, unless Nostradamus was such a bad poet that he could not see the discrepancy in his work. Connecting the "un" and "trahyr" would be impossible by the rules of caesura. It would be equivalent to singing "The Star-Spangled Banner" like this (try it!):

Say can you see by the,
Dawn's early light what so,
Proudly we hail'd at the,
Twilight's last gleaming whose broad.

Bleiler suggests that the correct reading is "By five-less-one." It's a cute way of saying "four." That may be the case, but I must respectfully reject this conclusion, however, since the literal meaning of "cinq sans un" would be "five *without* one." "Less" would be "moins."

On one point, I will give you some idea of how careful a researcher must be about accepting statements from others. Stewart Robb, one of the leading Nostradamians, tells his readers that in using the word "thuille," which he says refers to the famous palace of Tuileries, Nostradamus shows his powers, since he could not have known of the palace except by prophetic means. Robb says:

> 'Le thuille' means 'the place of the tiles.'* When Nostradamus wrote this prophecy, the site of the Tuileries was only an old tile kiln. The palace was not begun till after the prophet's death.

Let us examine that claim, as I had to do before accepting it. Basic history books provide the answers.

A Frenzy of Inspired and Expensive Expansion

In 1528 King Francis I of France, father of Henry II, had begun making extensive alterations to existing buildings in Paris and was creating new architectural wonders. The Louvre—already a marvelous royal residence—was being greatly expanded so that it would be more suitable as his palace. He also remodeled Saint-Eustache and Saint-Étienne-du-Mont at great expense, and the creation of a bigger and better capital city of France was under way.

What followed was a frenzy of building that seemed as if the monarchy were raising temples to itself as fast as possible, and each ruler was anxious to add to it all. The citizens of France knew that a big chunk of their tax money was going into these ego-building projects, and the construction spree was naturally a subject of great interest to everyone. This show of progress was doubtless also designed to take the minds of the *bourgeoisie*

*No printed reference, authority or scholarly source I have consulted gives this meaning—or *any* meaning—to "le thuille." "La tuile," the closest word, means "tile."

from the debilitating, cruel wars, both civil and religious, in which their country was so deeply involved, particularly with Italy.

With the assistance and inspiration of Catherine de Médicis, what is now the modern city of Paris began to take shape. At her order, plans for an extravagant new palace were drawn up by Philibert de l'Orme, the pre-eminent architect of the day. This was to be an extraordinary project of great scope to be built on the site of what was until then only a group of abandoned tile-factories, and it exists today as a monument to the architect's skill and Catherine's good taste. It became known by the name of the site: Tuileries.

Construction was well under way by 1564, and everyone in France was very much aware of it. With his royal patrons so much on his mind, and with his informers, the Seer of Salon could hardly have failed to know of the great project being planned in Paris, and it is no surprise that he worked it into one of his quatrains. Charles IX and the queen mother, Catherine, visited Nostradamus in 1565—*when the palace had already been under construction for a year,* and a year before his death. The first *authenticated* edition of the *Centuries* that contained this quatrain *did not appear until 1568,* four years after the building was begun.

It is not impossible that Nostradamus may have been refer-ring to the Tuileries in this quatrain, though I think it is not likely. Though admittedly the detail is not of prime importance in evaluating the verse as prophecy, my point is that Mr. Robb's declaration that Nostradamus could not have known about the palace except through a prophetic vision or his analysis of a particular configuration of the stars and planets is not well derived. He may have simply chosen to accept Charles Ward's declaration that

> the Tuileries . . . [was] not in existence when Nostradamus wrote this in 1555.

The quatrain, as Ward certainly knew, was not even in the 1555 edition. As stated above, it was not in print until 1568.

But that is a small matter, to which I may well have devoted too much time and space. This quatrain has in it a number of seemingly evidential references. The historical facts are that a full year after the royal family had been stopped at Varennes and returned to Paris, a mob broke down the gates to the Tuileries palace and entered to confront Louis XVI and his queen. In a farcical and cruel gesture, he was forced to don the red Phrygian bonnet (a sort of stocking cap) that was a symbol of the Revolution. Marie Antoinette, too, put on an identical cap. It would be comical to suggest that "mitred" refers to that event. The line must indicate that someone will be elevated to the position of bishop, since that is what the verb (miter or mitre) means. To equate it with the tragicomic spectacle of King Louis XVI wearing a silly hat is equally silly. Besides, attempts to explain the "single part afflicted" have failed, since Louis was still very much married, not single nor solitary, though he was certainly "afflicted."

Concerning the translation of line three, Le Pelletier says it means that

> The Marseillais Federates, five hundred of them, will direct the attack of the people, on August 10 of the same year [1792], against the Tuileries Palace.

This is an attempt to incorporate the "cinq cens" ("five hundred") of the quatrain with the storming of the Tuileries, by mentioning that the Marseillais Federates led that attack. The attempt fails miserably, for there were other groups of organized, armed men there as well, numbering in the thousands. Along with them was a huge mob of citizens brandishing every sort of weapon from knives to stones. Those who recorded the event estimated the mob at 20,000.

Unfortunately for the Nostradamians who wish to establish the Five Hundred, there exist in the Archives of France *many* highly dependable firsthand accounts of every event of the Revolution. Those were times when anyone's future could change within hours, and major historical turns in the destiny of France took place with great suddenness.

Those days of turmoil within the Tuileries when the royal family was defending its position under siege were written down in minute detail by the Abbé Gallois, the Royal Sacristan and a close friend of the family. He kept a diary in which actual conversations were recorded. He wrote that when the mob approached the Tuileries in the 1791 assault on that regal residence, and Pierre Louis Roederer, the Prefect of Paris, was begging the royal family to leave the palace and take refuge with the National Assembly, Marie Antoinette objected, "But Monsieur, we have troops." She was referring to the Swiss Guard, who were to be overcome in short order by the enormous mob outside. Replied Roederer, "Madame, all of Paris is marching." The citizens of Paris looted the Tuileries.

A Matter of Names

The name "Narbon" in this quatrain, to the interpreters, seems to fit the Revolutionary picture quite well. Says le Pelletier:

> Amongst the traitors who contribute powerfully to the ruin of Louis XVI, there will stand out, in the ranks of the nobility, the Count of Narbonne, his Minister of War. . . .

True, Narbonne was a "traitor," among thousands of them. I must point out that his name appears nowhere in the many history books I have consulted, and I must congratulate the Nostradamians for persevering until they found something— anything—to match "Narbon." Anything, that is, except the city of Narbonne, to which Nostradamus often referred. However, that reference does not suit them. And to follow le Pelletier further in his interpretation, he says:

> . . . amongst the people, a son and grandson of chandler-grocers, named Sauce, procureur-syndic of the commune of Varennes, who will cause him [Louis XVI] to be arrested in this town.

Again, true. And "Sauce" is not far from "Saulce."

I believe it would be difficult for the Nostradamians to explain why, if this quatrain describes the donning of the red bonnet by Louis *and* the flight via Varennes, Nostradamus chose to place the two events, a year apart, in reverse order.

But there is something else which has escaped (perhaps conveniently) the notice of the Nostradamians. Our hero had a strange tendency to group two, three or four towns together in quatrains, usually in very close proximity to one another. This close association of towns is done several places in the *Centuries,* as in 8-22, where "Gorsan" (Coursan), Narbonne, Tucham (Tuchan), and Parpignam (Perpignan) are named, all within a sixty-kilometer pattern. It will occur again when we discuss the famous "Napoleon" Quatrain, 8-1, and in 9-49, the "Charles I" prophecy. Nostradamus' cabalistic/Pythagorean tendencies are showing.

Since we are able to easily find the major city of Narbonne (formerly Narbo), as just mentioned, in the extreme south of France near the present Spanish border, we might look around a bit. Lo! Just forty kilometers south of Narbonne on the main coastal road is the town of Salces, also spelled "Salses."

Well, if Nostradamus was *not* describing Louis's flight, what *was* he writing about? Historian Louis Schlosser gives a detailed account of the siege of Metz, which occurred in 1553, two years before Nostradamus published. Here are the lines of 9-34, one by one, with historical facts of the Metz siege:

(1) Le part soluz mary sera mittré (The single part afflicted will be mitred). Embattled French ambassador Charles de *Mary*llac, Bishop of Vannes (thus he was already mitred and would soon again be mitred as Bishop of Vienna), was defeated in negotiations with his enemy at Metz.

(2) Retour conflict passera sur la thuille (Return conflict will pass over the tile). The defensive walls around Metz were made of tile, an uncommon material for this purpose. Henry II of France (Nostradamus' king) and Emperor Charles V were the two in conflict at Metz.

(3) Par cinq cens un trahyr sera tiltré (By five hundred, treason will be titled). The day following the failed negotiations with the traitor Marquis de Brandebourg, at Metz, it was recorded that the mayor despatched 500 soldiers to join the mercenaries there.

(4) Narbon & Saulce par coutaux avons d'huille (Narbon and Saulce by knives we have oil). At the siege of Metz, two officers, *D'Albon* and *Saulx*, were in charge of the commissary. A list of their supplies shows: *tiles*, casks of *oil* and pitch, rope and *knives*. The "x" as used in Saulx was often put in place of "s" in Provençal usage. The word "Narbon" is pretty close to "D'Albon," and Nostradamus had used such a gimmick in both quatrains 6-56 and 8-22, wherein both Narbon and Perpignan are mentioned. D'Albon was the besieger of Perpignan, and at the time that Nostradamus wrote this quatrain, he was one of the three commanders of the Catholic army.

Which correspondence seems better?

Everett Bleiler suggests that, as often happens, a correlation with this quatrain might be found in another event of Nostradamus' own day. This is his idea, based upon the possible use of "five-less-one" which he has suggested, and with which I close this examination:

A stronger explanation is to be found [for quatrain 9-34] in the life of Catherine de Médicis. 'Five less one' is 'quatre,' which is not far [in pronunciation] from [Catherine]. Catherine was involved in a case of simony concerning the Bishopric of Narbonne. A courtier named Saulce befriended Catherine by offering to take his knife and cut off the nose of Diane [de Poitiers], the King's mistress.

An interesting possibility indeed. I refer to the possible correlation, not the drastic rhinoplasty. . . .

(#6) THE EXECUTION OF CHARLES I OF ENGLAND
9-49

Gand & Bruceles marcheront contre Anuers.
Senat de Londres mettront à mort leur roy
Le sel & vin luy seront à l'enuers,
Pour eux auoir le regne en desarroy.

Ghent and Brussels will march against Antwerp,
The senate of London will put to death their king
The salt and wine will be against him,
To have them, the realm in disarray.

The Rigaud copy of the *Centuries* from which I have been taking most of this material, has "Envers," rather than "Anuers," in the first line. I believe this is a typographical error, and I go along with other editions, which show "Anvers." A "u" is often used for a "v." Anvers is the old name for Antwerp.

Nostradamian Charles Ward offers to handle all four lines of this quatrain together. He marvels over the fact that the Treaty of Westphalia in October of 1648 occurred just three months before Charles I of England knelt at the executioner's block in London. He says

. . . that the conjunction of the two events is extraordinarily definite and remarkable.

The Treaty, says Ward, ended Spain's attempts to establish rights to the Netherlands, and is well described by the words "Ghent and Brussels will march against Antwerp." This is total nonsense. No such action took place.

However, a quick perusal of history books reveals that ninety years previously, when Nostradamus wrote the *Centuries,* there was much activity going on in the area of Ghent, Brussels and Antwerp. In 1555,* Emperor Charles V of the Holy Roman Empire (which Voltaire said was none of those three designations) was attempting to consolidate a number of communities that included what is now Belgium, Luxembourg and Holland, and to control a peasantry who were very unhappy with the heavy taxes they paid to Spain, who claimed the area. Charles transferred his power to his son Philip, whose main interest was enforcing the Inquisition.

Nostradamus did well to predict strange events in that area, since it was a confusing time and likely to see armies marching about from city to city. We must recall that our hero was in the habit of naming three French towns or cities in close proximity to one another. Could he have done this here, too? Here we find him naming three cities located close together in an almost perfect equilateral triangle, for whatever reason.

James Laver, pointing out the apparently remarkable prediction when line two of this quatrain is taken alone, reminds us that in 1649 King Charles I was executed at the order of the English parliament. He declares that the prophet would have had to write a million quatrains to come up with that prediction just by chance. Not so. Given all of recorded time for this to occur, with the seer understandably believing that monarchies would continue throughout history, we cannot be surprised if occasionally he got lucky. The thousands of times that he was unlucky must also be counted.

As early as 1625, observer Gabriel Naudé wrote:

. . . The *Centuries* are so ambiguous, and so diverse, obscure and enigmatic, that it is not something to marvel at, if amongst a

*The year in which Nostradamus first published, though this quatrain was not in that printing. It appeared thirteen years later.

thousand quatrains, each of which speaks always of five or six different things . . . one finds sometimes a [line] which mentions [an event] as if all these things were extraordinary, and as though, if they didn't occur at one period, they couldn't occur at another.

But we must also look to events that had already taken place before Nostradamus' time, to see if perhaps the prophet was merely restating history for us, as he sometimes did. Everett Bleiler suggests that this quatrain might be just such an entity. He says,

Fifteenth century English history, however, can account for the verse fairly well. At about the time that Henry VI died in the Tower, without objection from Parliament, the English were driven out of Guienne, the region from which wine and salt were imported. There was much turmoil in England at the loss of the French territories.

Is this an explanation for Quatrain 9-49? Perhaps. But, given all the colorful metaphors used by Nostradamus, along with the obscurity of his writing, we may be falling into the same trap that the Nostradamians have entered so enthusiastically: We may be looking for a correspondence that is simply not there, in a verse with one line that came true.

(#7) NAPOLEON BONAPARTE & THE IMPRISONMENT OF THE POPES
8 - 1

PAV, NAY, LORON plus feu qu'à sang sera.
Laude nager, fuir grand aux surrez.
Les agassas entree refusera.
Pampon, Durance les tiendra enserrez.

PAU, NAY, OLORON will be more in fire than in blood.
Swimming the Aude, the great one fleeing to the mountains.
He refuses the magpies entrance.
Pamplona, the Durance River holds them enclosed.

Lest it be thought that I have gone off into Wonderland with this translation, I should explain some aspects of my version.

(a) Some editions of Nostradamus show "L'Aude" in place of "Laude." The Aude River runs just north of Narbonne near the southeastern edge of the French-Spanish border.

(b) West of that, near the southwestern border, are the three towns Pau, Nay and Oloron. Pau is now a large and prosperous city; Nay and Oloron are minor towns.

(c) The word "surrez" does not show up in French, of whatever vintage, but all through various dictionaries are derivatives suggesting that "surrez" could be "serrez," which denotes a range of jagged or "serrated" mountains. The Spanish word "sierra" refers to a range of mountains. "Serres" shows up in old French as a modifier meaning "hills," and in Nostradamus' time, an accepted practice was to use "z" in place of a final "s."

(d) "Durance" is clearly the Durance River, a prominent tributary which runs just north of Nostradamus' birthplace. It bore that name when he lived there, and it still does.

(e) "Pampon" is most likely a version of the modern name Pamplona, which appears in geographical texts and maps in a great variety of spellings such as: Pamplon, Pampelona, Pampelune and Pampeluna. This city, famous for its annual festival in which overly macho men are pursued in the streets by largely disinterested bulls, was within the kingdom of Navarre in the 16th century.

Note, in this map, the relationship of the four named towns and the Pyrenees range, which marks the border between modern France and Spain.

Here in Quatrain 8-1 we again have the strange device in which Nostradamus names towns or cities located close to one another, and often located in an almost perfect equilateral triangle. Perhaps he consulted maps of his day and merely used this gimmick for his own amusement, or he might have been titillated by the possible prophetic or magical significance of this geometric relationship. I like to imagine that it was one of his little jokes on the readers.

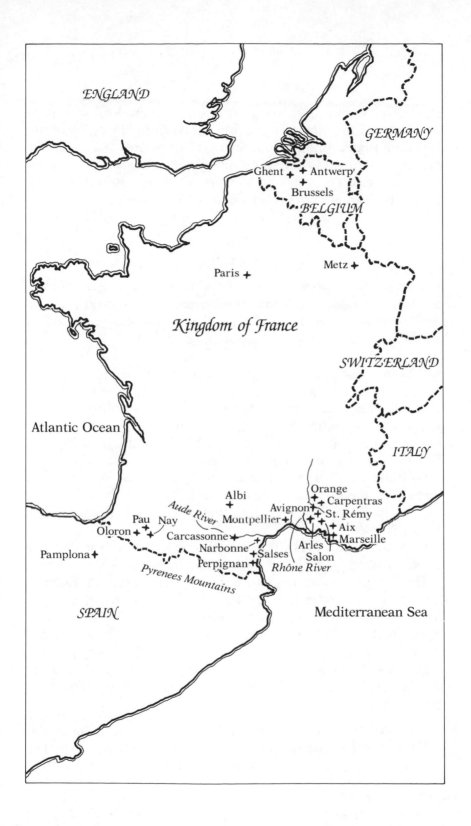

Other Points of View

But before I get into this logical interpretation, I must inform my reader of the miraculous explication offered by many of the Nostradamians, among them Stewart Robb. Ever searching for hidden meaning, Robb seizes upon the "anagram" gimmick with zeal, and gives it a great workout. I will summarize his ingenious (though borrowed) method of turning

PAV, NAY, LORON

into

NAPOLEON

First, I accept, as previously, that the "V" can become "U." In the Garencières book on Nostradamus, which was unknowingly derived from a spurious edition of the *Centuries* and which Robb used, those words are written as

Pau, Nay, Loron,

so I cannot understand why he chooses to replace the commas with periods, the presence of which he accepts as proof that Nostradamus meant these three words to constitute an anagram. The capitalization of these words has no significance, either, since this was always done with the first word(s) of the first line of each first quatrain of each "book" of quatrains.

So Robb has Pau, Nay and Loron from which to derive the name "Napoleon." Here's how he says it can be done:

(a) Take "roy" from it. That means "king" in French. That leaves Pau, Na, Lon.

(b) Rearrange into Na, Pau, Lon. You now have Napaulon roy or Napolaun roy, which is close enough for King Napoleon.

The fact that Napoleon was never a king is ignored. Equally unimportant, it seems, is the fact that he had to change two letters out of eight to get his anagram. In all fairness, I must mention that when the three *syllables* Na, Pau, and Lon are *pronounced* in French, the result is quite similar to Napoleon.

Perhaps the fuzzy thinking involved in these manipulations can be best expressed by Robb himself, as he offers this test of his process:

> . . . the odds against such a possibility are practically incalculable. The reader may judge of this for himself by experiment. Let him take down a book from his shelf, open it at the beginning,

pencil-mark off the text in groups of eleven letters apiece, and continue doing this till he finds a combination re-arrangeable to Napaulon roy. . . . If the Frenchman Nostradamus, prophesying on the kings of France, were working only by chance, the odds against his hitting off in an anagram the name of one of his own rulers would be as great as those encountered by the reader conducting this experiment.

I hardly know how to answer this incredible statement. Here are only a few points, which I simply must make:

   (a) Robb mentions "eleven letters" that make "Napaulon roy." But may we not also take eight (for just the word "Napoleon" or "Napaulon") or seventeen (for "Napoleon (Napaulon) Bonaparte") or nine (for "Bonaparte") or perhaps eight for just "Bonapart"? There are endless different selections to be made.

   (b) Who said this has to be Napoleon? Won't *any* leader of France, including De Gaulle (D'Gaul, DiGall, Degaul, etc.) be just as acceptable?

   (c) Add to the above variations the fact that 25 percent of any letters we find may be changed, and any extra little word may be excluded or included, whether it fits or not. Had "roy" been "roi" (the modern spelling of the French word for "king"), I am sure that Nostradamian Robb would have accepted it just as happily.

These are just a few observations on the faulty reasoning involved in this example, alone, of subjective validation in the subject.

Interpreters assign this quatrain to Napoleon for another reason, too. The old word "agassa" can refer to "magpie," which is expressed in modern French as "pie" (pronounced "pee"). This is also the French word for "pious" and it can refer to pilgrims or penitents. Since Napoleon imprisoned two popes named Pius, they obtain a connection. It seems a long reach.

I believe that this quatrain simply expresses Nostradamus' prophecies of: (1) heavy problems in the area of the city of Pau, (2) some prominent person escaping across the Aude River into the mountains, (3) something involving magpies or chattering persons, or possibly pilgrims, (4) something about the city of

Pamplona in Spain, and the Durance River offering an impediment to someone. I believe these were intended to be four separate predictions, since they are marked off by periods at the end of each line.

Before leaving this matter of Napoleon-in-Nostradamus, I will give you another example of a place where the Nostradamians have found Bonaparte. Quatrain 8-57 reads:

De souldat simple paruiendra en empire,
De robe courte paruiendra à la longue
Vaillant aux armes en eglise ou plus pyre,
Vexer les prestres comme l'eau fait l'esponge.

From a simple soldier he will attain to empire,
From a short robe he will attain to the long
Valiant in arms, in the church he is the worst,
Vexing the priests like water does the sponge.

Who is Nostradamus speaking of here? Most of the Nostradamians dearly want it to be Napoleon. Garencières, resident in Britain at the time he wrote and always a royalist, says that he

never knew nor heard of any body to whom this Stanza might be better applied, than to the late Usurper Cromwell. . . .

Garencières then gives a number of excellent supporting details for his decision. But the quatrain can apply to Mussolini, Hitler and others just as well. I leave it to my reader to find historical facts on these two that will satisfy the quatrain. They are certainly there to be found.

Wishful thinking aside, Nostradamus did not know Napoleon, nor the other corporal we will next bring up for examination.

(#8) ADOLF HITLER I
2-24

Bestes farouches de faim fleuues tranner,
Plus part du champ encontre Hister sera.
En caige de fer le grand fera treisner,
Quand rien enfant de Germain obseruera.

Beasts mad with hunger will swim across rivers,
Most of the army will be against the Lower Danube.

The great one shall be dragged in an iron cage
When the child brother will observe nothing.

In prophecy, it seems that the Antichrist is always imminent. There are different demons for different ages, with Napoleon being replaced by Hitler who in turn is squeezed out by Khomeni, a Khadafy, and so on. To discover a currently prominent devil in Nostradamus is the dearest wish of each devotee of the prophet.

On Roman maps of the area, the lower portion of the Danube River is known as either "Ister" or "Hister." Nostradamus, as we have seen, often used Latin words and names. (In the next quatrain we will discuss, "Hister" is joined with the Rhine River, strengthening our right to believe it to refer, certainly in that verse and very likely in this one, too, to the Lower Danube.)

The Nostradamians sorely need to find an important figure like Adolf Hitler in the prophecies; he just could not have been missed by their hero. Though Nostradamian Stewart Robb recognizes the real meaning of "Hister," he admits the fact then rationalizes it by saying:

> Hister is an old, old name for the Danube, old even when Nostradamus resuscitated it for some good reason of his own. But the passage of the centuries has brought it up to date. It was the obvious word for the prophet to use. It meant the Danube: it also served as an anagram for Hitler. . . . The change of one letter was permissible in anagram writing (see Dictionnaire de Trevoux). What other word could serve better than *Hister* to specify both the name, and the place of origin of [Hitler]?

I have searched diligently to discover the source of this "change of one letter" rule, and cannot locate the "Dictionnaire de Trevoux," either. *All* of the definitions and discussions of the word "anagram" that I have found omit any mention of this practice. I leave it to my readers to answer Mr. Robb's question as posed above.

The most astonishing fact about Mr. Robb's discussion on what he calls the "Three Hister Quatrains" is that he admits "Hister" refers to the Lower Danube, but claims it is used here to represent Adolf Hitler, then he proceeds to point out the relationship of the Lower Danube to the Hitler story. He is using "Hister" *both* ways!

As for "de Germain," it is easy to interpret that as meaning "of Germany." Such a usage is reasonable enough, given the strong influence on modern France of English vocabulary, and it can be found in modern French dictionaries. But from the 12th to the 16th century, "de germain" meant "brother" or "near relative" and nothing else. The word "German" came to be used in France only after World War II, to mean an inhabitant of Germany.

Everett Bleiler, as Liberté E. LeVert, suggests that though the Nostradamians have chosen to associate Hitler with this quatrain, it was evident to those of the 1550s that something else was being hinted at. His printing of line four uses "Rin" in place of "rien," thus giving the meaning "child of the Rhine." I believe a better translation of his printing would be "When the child brother will observe the Rhine." However, Mr. Bleiler says:

> For Nostradamus's contemporaries . . . [the verse] embodied clear references to recent advances by the Turks, in which much of the Hungarian plain was lost and Austria was gravely threatened.

Mr. Bleiler goes on to say that

> The 'child of the Rhine' was Charles V, in Flanders, and his brother was Ferdinand, titular King of Hungary.

His analysis is based upon what I believe (because of the Rigaud version which I have consulted) to be a faulted printing of line four, which he translates as, "When a child of the Rhine shall keep watch over his brother."

Bleiler's idea of the Turkish action is quite interesting, though, since in 1529 the Turks had encamped along the Lower Danube and threatened the city of Vienna. Emperor Charles V, the largely absentee ruler of Germany, stopped the Turks at that point. Later, seeing that Henry II, Nostradamus' monarch, had invaded Germany from the west, he tried to regain that territory and failed. His brother, Ferdinand, arranged the Peace of Augsburg in 1555, the year that the *Centuries* (containing this quatrain) was published.

Mr. Bleiler's suggestion, that Quatrain 2-24 is a Q3K, may quite possibly be valid. But where is the Man in the Iron Cage?

(#9) A D O L F   H I T L E R   I I
4-68

En l'an bien proche non esloigné de Venus,
Les deux plus grans de l'Asie & d'Affrique
De Ryn & Hister qu'on dira sont venus,
Crys, pleurs à Malte & costé ligustique.

In the year very near, not far from Venus,
The two greatest of Asia & Africa
From the Rhine & Lower Danube, which will be said to have
come,
Cries, tears at Malta & the Ligurian coast.

James Laver sees in this quatrain that

> If Mussolini might be called the greatest one in Africa and Japan the greatest one in Asia, then the second line refers to the Tripartite Pact. Both, says the third line, will make themselves Hitler's accomplice, and the fourth may be taken to refer to the bombing of Malta and the bombardment of Genoa.

The Tripartite Pact created the Axis powers (Germany, Italy and Japan) in December of 1941. To author Laver, that event was less than a year old when he wrote his analysis. Genoa is the central port city of the Ligurian coast, and was bombarded along with most of the rest of that coast. Hardly any further comment is needed on the lengths to which Laver has reached for this analysis.

I cannot resist the feeling that Nostradamus could not resist the temptation in this quatrain to rhyme "Venus" (the planet or goddess) and "venus," (in French, the plural past participle of the verb "to come"). The "Venus" in line one probably refers to Venice, which is located on the eastern coast of Italy, mirrored by the "Ligurian coast" on the western side. "Hister," as we have seen in the previously discussed quatrain, does not refer to Adolf Hitler, but to the Lower Danube, particularly in view of its association here with the Rhine.

(#10) L I F E   &   D E A T H   O F   E L I Z A B E T H   I
6-74

La deschassee au regne tournera,
Ses ennemis trouués des coniurés:

Plus que iamais son temps triomphera,
Trois & septante à mort trop asseurés.

Minimally corrected for modern usage, this becomes:

La dechassée au regne tournera,
Ses ennemis trouvés de conjurés:
Plus que jamais son temps triomphera,
Trois & septante à mort trop assurés.

She who was chased out shall return to the kingdom,
Her enemies found to be conspirators:
More than ever her time will triumph,
Three and seventy to death much assured.

We must bear in mind that Nostradamus' sovereign was Henry II, archenemy of Elizabeth. Nostradamus was not unaware of the service he could perform for his sovereign by creating discontent in England, which he certainly managed to do with some of his annual almanacs. As taken from Nostradamian Charles Ward's book, line four of Quatrain 6-74 reads:

Trois, et Septante, la mort, trop asseurez.

It appears that Ward made slight alterations from the original here in order to make it not only a reference to Elizabeth, but an accurate prophecy of her future death. He has broken up the last line but explains

The fourth line is a very singular one. It has no punctuation in the edition of 1558; so I introduce a comma between *trois* and *septante*. . . . *Trois* stands for 1603. Nostradamus often drops the thousands and hundreds from a date. . . . The nought in 1603 cannot be given, so that, omitting the figures in the tens, hundreds, and thousands, the *trois* remaining gives the date; so that the line remains 'In the third year (of the seventeenth century) and seventy years old, assured death comes.'

This quatrain may well have actually been a direct reference to Elizabeth by Nostradamus, since it seems to describe the conditions of her ascent to the throne. This can be classified as an assured hit by Nostradamus since that event occurred the same year that the quatrain was first published. It is quite clearly a "Q3K."

Obviously, it is the last line that has delighted the Nostrada-mians. Elizabeth died in 1603, at the age of *seventy*. But that line clearly says "three and seventy." In the original Old French, the word "septante"—seventy—is used. (It would be represented by "soixante-dix" in modern French.) "Seventy-three" would thus be "septante-trois," which would not fit the meter of the verse, so it appears that "trois et septante" was used. But "seventy-three" does not fulfill what the Nostradamians require for a working prophecy. Thus, a comma is inventively inserted into the line. Such manipulation to serve the cause is quite common among the Believers.

To perpetuate their needs, in 1715 the Nostradamus fans liber-ally retranslated and expanded the quatrain thus:

(1) The Rejected shall for all that come to the Crown;
(2) Her Enemies will be found to have been a band of Traitors forsworn against Her.
(3) The Time of her Reign will be more Happy and Glorious than any of her Predecessors
(4) In the 3rd Year of the Century, at the Age of Seventy She dies, of which I am but too much assured.

I find it astonishing how French expands so dramatically to reveal its hidden meanings when merely translated into En-glish!

I must mention the very important fact that this same qua-train has been interpreted in radically different ways by other prominent Nostradamians. Consider how many novel ways have been found to make this Nostradamus quatrain work ac-cording to expectations:

(1) Garencières, ever the Royalist, says it predicts that Charles II will return to the English throne.
(2) De Fontbrune discovers here the advent of communism in France, which he says will last just three years and sev-enty days.
(3) Henry C. Roberts tells us he gets a clear picture of liberal Nazis [!?] returning to Germany following World War II.
(4) Vlaicu Ionescu is convinced that it portends that for seventy-three years communism will rule in Russia after being chased there out of France by Napoleon.

(5) Le Pelletier finds here an allegorical reference to events in the French Revolution.

Once more, various interpreters—six of the major figures in the field—believe they have each solved one of the Nostradamus puzzles, and they all have quite different answers. At best, only one can possibly be right, and all appear to be wrong, but their pronouncements have been taken seriously by the Believers.

CHAPTER TWELVE

The Legend Begins

What is the end of Fame? 'tis but to fill
A certain portion of uncertain paper;
Some liken it to climbing up a hill,
Whose summit, like all hills, is lost in
vapor;
For this men write, speak, preach, and
heroes kill,
And bards burn what they call their
"midnight taper,"
To have, when the original is dust,
A name, a wretched picture, and worse
bust.
—LORD BYRON, 1788–1824

NOSTRADAMUS WAS, ABOVE ALL, a medical man. He spent much of his life caring for the sick in an age when experienced observation, a gentle touch and the traditionally expected rituals were the major real tools of the physician.

Nostradamus' own health was generally poor during his last years. Gout, a crippling affliction of old age common in his time, incapacitated him severely. His steadily deteriorating condition must have clearly indicated to him that he had not long to live when in June of 1566 he called in a notary to record his will.

He died in his sleep of congestive heart failure (then known as dropsy) after a week of torment. He was sixty-three years old, a respectable age. By the standards of his day, he was moderately rich. He left his heirs an amount of property and currency that seems to indicate he had been professionally successful.

Early in the 19th century, the citizens of Salon, having managed to save most of his homesite, erected a marble plaque at the front of the house inscribed with these words:

DANS CETTE MAISON
VECVT ET MOVRVT
MICHEL NOSTRADAMUS
ASTROPHILE
MÉDECIN ORDINAIRE DV ROI
AVTEVR DES "ALMANACHS" ET
DES IMMORTELLES "CENTURIES"
MDIII   MDLXVI

Translation:

IN THIS HOUSE
LIVED AND DIED
MICHEL NOSTRADAMUS
ASTROLOGER
PHYSICIAN-IN-ORDINARY TO THE KING
AUTHOR OF THE "ALMANACS" AND
OF THE IMMORTAL "CENTURIES"
1503   1566

The plaque may still be seen by visitors to the site, which is now a museum dedicated to the work of the seer.

A Dedicated Biographer

A disciple named Jean-Aimé de Chavigny from Beaune, a town to the north near Dijon, had attached himself to Nostradamus many years earlier, perhaps in 1554. A doctor in theology and in law and a former mayor of Beaune, de Chavigny promptly announced that he was his master's successor as an astrologer and prophet and also his literary heir. The considerable fame that Nostradamus had enjoyed while he lived now took a different though not surprising turn. De Chavigny began recording the life of Nostradamus, recalling every detail that had been told him by his master.

Since de Chavigny is not mentioned at all by Nostradamus'

early biographers nor in his will, there is some doubt that he enjoyed the confidence of the prophet that he claimed. In any case, he wrote copiously on his subject, spending twenty years at the job. He freely accepted outrageous contradictions and paradoxes that turned up in the material left behind by Nostradamus, even publishing precise predictions that had already been proven wrong by history.

De Chavigny wisely allied himself with King Henry of Navarre, the as-yet-uncrowned King (Henry IV) of France, who came into line for the throne when the Valois family became extinct. De Chavigny applied every possible past comment of the seer to the coming career of Henry IV, even some that Nostradamus had obviously intended to flatter Henry II. To his credit, the very sober and hard-nosed Henry IV seems to have taken all this Gallic blarney without too much excitement or expectation. Years passed, and the prognostications, whether applied to either of the Henrys, failed to be realized.

Though many additional works about Nostradamus were promised by de Chavigny, only a small fraction ever appeared. A section of 141 "Presages" gave actual months and years of application for each, but de Chavigny chose to ignore that inconvenient fact, especially since these prophecies had already failed. He decided that the master had cleverly coded those dates to represent *other* future dates. He also gave his own interpretations of 126 formerly published quatrains. These interpretations have been copied by almost every Nostradamian ever since. And there are a number of Q3K items here with detailed and—not surprisingly—successful interpretations.

One de Chavigny interpretation that decidedly identifies a QWK that tried for Q2K status, said that:

(1) Paris will surrender to Henry IV after a battle. (The city was already under siege from Henry when de Chavigny did his interpretation.)

(2) That event will occur in May or June of that year.

(3) Almost every inhabitant of Paris will be dead as a result of the siege.

(4) A named enemy of Henry will go into exile.

(5) Following these events, Henry will conquer Italy.

(6) Henry will invade and conquer Turkey.

(7) Turkey will be converted to Christianity.

(8) Henry will become Emperor of the World.

Both de Chavigny and Nostradamus lost this brave try by a score of eight to nothing. Rather than going into exile, Henry's enemy retired loaded with honors and appointments, Paris quietly gave up well before May, and none of the other glorious prophesied activities happened.

Some More Embarrassing Evidence From Early Days

We need not go further than Nostradamus' early local activities at home in Salon to see just how bad a prognosticator he was. Unfortunately for his reputation, we have a detailed account of a horoscope he drew up for a High Justice in Salon de Provence, and the statement of that man's son that shows *not one* correct astrological prediction by Nostradamus. He was strikingly wrong in every respect, especially in missing the subject's death date by twenty-one years.

In the prose section of the *Centuries,* Nostradamus wrote very clearly and in excellent French, unlike the crabbed, mystical words and construction of the quatrains. *Not one* of the many predictions contained in the prose was correct, and they were all made for dates that are now past, except the end of the world, which is happily placed in the year 3797, according to some, and in 1999 by others. One notable item failed spectacularly. It is for June 22, 1732, a specific day and year on which the seer clearly predicted that

> through Pestilence, Famine, War, and for the most part Inundations, the World between this and that prefixed time, before and after for several times shall be so diminished, and the people shall be so few, that they shall not find enough to Till the Ground, so that they shall remain fallow as long as they have been Tilled.

As Leoni points out, on that date Europe was in the very center of several decades of rare relative peace and prosperity.

Author Hans Holzer, in his book *Predictions: Fact or Fallacy,* faced with facts which he cannot successfully weave into his evidence for the reality of the phenomenon, makes this inane statement:

The perplexities of predictions include the fact that some simply do not come true and many come true at a much later time than the date given by the psychic.

It follows, even by the logic embraced by the Believers, that if no date is given, as with the vast majority of the Nostradamus prophecies, not coming true is no impediment at all to acceptance of the man's writings as true prophecies, since they *might* come true sometime in the future.

The legend of Nostradamus, faulty as it is, will survive us all. Not because of its worth, but because of its seductive attraction, the idea that the Prophet of Salon could see into the future will persist. An ever-abundant number of interpreters will pop up to renew the shabby exterior of his image, and that gloss will serve to entice more unwary fans into acceptance of the false predictions that have enthralled millions in the centuries since his death. Shameless rationalizations will be made, ugly facts will be ignored and common sense will continue to be submerged in enthusiasm.

There will always be those who will point to some quatrain that I have not treated in this book, and jeer that the prophetic powers of Nostradamus are proven in that instance. Let them consult the same sources that I have, and come to their own conclusions, which will probably not change in any case.

An historian of France in 1682 provided an appropriate epitaph for our subject in his review of the year 1566:

> This year there died that trifler, so famous throughout the world, Michel Nostradamus, who boasted while he lived that he knew and could foretell future events by the influence of the stars, in whose name afterwards many ingenious men have put forth their imaginings. . . .

I cannot improve upon that comment.

The Royal Lineage

	LIVED	RULED FRANCE
Henry II	1519–59	1547–59
Francis II	1549–60	1559–60
Elizabeth (Queen of Spain)	1545–68	
Claude (Duchess of Lorraine)	1547–75	
Charles IX	1550–74	1560–74
Henry III	1551–89	1574–89
Marguerite (Queen of Navarre)	1552–1615	
Francis (Duke of Alencon)	1554–84	

The Anonymous Document Concerning the 1555 Edition

THE NEW YORK PUBLIC LIBRARY has a twelve-page manuscript-style typewritten essay, circa 1930, by an anonymous author who suggests that there never was a 1555 edition of the *Centuries!* I find this rather unsupported, since as Everett Bleiler observed when I informed him of this document, to create the trail of a nonexistent book is rather difficult, and there are a great many books that are definitely known to exist but of which the first editions are now totally lost. In any case, any quatrains from the 1555 edition that I have found to be Q3Ks did not need a later printing date to work. To quote from this essay as the author asks about the 1555 edition of the *Centuries:*

> When shall appear the much-quoted, never seen *Editio Princeps* of this unaccountably rare publication of the Nostradamus Prophecies? What is it like in appearance? Where, and by whom has it ever been printed?
>
> The Nostradamites have their reply ready. Not only one conclusive reply, but a number of them. The little book had at first appeared in the year of 1555, with three chapters and 45 verses. ... Or, perhaps the first one came in 1556. After two or three years there appeared the complete edition of ten chapters. Both of them were published by Macé Bonhomme in Lyons, France, in a small format (18°). So say the first ones.
>
> Other folk again ... maintained that the first edition had contained seven chapters, and was of an octavo size (8°) [6″ × 9½″].
>
> Thus there were two editions of ... [this] little book?
>
> For the last hundred years there was no one to maintain that

he had seen a copy of the first edition, let alone that he had one in his possession. At no former time, either. However, in the year 1840 there appeared Eugene Bareste's work dealing with Nostradamus, and the author was explaining that he had borrowed, from a certain Mr. James, a copy of the first edition, the one with the three chapters in small format. And of the other edition we know only through a second, a third and a twelfth hand. The French Bibliothèque Nationale possesses, among others, yet another 'very old edition.' It has, however, refused repeatedly to give any guarantee at all as concerns its date. One edition, dating from 1568, likewise there, has been pointed out by a professional authority—concerning this there is more below—as a falsificate from the Seventeenth Century, insofar as touches the date. The not exactly devoid of means J.P. Morgan—well known as an inspired adherent of Astrology—has in his splendid library but a single exemplar from the second half of the Seventeenth Century. . . .

The writer goes on to say that one celebrated Nostradamian at the beginning of this century, Count von Klinkowström, had traveled over Europe searching for a first edition of Nostradamus, only to be disappointed. He points out that nearly all the 16th-century editions were printed by the Benoist Rigaud press, and that Pierre Rigaud, who inherited the business, used his father's name on further editions. He suggests that perhaps César Nostradamus, the son of the prophet,

> set up the renowned Centuries himself, providing them, afterwards, with falsified dates. Was the first one also among the lot? The [suspicion] could be lifted only by means of one unobjectionable, genuine first edition.

Klinkowström, apparently, was unable to find any trace of the *Privilege du Roy* (royal permission to print) for the first edition, in Lyon or elsewhere. That permit would have been required, and would certainly be on record. There are records of other permits for other books from the presses of Lyons.

Our anonymous author continues:

> The many successors and adherents of Nostradamus have come to raise a school of copy-writers. A scarlet thread of swindle winds itself, clearly perceptible, through all this literature. And

whenever, as occasionally happens, it is not a known swindle, it is still an undiscriminating, exaggerated zealotism by the fanatics. All the biographies of the clairvoyant have been copied from the one that the son has written, independent investigations never having been instituted.

The suggestion that the "first" edition of the *Centuries* never existed in 1555 is fascinating indeed. Since a great number must have been printed, and it was such a celebrated work, why is there not a single copy in existence?

One wonders.

APPENDIX III

Important Dates in the Nostradamus Story

1478 A book (the first) on business mathematics, *Treviso Arithmetic,* was published near Venice. There was no mention of astrology as such, but methods for calculating calendars and holidays were a prominent part of the text, and the process for determining religious holidays used the same tables and methods as the astrologers. The Inquisition was established by Pope Sixtus IV.

1482 Provence was given to France. Until the reign of Charles VIII, it was not officially a part of France, but existed as a fiefdom ruled by its own laws—essentially Roman laws. Stiff regulations requiring Jews to convert to Christianity were now established.

1492 America was discovered. All Jews were legally expelled from Spain, many going across the Pyrenees to take refuge in Provence.

1501 An edict was issued giving Provençal Jews three months to convert to Catholicism or be expelled, with loss of property. Guy Gassonet, who would become the grandfather of Michel, took the name Pierre de Notredame.

1503 In St. Rémy de Provence, Michel de Notredame was born, on December 24 (new calendar).

1517   Michel went to Avignon, city of the popes, to begin his secondary education.

1522   Michel attended the University of Montpellier to study medicine.

1523   A severe winter hit France, freezing the wheat crop and bringing about widespread famine and sickness. Michel treated people in his area.

1525   A prodigious student, Michel received his baccalaureate degree and his license to practice medicine after a remarkably short period of study. Plague hit the area. He visited Narbonne, Toulouse, Carcassonne and Bordeaux, treating plague victims, then returned to Avignon.

1528   Another bout of plague, more severe, hit Provence.

1529   Having traveled about France and northern Italy as a physician, Nostradamus returned to Montpellier and obtained his full medical degree, which was granted October 23, 1529. He taught there for two years.

1532   Nostradamus received a letter from famous scholar Jules-César Scaliger and went to Agen to study with him.

1533   Nostradamus settled in Agen, where he established a medical practice, married, and had two children. He broke off his association with Scaliger.

1537   The plague visited Agen in full force. Nostradamus was active treating victims. His children died of the plague, and his wife soon after.

1538–44   Mourning his loss and suffering from criticism for being unable to save his family, Nostradamus heard that the officials of the Inquisition wanted to question him, and wisely left Agen on a tour. He practiced briefly at Aix-en-Provence and at Lyons. The edict against heretics was beginning to be fully enforced by the French Inquisition.

1544 Nostradamus was in practice at Marseille.

1546 At Aix-en-Provence, Nostradamus was highly successful fighting the plague.

1547 Nostradamus went to Salon, where he married widow Anna Ponce Gemelle and settled down for life. They had six children. King Francis I died and Henry II ascended the French throne.

1548 Nostradamus was reported to be in Venice, Geneva and Savona.

1550 Nostradamus published his first astrological almanac.

1552 Two of his books, *Traicté des Fardemens* and *Vray et Parfaict embellissement de la Face* were published.

1555 Another book, on cosmetics, gastronomic and medical recipes, *Excellent et Moult utile Opuscule,* was published. It was largely a combination of the two 1552 books. In May or June, the first edition of the *Centuries* appeared, printed by Macé Bonhomme in Lyons.

1556 Nostradamus left Salon for Paris at the invitation of Queen Catherine. He left on July 14 and arrived in Paris August 15. He received several royal appointments, and returned to Salon.

1556–7 Nostradamus is said to have traveled in Italy sometime during this period.

1557 Nostradamus' translation of the classical anatomist Galen was published. Another edition of the *Centuries* adding 4–54 to 7-40 also appeared.

1558 Nostradamus wrote centuries 8, 9 and 10, including the Epistle to Henry II.

1559 King Henry II died in a joust. It was felt his death had been predicted by Nostradamus, and it became a matter of widespread interest. The Duke of Savoy visited Nostradamus in Salon.

1564 King Charles IX and Catherine set out on a Royal Progression across France.

1565 The royal pair visited Salon, and called for Nostradamus to confer with them. He was appointed Physician-in-Ordinary to the king.

1566 Nostradamus, in poor health, had his will drawn up and died of congestive heart failure at age sixty-three.

1568 The Benoist Rigaud edition of Nostradamus was published in Lyons.

1594 Henry IV of Navarre became King of France. Thus ended the Valois line.

Some End-of-the-World Prophecies—That Failed

Divine prophecies being of the nature of
their Author, with whom a thousand years
are but as one day, are not therefore
fulfilled punctually at once, but have
springing and germinant accomplishment,
though the heightfulness of them may refer
to some one age.
    —SIR FRANCIS BACON, 1561–1626

A FAVORITE SUBJECT of prophets has always been the end of Mankind and/or the demise of our planet and/or the collapse of the entire universe. Part of the technique, for some, is to place the date far enough ahead that when The End fails to arrive, the oracle is no longer around to have to explain why. Others, often to encourage the surrender of property and other worldly chattels by the Believers, prepare excuses well in advance and manage to survive the great disappointment that often follows a failed prediction.

Here is a short list of some rather interesting end-of-the-world prognostications, beginning with biblical references and ending with some contemporary seers and their doomsayings. Judging from the record earned by the soothsayers in this matter, we may safely assume that our planet will continue very much the same as it is for some considerable period into the future. I, for one, am not worried.

*   *   *

235

B.C.–A.D. According to the New Testament, The End should have occurred before the death of the last Apostle. In Matthew 16:28, it says, "Verily, I say unto you, there be some standing here which shall not taste of death, till they see the Son of Man coming in his kingdom." One by one, all the apostles died. And the world rolled on for everyone else. . . .

A.D. 992 In the year 960, scholar Bernard of Thuringia caused great alarm in Europe when he confidently announced that his calculations gave the world only thirty-two more years before The End. His own end, fortunately for him, occurred before that event was to have taken place.

A.D. December 31, 999 The biblical Apocrypha says that the Last Judgment (and therefore, one supposes, the end of the world) would occur one thousand years after the birth of Jesus Christ. When the day arrived, though it is doubtful that there was all the panic that was reported by later accounts, a certain degree of apprehension was probably experienced. It was said that land was left uncultivated in that final year, since there would obviously be no need for crops. According to the *Encyclopedia of Superstitions,* public documents of that era began, "As the world is now drawing to a close. . . ." Modern authorities suspect that historians Voltaire and Gibbon created or at least embellished this tale to prove the credulous nature of medieval Christians.

September 1186. An astrologer known as John of Toledo in 1179 circulated pamphlets advertising the world's end when all the (known) planets were in Libra. (If the sun was included in this requirement, I have determined this should have occurred on September 23 at 16:15 GMT, or at that same hour on October 3 in the new calendar.) In Constantinople, the Byzantine Emperor walled up his windows, and in England the Archbishop of Canterbury called for a day of atonement. Though the alignment of planets took place, The End did not.

February 1, 1524. This was one of the most pervasive Doomsday-by-Flood expectations ever recorded. In June of 1523, astrologers in London predicted that The End would begin in London with a deluge. Some 20,000 persons left their homes, and the

Prior of St. Bartholomew's built a fortress in which he stocked enough food and water for a two-month wait. When the dreaded date failed to provide even a rain shower in a city where precipitation is very much to be expected, the astrologers recalculated and discovered they'd been a mere one hundred years off. (On the same day in 1624, astrologers were again disappointed to discover that they were still dry and alive.)

The year 1524 was full of predicted disaster. Belief in this date was very strong throughout Europe. An astrologer impressively named Nicolaus Peranzonus de Monte Sancte Marie, found that a coming conjunction of major planets would occur in Pisces (a water sign) that year, and this strengthened the general belief in a universal final deluge.

George Tannstetter, another astrologer/mathematician at the University of Vienna, was one of very few at that time who denied The End would occur as predicted. He drew up his own horoscope, discovered that he would live beyond 1524, and denied the other calculations were correct. But George was considered a spoilsport, and was ignored.

A "giant flood" was prophesied for February 20 (some say the 2nd) of 1524 by astrologer Johannes Stoeffler, who employed his skill to establish that date in 1499. Such was the belief in his ability that more than one hundred pamphlets were written and published on his prediction.

(I have determined that the planets involved in this dire conjunction were Mercury, Venus, Mars, Jupiter and Saturn, along with the sun. Neptune, unknown then, was also in the sign Pisces. Other major influences, Uranus and the moon, were not. Nor was Pluto, also unknown then. But the date of this conjunction was February 23 (old calendar), not the 20th. Interestingly enough, this congregation of heavenly bodies was far, far more powerful than the recent one described in a silly book titled *The Jupiter Effect*, written by two otherwise sensible astronomers who, in 1974, predicted dreadful effects on our planet as a result of a March 10, 1982, "alignment" of planets. Other astronomers denied any effect would be felt, and when the date came and went, as you may have noticed, no one noticed. One of the authors reported that some earthquakes which had occurred in 1980 had been the "premature result of The Jupiter Effect," and the public yawned in amazement.)

In response to the 1524 prophecies, in Germany, people set about building boats, while one Count von Iggleheim, obviously a devout believer in Stoeffler's ability, built a three-story ark. In Toulouse, a man named Aurial also built himself a huge ark. In some European port cities, the populace took refuge on boats at anchor. When it only rained lightly on the predicted date where von Iggleheim had his ark, the crowd awaiting the deluge ran amok and, with little better to do, stoned the count to death. Hundreds were killed in the resultant stampede. Stoeffler, who had survived the angry mob, re-examined his data and came up with a new date of 1528. This time there was no reaction to his declaration. Sometimes people actually get smart.

Incidentally, the 1878 *Encyclopaedia Britannica* described 1524 as "a year, as it turned out, distinguished for drought."

1532. A bishop of Vienna, Frederick Nausea, decided a major disaster was "near" when various strange events were reported to him. He was told that bloody crosses had been seen in the skies along with a comet, that black bread had fallen from mid-air, and that three suns and a flaming castle had been discerned in the heavens. The story of an eight-year-old girl of Rome whose breasts, he was told, spouted warm water, finally convinced this scholar that the world was due to end, and he so declared to the faithful.

October 3, 1533, at 8 a.m. Mathematician and Bible student Michael Stifel (known as Stifelius) had calculated an exact date and time for Doomsday from scholarly perusal of the Book of Revelation. When they did not vaporize, the curiously ungrateful citizens of the German town of Lochau, where Stifel announced the dreaded day, rewarded him with a thorough flogging. He also lost his ecclesiastical living as a result of his prophetic failure.

1533. Anabaptist Melchior Hoffmann announced in Strasbourg, France, a city which had been chosen by him as the New Jerusalem, that the world would be consumed by flames in 1533. He believed that in New Jerusalem exactly 144,000 persons would live on while Enoch and Elias would blast flames from their mouths over the rest of the world. The rich and pious who hoped to be included in that number saved destroyed their rent records, forgave their debtors, and gave away their money and goods to the poor. How those commodities were to be used among the flames was not explained, nor did anyone point out that such sacrifices so near The End were hardly meritorious.

The time of cataclysm by fire came and went, and a new apostle named Matthysz arose to encourage those who now expressed slight doubts. In February 1534, more than one hundred persons were baptized in Amsterdam in anticipation of the still-expected event. As it turned out, the years 1533 and 1534 were noted for their lack of conflagrations, a fact that might be explained by the public's suddenly increased awareness of danger from fire.

1537. (And also in 1544, 1801 and 1814) In Dijon, France, a list of prophecies by astrologer Pierre Turrel were published posthumously. His predictions of The End were spread over a period of 277 years, but all were fortunately wrong. He had used four different methods of computation to arrive at the four dates, while assuring his readers that he had strictly orthodox religious beliefs—a very wise move in his day.

1584. Astrologer Cyprian Leowitz, who had the distinction in 1559 of being included in the official Index of prohibited writers by Pope Paul IV, predicted the end of the world for 1584. Taking no chances, however, he then issued a set of astronomical tables covering celestial events all the way to the year 1614, in the unlikely event that the world would survive. It did.

1588. The sage Regiomontanus (Johann Mueller, 1436–1476), posthumously a victim of enthusiastic crackpots who delighted in attributing occult and magical powers to him, was said to have predicted The End for the year 1588 in an obscure quatrain, but in 1587 Norfolk physician John Harvey reassured his readers that the calculations ascribed to the master were faulty, and the resulting prophecy false. Harvey was right.

1648. Rabbi Sabbati Zevi, in Smyrna, interpreted the cabala to show that he was the promised Messiah and that his advent, accompanied by spectacular miracles, was due in 1648. By 1665, regardless of the failure of the wonders to appear, Zevi had a huge following. Citizens of Smyrna abandoned their work and prepared to return to Jerusalem, all on the strength of reported miracles by Zevi. Meeting a sharp reversal when arrested by the Sultan for an attempted coup and brought in fetters to Constantinople, the new Messiah sat in prison while followers as far away as Holland, Germany and Hungary began packing up in anticipation of Armageddon. Unfortunately for these faithful, the Sultan converted the capricious Zevi to Islam, and the movement ended.

1654. Consulting his ephemeris and considering the nova of 1572, physician Helisaeus Roeslin of Alsace decided in 1578 that the world would surely terminate in flames in another seventy-six years. He did not survive to see his prophecy fail.

That should have been an evil year indeed. An eclipse of the sun was predicted for August 12 (it actually occurred on the 11th) and that was also widely believed to bring about The End. Many conversions to the True Faith took place, physicians prescribed staying indoors, and the churches were filled.

1665. With the Black Plague in full force, Quaker Solomon Eccles terrorized the citizens of London yet further with his declaration that the resident pestilence was merely the beginning of The End. He was arrested and jailed when the plague began to abate rather than increasing. Eccles fled to the West Indies upon his release from prison, whereupon he once again exercised his zeal for agitation by inciting the slaves there to revolt. The Crown fetched him back home as a troublemaker, and he died shortly thereafter.

1704. Cardinal Nicholas de Cusa, without Vatican endorsement, declared The End was to arrive in 1704.

May 19, 1719. Jacques Bernoulli, the first of a famous line of Swiss mathematicians who made their home in Berne, predicted the return of the comet of 1680 and earth-rending results therefrom. The comet did not come back, perhaps for astronomical reasons, but Bernoulli went on to discover a mathematical series now called the Bernoulli Numbers. He is renowned for this and for the eight exceptional mathematicians his line produced in three generations, but not for Doomsday nor for his astronomical calculations.

October 13, 1736. London was once again targeted for the "beginning of the end," this time by William Whiston in 1736.

1757. Mystic/theologian/spiritist and supreme egocentric Emmanuel Swedenborg, ever willing to be a center of attention for one reason or another, decided after one of his frequent consultations with angels that 1757 was the terminating date of the world. To his chagrin, he was not taken too seriously by anyone.

1774. English sect leader Joanna Southcott had the notion that she was pregnant with the New Messiah, whom she proposed to name Shiloh. History records that her pregnancy "came to nothing," nor did the world end. She left behind a box of mystical notes that were to be opened only after her death with twenty-four bishops present. Perhaps because of a failure to interest that many ecclesiastics of high rank in attending the occasion, the box was not opened and vanished somewhere. (One box claimed to be genuine was recently opened. It produced nothing but a few junk items of little interest.) She was succeeded by several would-be prophets, all of whom tried other End-of-the-World predictions, with the same result. One successor, John Turner, we will meet up ahead.

April 5, 1761. When religious fanatic and soldier William Bell noticed that exactly twenty-eight days had elapsed between a February 8 and a March 8 earthquake in 1761, he naturally concluded that the entire world would crumble in another twenty-eight days. Many credulous Londoners believed him and snapped up every available boat, taking to the Thames or scurrying out of town as if those actions would save them. History records nothing more of Bell after April 6, when he was tossed into London's madhouse, Bedlam, by a disappointed public.

October 14, 1820. Prophet John Turner was leader of the Southcottian movement in Bradford, England. The specialty of this sect was End-of-the-World prophecies, the first one having been made by the founder of the group, Joanna Southcott, whom we have already met back in 1774. His failed prediction turned his congregation against him, and John Wroe (see 1977, up ahead) took over the movement.

April 3, 1843. (And also July 7, 1843, March 21 and October 22, 1844) William Miller, founder of the Millerite church, spent fifteen years in careful study of the scriptures and determined that the world would conclude sometime in 1843. He announced this discovery of what he called "the midnight cry" in 1831. When there was a spectacular meteor shower in 1833, it seemed to his followers that his prediction was close to being fulfilled, and they celebrated their imminent demise. Then, as each date he named failed to produce Armageddon, Miller moved it up a bit. The faithful continued to gather by the thousands on hilltops all over America each time one of the new dates would dawn. Finally, on October 22, 1844, the last day that Miller had calculated for The End, the Millerites relaxed their vigils. Five years later, Miller died, still revered and not at all concerned at his failed prophecies.

The movement eventually changed its name and broke up into a number of modern-day churches, among them the Seventh-Day Adventist Church, which today has over three million members.

1881. Those who delighted in measuring the various passages of the Great Pyramid at Ghiza, presumed to be the tomb of Cheops, calculated that all would be over in 1881. Careful remeasuring and some imagination gave a better (but not much better) date of 1936. That was improved upon by other students who decided upon 1953 as the terminal year. Further refinements and improvements of technique are still being made. If I get a new date, I'll let you know.

1881. Mother Shipton is supposed to have written:

> *The world to an end will come*
> *In eighteen hundred and eighty-one.*

The prediction, as well as the rhyme, are faulted. A book titled *The Life and Death of Mother Shipton,* written in 1684 by Richard Head, was reprinted in a garbled and freely "improved" version in 1862 by Charles Hindley. In 1873 Hindley admitted having forged that rhyme and many others, but his confession caused no lessening of the great alarm in rural England when 1881 arrived.

The world not having ended in that year, the above spurious verse has since been published in a refreshed version which substitutes "nineteen" for "eighteen" and "ninety" for "eighty." I predict that in 1991, there will be adequate material for the journalists to once more develop a minor panic over this dreadful pronouncement.

1947. In 1889, "America's Greatest Prophet," John Ballou Newbrough, said that for sure in 1947

> all the present governments, religions and all monied monopolies are to be overthrown and go out of existence. . . . Our present form of so-called Christian religion will overrun America, tear down the American flag, and trample it underfoot. In Europe the disaster will be even more terrible. . . . Hundreds of thousands of people will be killed. . . . All nations will be demolished and the earth be thrown open to all people to go and come as they please.

It wasn't a *great* year, but it wasn't all *that* bad.

1977. John Wroe, who is described by the kindliest historian I can find as a "foul-mouthed, ugly, dirty lecher," in 1823 inherited the leadership of the Southcottian sect in England when an End-of-the-World prophecy by John Turner failed. Learning from the example, Wroe took no chances. He made his Armageddon prophecy for 1977. A 1971 book, *Prophets Without Honor,* says of Wroe,

> At a time when thermo-nuclear powers face each other across the Iron and Bamboo Curtains, it is well to remember that—as far as can be judged from the scanty records—John Wroe, indeed, was a true prophet!

1980. A very old Arabic astrological presage of doom specified that when the planets Saturn and Jupiter would be in conjunction in the sign Libra at 9 degrees, 29 minutes of that sign, we could kiss a big bye-bye to everything—camels, sand, mosques, the whole bag. That astronomical configuration *almost* took place at midnight of December 31 (new calendar), 1980, a date calculated by astrologers many years ago as the one spoken of. Jupiter was at 9 degrees, 24 minutes, and Saturn was at 9 degrees, 42 minutes, so it was close to correct. Nary a camel blinked an eye.

1980s. The unsinkable Jeane Dixon, ever optimistic and daring, predicted in 1970 that a comet would strike the earth in the "mid-80's" at a place that she knew, but did not deign to tell. That information was to be held until a "future date." Perhaps she is *now* prepared to tell us? She said of this event that it "may well become known as one of the worst disasters of the 20th century." But then Jeane also said that, "I feel it will surely be in the 1980's that [an un-named person] will become the first woman president in the United States."

1996. It has been reasoned by biblical scholars that since one day with God equals one thousand years for Man, and that God labored at the creation of the universe for six days, Man should labor for six thousand years and then take a rest. Thus, using other scripturally derived numbers, the world should end sometime in 1996. With any luck at all, we'll see. . . .

July 1999. In Quatrain 10-72, Nostradamus declared:

L'an mil neuf cens nonante neuf sept mois
Du ciel viendra grand Roy deffraieur
Resusciter le grand Roy d'Angolmois.
Auant apres Mars regner par bon heur.

The year 1999, seven months,
From the sky will come a great King of Terror:
To bring back to life the great King of the Mongols,
Before and after Mars to reign by good luck.

Ho hum.

Bibliography

Bleiler, E.: see LeVert

Boïelle, James: *Heath's French and English Dictionary*. Boston, 1905.

Boswell, Rolfe: *Nostradamus Speaks*. New York, 1941.

Castelot, André: *Queen of France*. New York, 1957.

Cavendish, Richard: *A History of Magic*. London, 1977.

Cheetham, Erika: *The Final Prophecies of Nostradamus*. New York, 1989.

————: *Further Prophecies of Nostradamus*. New York, 1985.

————: *Prophecies of Nostradamus*. London, 1972.

Cournos, John: *A Book of Prophecy*. New York, 1952.

Crombie, A.C.: *Medieval and Early Science*. New York, 1959.

De Fontbrune, J-C.: *Nostradamus 1: Countdown to Apocalypse*. London, 1983.

————: *Nostradamus 2: Into the Twenty-First Century*. London, 1984.

————: *Nostradamus: Historien et Prophète*. Monaco, 1980.

De Fontbrune, Dr. Max.: *Ce que Nostradamus A Vraiment Dit*. Paris, 1937.

————: *Les Prophéties de Maistre Michel Nostradamus*. Sarlat, France, 1939.

Dupèbe, Jean: *Nostradamus—Lettres Inédites*. Geneva, 1983.

Festinger, Riecken, and Schachter: *When Prophecy Fails*. Minneapolis, 1956.

Forman, Henry James: *The Story of Prophecy*. New York, 1940.

Gardner, Martin: *Fads and Fallacies in the Name of Science*. New York, 1952.

Garrison, Omar V.: *The Encyclopedia of Prophecy*. Secaucus, NJ, 1979.

Glass, Justine: *They Foresaw the Future*. New York, 1969.

Greenhouse, H.B.: *Premonitions: A Leap Into the Future*. New York, 1971.

Hassell, Max: *Prophets Without Honor*. New York, 1971.

Hogue, John: *Nostradamus and the Millennium*. Garden City, NY, 1987.

Ionescu, Vlaicu: *Nostradamus: L'Histoire Secrète du Monde*. Paris, 1987.

Langer, W.L.: *An Encyclopedia of World History*. Boston, 1940.

Laver, James: *Nostradamus; or, The Future Foretold.* London, 1942.

Leoni, Edgar: *Nostradamus and His Prophecies.* New York, 1961.

Leroy, Dr. Edgar: *Nostradamus—Ses Origines, Sa Vie, Son Oeuvre.* Bergerac, France, 1972.

LeVert, Liberté E.: *The Prophecies and Enigmas of Nostradamus.* Glen Rock, NJ, 1979.

Lewinsohn, Richard: *Science, Prophecy and Prediction.* New York, 1961.

Littlefield, Henry W.: *History of Europe, 1500–1848.* New York, 1939.

McCann, Lee: *Nostradamus, the Man Who Saw Through Time.* New York, 1941.

Nostradamus, M.: *Les Prophéties de M. Michel Nostradamvs.* Lyon, 1568.

Robb, Stewart: *Nostradamus on Napoleon, Hitler and the Present Crisis.* New York, 1942.

———: *Prophecies on World Events by Nostradamus.* New York, 1961.

Roberts, Henry C.: *The Complete Prophecies of Nostradamus.* New York, 1947.

Robinson, H.R.: *History of Western Europe.* Boston, 1902.

Schevill, Ferdinand: *A History of Europe.* New York, 1925.

Schlosser, Louis: *La Vie de Nostradamus.* Paris, 1985.

Schumaker, Wayne: *The Occult Sciences in the Renaissance.* Berkeley, 1972.

Sladek, John: *The New Apocrypha.* New York, 1973.

Smith, Richard F.: *Prelude to Science.* New York, 1975.

Stearn, Jess: *The Door to the Future.* New York, 1963.

Stevenson, David L.: *The Elizabethan Age.* New York, 1966.

Thorndike, Lynn: *History of Magic and Experimental Science.* New York, 1941.

Toonder, J.G., and West, J.A.: *The Case for Astrology.* New York, 1970.

Ward, Charles A.: *Oracles of Nostradamus.* London, 1891.

Index